Remaking China Policy

Remaking China Policy
U.S.-China Relations and
Governmental Decisionmaking

Richard Moorsteen
and Morton Abramowitz

Harvard University Press
Cambridge, Massachusetts
1971

To Keren, Peter, Michèle, Kay, and Esther
and
To S.

Contents

Part II | Some Problems of Governmental Decisionmaking

Appendix | Selected Documents on U.S.-China Relations 87

Foreword

John K. Fairbank

The authors of this book got their graduate training as economists, people who esteem theory but most prize quantification and precision. Responsive to high challenges, they also studied China, including its language, and acquired a proper humility. During a decade of work on China policy they have trained themselves to think like historians, comprehensively and synthetically, but as historians dealing with the future, since policy is the effort to influence the future before it becomes history. What they offer us is a case study of "how to make policy in conditions of great uncertainty."

These are men worth following, for they know that they can't see where they are going, and they are accordingly skeptical and prudent. They offer to teach us a way of thinking about China policy, a way that is imaginative, thorough, and as objective as possible. Richard Moorsteen began as a specialist on the Soviet economy. He and Morton Abramowitz are asking their readers to join in the process of all-around evaluation normally followed in Washington policy studies.

The first merit of their approach is to keep China in perspective: "Better relations with China are a desirable, but not our most important, objective in Asia. We have other interests of greater priority there." Such realism is a salutary corrective to the kind of study that focuses on China, much as the Chinese do, and brings in the outer barbarians only peripherally. Indeed, too many barbarians still follow the tradition by which the nineteenth-century Sinologue, the modern Sinologist, and the recent China-watcher have been assumed to possess arcane knowledge. All China questions except the important ones could be referred to the "China experts," leaving the rest of us free of the intellectual burden of trying to understand China. Though obviously convenient, this system had its limitations. When the most vital decisions had to be taken at top levels by an Ambassador Patrick J. Hurley or a Secretary of State Dulles or a President Johnson, China experts were seldom considered of sufficient standing to participate. Having "experts," but not having them present, left the decisionmakers intellectually pauperized, and we got results accordingly. The first premise of this book is that China is too important to be left to "China experts"; our China problems must be seen in the context of our other East Asian and world problems, and this perspective must and can be attained by top policymakers.

The second premise is that the government's fund of information, its understanding of problems, must be systematically improved. The need is for "information about China that is relevant to policy issues." In a given situation, what is Peking's and what is our order of priorities? What are our respective interests? How will Peking react? The military classic of the fourth century B.C., the *Sun-tzu*, phrased this tersely as *chih-chi chih-pi, pai-chan pai-sheng,* "know ourselves, know them; hundred battles, hundred victories." You can win if you thoroughly comprehend the

situation of both sides. Moorsteen and Abramowitz respond
to this need by asking a multitude of questions that call for
studied answers. Further, they suggest policies that we
might move toward, from our present positions, and thus
they doubly stimulate study and discussion.

Here, for better or worse, we come back to the China
specialist, for the fact is that peoples are products of their
history, China's history has been different from ours, and we
have only begun to study it. Our greatest need is for a mental
image of China's experience commensurate with our image
of our own historical development in the West. Lacking it,
we must still think of China in Western terms. For example,
Chairman Mao in putting the new China together sets an
example some have called "puritanical." His predecessor the
K'ang-hsi Emperor of the Ch'ing put China together in the
seventeenth century. But we know less of K'ang-hsi than we
do of his contemporary Oliver Cromwell, and "puritanical"
evokes an image of a Chinese Cromwell somewhere in the
Chairman's background.

Remaking China Policy, in short, is a seminal study that
sets in motion ideas that may outdistance even the authors,
for it clearly implies that we need historical studies "structured to fit the preoccupations of the policymaking level."
"The China Group" that they so cogently advocate as a de-
vice to pull together Washington's wisdom on China policy
will have to include historians, or rather ex-historians, who
have developed their knowledge and skill to the level of
perceiving the Sino-historical dimensions of current policies.
Such people are so scarce they will have to be specially produced. Without presuming to be one, let me try to suggest
the kind of historical resonance that such policy historians
might provide.

Take the question of China in the UN: Peking and Taipei
agree on "One China" because China began as a culture

island and spread outward, civilizing the uncouth and incorporating all Chinese in a single civilization; and for two thousand years the unity of this Chinese realm has meant peace; its disunity, war. Reinforced by history, China's national-culturalism today is monolithic, whereas European nationalisms are mere political subdivisions within European culture. After a century of humiliation, China's claims to sovereignty express this resurgent unity, and "Two Chinas" is an utter blasphemy.

But now watch carefully. China's sovereignty has frequently covered autonomous regions that were not under central control, such as warlord provinces or border enclaves like Tibet, Mongolia, or Manchuria. Autonomy recognized as a fact does not destroy sovereignty as the unitary ideal. After the fall of the Ming in 1644, Taiwan was autonomous for four decades. Today Peking can wait and solve its Taiwan problem by degrees.

International law buffs who see inconsistency in the preceding two paragraphs will only make trouble for themselves and us. The Chinese are not descended from Aristotle nor do they worship the syllogism. But in the last hundred years of contact with us, they have learned how to use our rules flexibly in self-defense. In fact they accepted the unequal treaties of the 1840s as a list of privileges that could be used to limit as well as to facilitate Western activity in China. The use of ping pong for people's diplomacy is not the last surprise we shall enjoy. The rejection of "Two Chinas" and acceptance of Taiwan's autonomy under Peking's sovereignty, if it occurs, should not surprise us.

All this may be stated, to suggest the sort of historical considerations that may be put forward as factors influencing Peking's policy views, but Moorsteen and Abramowitz will call us back to bureaucratic reality. As they point out, "Hard information (usually numbers) tends to prevail over soft (usually political)." Government seminars on China have been "attended by over 200 specialists.... But how much of their output really influences policy? Too little of it is used, but also too little is 'usable' for this purpose." Like all advocates of history as the usable past, we are challenged to show its utility, and can also expect attack from the equally valid history-for-its-own-sake school.

Perhaps the most interesting contribution of this book is not its cool dissection of policy problems but its concern for the policymaking process. The authors tick off the many pitfalls that await unexpected information or a novel idea on its way to the policymaker's desk, eyes, and mind. Few get through. They suggest a remedy—no panacea but a forward step. Plainly they are hardbitten optimists, determined to keep on trying, good men to go along and argue with.

Foreword

Nicholas deB. Katzenbach

Remaking China Policy is a unique and valuable book. It lays before the general public what is in essence a memorandum for the President (or the National Security Council), recommending both substantive and procedural courses of action—just as a real memorandum on the subject would do. As such a paper should—but too seldom does—it analyzes almost brutally the complexity, the uncertainties, the political constraints and risks involved in the course of action suggested. It has, therefore, the honesty and candor that a highly classified intragovernmental policy paper must have to support an important foreign policy initiative. These almost never exist, or can exist, when the President or his cabinet attempts to explain our foreign policy in public.

In a free and open society the general public should know why its elected representatives act the way they do. On domestic matters there is seldom a convincing reason for statements that do not put the policy considerations squarely before the public. It is not so easy in foreign affairs —and the fact that it is not unavoidably contributes to misunderstandings and a credibility gap. I believe that there is more secrecy in foreign affairs than there need be and that the need for secrecy can cover up poor judgments. But this book illustrates, without ever raising the issue, why foreign policy decisions are seldom candidly discussed in public, even on a deep background basis. It shows why the Congress must yield leadership in foreign policy to the President, why the President is concerned about being the victim of a foreign policy bureaucracy, and why the public is too seldom sure about where we are going in our foreign relations.

Posing a foreign policy proposal as realistically as does this book requires the discussion of complexities seldom recognized by the public or even the Congress—and, if the policy is to succeed, is unmentionable by the administration. Indeed, the public statements by the administration are an operative part of the policy itself. They are designed for a particular audience which is not only—or even primarily in all cases—the American people. On important matters, it inevitably ends up as a rather bland, unsophisticated, rarely candid explanation.

How, for example, can an administration possibly state to the general public that what we are doing and saying with respect to China is aimed as much at influencing the decisions of Japan, Korea, and Southeast Asia as it is aimed at the People's Republic of China? Recognizing this fact, rarely emphasized in the current literature, is in itself a contribution to thought about our China policy.

It may or may not be useful to have the press speculate on such matters, but it is almost impossible to state all of the relevant considerations without seriously impairing the policy itself. It is often not possible to say much at all. One cannot avoid recalling in this connection George Kennan's famous "X" article in *Foreign Affairs* which anonymously laid the basis for our policy with regard to Russia at the beginning of the Cold War.

It follows that the real significance of this book is in giving the general public a rare insight into the process whereby important decisions of foreign policy are made. It should suggest to its readers that there is more thought and rationality in the making of foreign policy than is apparent on the surface. It should suggest that there is—or at least can be—an objective, reflective, and rational decisionmaking process and that this process does in fact go on—behind the scenes and unfortunately rarely exposed to public debate.

Both Mr. Moorsteen and Mr. Abramowitz are experienced bureaucrats as well as China experts. I am biased because both worked with me when I was in the State Department. Both have in fact written memoranda to the President that he has acted on. Both have been directly responsible for foreign policy decisions of the United States.

I wish they had done this analysis as my subordinates. Had they done so I could have taken my part and acquired in history some of the credit they deserve for a perceptive and objective look at U.S. policy toward China.

Mr. Nixon has made some imaginative moves in our China policy. He is currently faced with some very tough—and very significant—decisions. He may or may not follow the recommendations of this study. But whether he does or not he will be the wiser for having considered them.

And that statement raises one point not raised in this book. If this study had in fact remained a private recommendation of the authors, even endorsed by the Secretary of State, would it have had the same impact on our China policy that it will have as a public document? Does the President pay the same attention to unpublicized policy recommendations that he does to public ones? And does not the public analysis of a possible course of action make his decisions easier? Most Presidents like to know the temperature of the water before plunging in. Perhaps this book will help the President to know.

In any event, whether he agrees with its conclusions or not, he is much too perceptive to ignore them.

Why This Book Turned Out As It Did

Authors' Note

Our study started with a working hypothesis that did not quite survive. The hypothesis seemed reasonable enough. A great deal of work has been done on China by U.S. specialists since the Korean War. Had not our understanding of China outrun our policies? The work was begun, therefore, in the spirit of a search-and-rescue operation for insights and judgments widely shared among China specialists but not yet percolated through to the policymaking levels of the government.

Much searching was done, but few rescues were made. The United States has learned a lot about China, but our information is still swamped by the uncertainties that remain. The specialists disagree on a variety of important topics, the most important being Chinese intentions and perceptions.

No doubt this marks the beginning of wisdom. The United States certainly needs a more complex understanding of how the Chinese look at themselves, their history, and their relations with other nations. They do indeed see things differently than we do. But there is also great diversity among the Chinese themselves. We are just starting to understand their differences with each other. And those uncertainties compound the problems for the American specialist in forecasting the likely actions of China. Furthermore, much of what the specialist community does "know" is of little use to U.S. policymakers because it is not structured to fit the preoccupations of the policymaking level. The reasons for this are a major theme of the book.

On balance, we came to feel it probable that past U.S. policies were based on excessive fear of the aggressiveness of the Chinese Communists. Even this is uncertain because of the self-fulfilling nature of such policy premises. Especially since the Korean episode, apprehension and hostility on each side have stoked apprehension and hostility on the other. Justified or not, the self-fulfilling premises of the past become the realities of the present.*

Even if our past notions of Chinese aggressiveness have been exaggerated, it is still uncertain what practical changes in policy would be implied. A conclusion as general as this does not automatically translate itself into concrete, workable policies. Judging from the recent increase in the flexibility of U.S. policy toward China, the Administration has reached a similar conclusion. Yet, it too is clearly having problems moving from a very general, still highly tentative conclusion to a forceful new policy stance.

Our quest for verities, therefore, turned into a study of how to make policy under conditions of great uncertainty. We propose two lines of attack. One has to do with increasing

---

*Dean Acheson's memoirs recall in detail how Washington's firm intention to avoid fighting China during the Korean War came to naught in an atmosphere of misapprehension and poor communication. See Dean Acheson, *Present at the Creation: My Years in the State Department* (New York, Norton, 1969, Chapters 46-48, especially pp. 452-454), and also Documents 1 and 2 in the Appendix to this book.

the policy relevance of what we do know or can find out about China through intelligence and research. But in the end, if the United States really wants to know more about China, it will have to go to the Chinese to find out. Our second approach, then, proposes exploratory policy moves toward China. Peking's responses (or lack of response) would help us learn more, and what we learned would then be incorporated into further studies and policies. In the course of time, it may be hoped, this process would substantiate (or dispel) our underlying premise, that better U.S.-China relations are possible.

Initially this study was written as essentially unsolicited advice to the government from the authors, acting as individuals.* This means, of course, that the views in it are purely personal and have no official standing whatsoever. The argument is the authors', and not that of The Rand Corporation or of the sponsors.

Another consequence is that the study was drafted and organized to suit the concerns and working style of its target audience, high level policymakers and the community of China specialists within the government. These people have very little time. They typically start their reading of papers at the end, to judge whether the conclusions merit plowing through the rest. Our study is therefore tersely argued. The language is often blunt. And the order in which subjects are taken up is sometimes unusual. In publishing it, we decided it would be better not to modify it, except for that minimum required for intelligibility. The most obscure governmentese

---

*Richard Moorsteen is a Rand Consultant. Morton Abramowitz is a Foreign Service Officer now on leave at the Institute for Strategic Studies, London; his participation in this study reflects the State Department's new emphasis on encouraging officers to "engage freely in public discussion" on an individual basis. See *Diplomacy for the Seventies—A Program of Management Reform for the Department of State* (Washington, D.C., Department of State Publication 8551, 1970).

has been put into English or explained, but much of the argot and all the original tenor and argumentation has been left as is. The result inevitably has its peculiarities. We think they are outweighed by the interest to the public in an actual specimen of this kind of paper, one that is tailored to the preoccupations and time constraints of those with operational responsibility for conducting foreign policy. For the use of the general reader, we have added an appendix of documentary material to give additional context for particular points made in the text.

Finally, we are aware and in fact very appreciative of new modes of analyzing foreign policy, in which explicit account is taken of the fact that governments are not unitary beings but congeries of diverse individuals and institutions. A government's behavior may be the result of diverse pressures and views interacting within it, rather than a rational expression of a well integrated set of values, objectives, and perceptions. Recognizing this in principle is a major advance in cognition, but applying it practically depends on the depth of one's knowledge of the internal workings of the governments involved. In our thinking, we have given explicit consideration to these factors where we felt we could. To keep the language of the book from an elaborateness exceeding the underlying thought, though, we have not referred expressly to these matters except when we had something of substance to say about them. Where nothing is to be gained by complexity, we use such simple terms as "Peking" or the "Chinese" without meaning to imply the predominance of a single overwhelming being, even one so luminous as Chairman Mao.

Richard Moorsteen   *Morton Abramowitz*
Santa Monica   *London*

Acknowledgments

The research on which this study is based has been supported by the Advanced Research Projects Agency of the Department of Defense, the State Department, and the Ford Foundation (under a grant to Richard Moorsteen to study problems of governmental organization). That help is gratefully acknowledged. The views expressed here are those of the authors, and not those of The Rand Corporation or of any of the sponsors.

The thoughts in this study as it finally came out are our private thoughts. That they are not necessarily original with us will be apparent from the many people we are indebted to for talking with us and reading and commenting on our drafts as the work progressed. Friends in the China specialist community of the government contributed anonymously on a personal basis. In addition, we were helped by: Doak Barnett, Robert Barnett, Abraham Becker, Ralph Clough, John Despres, Leslie Gelb, Herbert Goldhamer, Melvin Gurtov, Morton Halperin, James Hayes, Hans Heymann, Philip Heymann, Malcolm Hoag, Frank Hoeber, Oleg Hoeffding, Fred Hoffman, Arnold Horelick, William Jones, Konrad Kellen, Joseph Kirchheimer, Paul Langer, Andrew Marshall,

Thomas Robinson, Henry Rowen, Allen Whiting, William Whitson, Albert Williams, Charles Wolf, Jr., Joseph Yager, K. C. Yeh, and Charles Zwick. We are also greatly indebted to John Hogan, Jean Martin, Malcolm Palmatier, and Helen Turin for helping us in each stage of moving from inchoate thoughts to a publishable manuscript.

Summary

This study deals with a process—the development of long-term U.S. policy toward China. It recommends:

- Points of departure for moving policy in desirable directions.
- Improved procedures for managing policy development.

It does not chart a course over the long run.

A. Southeast Asia offers Peking its greatest potential for pressuring the United States and challenging the Nixon Doctrine. Because Peking's risk would be small, any efforts it chose to make would be hard for U.S. policies to cope with *in a context confined to Southeast Asia alone.* However, Peking has other interests with higher priority than dominating Southeast Asia. And U.S. policy has a central influence on each of them. There may be some grounds for mutual accommodation, therefore, if we bring these other interests into the picture.

B. Taiwan's status figures in Peking's public declarations as its most important issue with the United States. At present the United States holds most of the levers. The Japanese role is also crucial. But even though constrained by this and other important interests, we have room for maneuver on this issue. Unless we are quite ingenious, however, this flexibility may be sharply limited for the long run by our short-term handling of CHIREP.*

C. Japanese rearmament, including Japanese nuclear acquisition, has shot upward in Peking's publicly expressed concerns since the Nixon-Sato communiqué of 1969 expressing a Japanese "security" interest in Taiwan's future. Peking openly fears the inclusion of Taiwan and South Korea in a Japanese sphere of influence. It fears that U.S. policy is promoting this. It does not publicly recognize a mutual interest between China and the United States in non-proliferation, including non-acquisition by Japan. It speaks—shrilly but unconvincingly—of overturning "Japanese militarism" and the Mutual Security Treaty through social revolution in Japan. It would be useful if Peking one day could see that an atmosphere of conflict throughout Asia stimulates the political and hence military processes it opposes in Japan—and that U.S.-China relations weigh heavily in Japanese decisions on military and nuclear matters.

D. The Sino-Soviet dispute has been China's most active external concern. We can, if we choose, work on China's fears of U.S.-Soviet collusion at its expense. Or we might in time find ways to lessen China's apprehensions, if there were

---

*CHIREP is government jargon for the complex of issues concerning Chinese representation in the United Nations. Contractions such as this originated in the effort to minimize the costs of cable traffic between Washington and our embassies abroad. Gradually, they became a part of the spoken as well as the written language within the government. They are still widely used, even though the introduction of leased cable lines has removed their economic raison d'être, because they save time in reading, writing, and talking.

progress in Peking's dealings with us. Peking also sees (but not optimistically) a possibility for somehow using the United States against Russia. We have a similar, if equally ill-defined, interest in using relations with China to limit troublesome Soviet tendencies.

E. The problem for U.S. policy is pulling together these highly diverse considerations. The United States and China can each make life easier or more difficult for the other. How can we encourage movement in the desired direction? One requirement is that we look at the whole of U.S.-China relations—something hard to do under present governmental procedures.

F. This study proposes some points of departure for U.S. policy with enough promise to merit more detailed study within the government. For that purpose, they are presented in the form of policy planning exercises. They include ways by which, in very fine slices, the United States and China could get a better picture of each other and start moving gradually toward reducing tensions: The United States by showing concern for Peking's fears over Taiwan and U.S.-Soviet "collusion"; Peking by showing restraint in Southeast Asia; both governments by edging toward an environment that does not stimulate Japanese nuclear acquisition. Our steps should be taken as circumstances merit, after feeling out other governments—and particularly in the closest collaboration with Japan. More specifically they could include:

- A "clarification" of the U.S. attitude on Taiwan's status which would decouple three issues now badly intertwined: CHIREP, government recognition, and the territorial integrity of China. It would move us ever so slightly toward Peking's preferred "one China," without ending our defense commitment to the GRC.* We could make further small moves if Peking's responses warranted them. This prospect should be used to motivate Peking.

• A U.S. position on CHIREP that could allow us to acquiesce in Peking's admission, tacitly or overtly. It would be consistent with future U.S. movement toward a "one China" position, whether or not Taipei remains in the UN.

• Quiet but explicit U.S. encouragement to both Bangkok and Peking for a modest improvement in relations between them.

• An effort, directly or through an appropriate third party, to convey U.S. views (and explore Peking's) on the value of non-proliferation in Asia.

• An approach that could offset some Peking apprehensions about SALT.**

G. The government has special bureaucratic difficulties in dealing with China policy. China-related questions usually come to the policymaking level as part of another problem. Someone charged with Japan or Southeast Asia or military deployments has the action responsibility and structures the problem for decision. China as a whole does not come into focus. This makes it hard for senior policymakers to consider our long-term relationship with China as a basic element in overall policy. It also means that they too seldom demand the information, analysis, and explanations from China specialists needed as a basis for China policy. The result is much information from the specialists but too little policy relevance. To alleviate this problem, we propose:

• **The creation of a China Group at the policymaking level.** The group would meet periodically for discussions

---

*Government of the Republic of China, on Taiwan.

**Strategic Arms Limitation Talks, now underway between the Soviet Union and the United States.

and recommendations on China-related matters. Given the time limitations on its principals, the group's value will depend largely on the quality of its staff's work and their interactions with the specialist community.

- **Some papers for bridging the information gap.** These are intended as a simulation of the kinds of information and analytic demands that should be generated at the policymaking level. But better information processes alone will not provide an adequate basis for policy toward China.

H. To go further will also require that the United States and China deal with each other on matters affecting their important interests, however tentative and exploratory the initial moves. The policy departures recommended above are intended to begin this process. They are designed to have enough substance to evoke a meaningful response from Peking—without our paying a high price only to learn that Peking's attitude is unacceptable. They may not evoke such a response.

I. Better relations with China are a desirable, but not our most important, objective in Asia. We have other interests of greater priority there. But our ability to deal with China, for better or for worse, will affect all of them.

will be important if not dominating. China is acquiring nuclear weapons, and this will have its impact too. Finally, China is a major factor influencing U.S.-Soviet relations. As will be explained in more detail, a successful policy toward China could contribute in a major way toward attaining such important objectives as halting the proliferation of nuclear weapons, reducing the challenge to U.S. security interests posed by the Soviet Union, and minimizing the costs and risks of fulfilling our defense commitments in Southeast and Northeast Asia. These are the more compelling reasons for looking hard at our ability to develop long-term policy toward China.

A. Are better relations with China important to U.S. interests? There are too many sources of conflict between the United States and China for friendly relations between us to be a realistic prospect, even after a considerable period. On the other hand, "better" relations with China do not have to be "friendly" ones. Adversarial relations can take very different forms, some more advantageous to us than others. Our experience with the Russians illustrates this. They still pose the single most serious threat to our security. But the world would be much more dangerous today if U.S.-Soviet relations had remained as purely hostile in content as in the early postwar era (say, 1948-1952).

"Better" U.S.-Chinese relations mean improving the capability of the two countries to deal with each other on matters affecting their important interests. These interests are complex. Some are subject to the most fundamental kinds of misunderstandings, the kinds that lead to war. Who threatens whom? Peking and Washington look differently at Southeast Asia, Japan, Taiwan, the two Koreas, and U.S.-Soviet efforts toward détente.

Improved communications alone, however essential, will

not suffice to deal with such issues. To get by the ideological and bureaucratic barriers now separating the two governments, there must be some evidence that *give-and-take* is a practical matter for them. But give-and-take (as opposed to brinkmanship) also demands a more rounded relationship than we have had so far. As later chapters will show, achieving such a relationship is no simple matter. Yet lacking it, communications alone are likely to be a diatribe without positive results.

In the past, problems with China have come up unexpectedly and with great intensity. Examples are Chinese entry into the Korean war in 1950, the Taiwan Straits crises of 1954-1955 and 1958, and the Sino-Indian border dispute of 1962. Some of these episodes were agonizing for us (and for China too, no doubt). All had to be handled by improvisation, with little insight into Chinese motivation and few means in hand to influence their course other than nerve and military strength. The future may hold more such cases as the Indochina war grinds down, as China acquires nuclear delivery means, and as the Nixon Doctrine is tested and challenged in Asia.

Cultural or athletic exchanges, trips by journalists and other visitors, intergovernmental talks about unimportant matters may lead to improved communications and have side benefits of their own. But they do not get at political and military matters and should not be taken as substitutes for a serious effort to achieve a more rounded relationship. Furthermore, dealings in relatively unimportant matters influence the atmosphere more than the fundamentals of the relationship. For this reason they tend to be used tactically by both sides and are subject to sudden reversal when more basic objectives require or unrelated events intervene. For example, a blossoming of atmospheric warmth in U.S.-China relations might, among other things, increase the willingness of UN members to vote Peking in and Taiwan out. Would this be followed by more warmth and a more basic improvement in our relationship? Perhaps it would. But the opposite might happen if Peking then changed tactics to achieve some other interim objective. Atmospherics, like communications alone, lack the self-sustaining momentum of serious dealings about the more fundamental issues. What is needed is an effort to begin to compose our differences with Peking on these fundamentals.

B. Are the potential benefits of better relations worth the cost of seeking them? Posed abstractly, there is no simple answer, because the benefits tend to be distant and uncertain, the costs often present and real. The solution for policy, therefore, is to set a very modest limit to the costs we should initially be willing to incur. Subject to that constraint, we want to find policy moves that maximize the likelihood of evoking a useful response from Peking. Two essential ingredients for this effort are information about China that is relevant to policy issues and ingenuity in policy design. This study is a search for these two ingredients, through both the evaluation of substantive policy issues and a critical analysis of present policymaking procedures.

These ingredients, of course, are necessary but not sufficient to produce good policy. There are a host of other factors, domestic as well as foreign, that may dominate policy decisions in the end. But the policymaker is entitled to the tools of his trade: good information and good policy options to consider.

C. Purpose and organization of the book. The study makes three kinds of recommendations:

1. Policy proposals. These are steps we think the United States probably should take soon. "Probably" implies an uncertainty that can be resolved by the kind of multi-factor scrutiny only the government can do. For this reason, these proposals are cast in the form of policy planning exercises, to be carried out more comprehensively within the government.

2. Organizational proposals. We consider these the most important, perhaps the only really important, recommendations. The U.S. government is action oriented and, typically, reactive to external events more often than innovative in its policymaking. All of this gives it a short time horizon for practical planning and too little opportunity for contemplation or hard-headed appraisal of long-term developments. But dealing adequately with U.S.-China relations requires precisely this long perspective, both in the intellectual building blocks needed from the China specialists and in the way that policymakers address their problems. Without changes in organization and procedures, we doubt that the government could adopt the other proposals we make, even if it very much wanted to.

3. Research and intelligence studies. Some of these would mainly repackage information already known to specialists by putting it into a form that policymakers will find intelligible and useful. Others would aim at adding missing pieces to a picture largely known, so as to move it from "interesting" to "policy relevant." The work needed for both of these kinds of studies can be specified in advance with reasonable precision.

A third kind of study would attempt to break new ground. It is the most important kind and also the most difficult. We may feel some confidence that the subject matter contains pay dirt, but until we explore further we will not be able to specify the best questions to ask or the best research design for answering them. For these, we propose "starter sets" of questions, understanding that future work, if it is good, should turn up new lines of attack and new subject matter more promising than our points of departure.

The discussion that follows is divided into two parts. Part I deals with the policy problems of interacting with Peking: with respect to Taiwan, Northeast Asia, Southeast Asia, and the Sino-Soviet dispute (Chapters 1-4) and in more general terms (Chapters 5-7). Each of the first four chapters lays out the main policy issues affecting the United States and China. Each recommends some research and intelligence studies and identifies some areas in which the prospects for beginning a more rounded relationship with China can probably be discovered only through active policy explorations by the United States. For such explorations we recommend tactical approaches, formulated as policy planning exercises. Some special complexities of U.S.-Chinese interaction are appraised in Chapter 5. Where all these moves might lead us is sketched briefly and tentatively in Chapter 6. The pace at which we should move is discussed in Chapter 7.

Part II analyzes some of the bureaucratic difficulties posed for the U.S. government by China policy. It treats the problems of developing policy-relevant information about China (Chapter 8) and the necessity to use policy explorations as well as research and intelligence means (Chapter 9). It concludes with recommendations for improved procedures (Chapters 10 and 11).

Part I | Problems of Policy

1 | Taiwan

The United States is not about to abandon its commitment to the Government of the Republic of China (GRC) to defend Taiwan and the Pescadores. Yet Peking again and again insists that our accepting its claims to Taiwan must be the starting point for any improvement in relations. In seeking such an improvement, then, are we simply trying to eat our cake and have it, too? Or is there a route for seeking better relations that still permits the Taiwan problem to be passed on to the uncertainties of a distant future? Perhaps there is, though the passage of time need not make it easier to *start* down this route, as some believe.

A. Peking's position. Peking maintains that Taiwan is part of China and that the United States forcibly deprives it of access to its own territory. It supports this argument by quoting our official pre-Korean war position, which did specify Taiwan as Chinese and the fighting between the Communists and the GRC as a civil war.* "Solution of the Taiwan

---

*See Documents 3-6 for the evolution of the official U.S. position on Taiwan's status.

issue in principle" is demanded by Peking as the test of our sincerity.

Specifically, Peking has officially formulated two "principles": "1. The United States must withdraw all its armed forces from the Taiwan Straits; 2. Sino-U.S. relations must be based on the Five Principles of Peaceful Coexistence." Since one of the Five Principles is respect for territorial integrity—and Peking claims Taiwan as Chinese territory—this is a tricky package to interpret. Much that is crucial is left unspecified. Does this convey Chinese flexibility? Or craftiness?

Whatever its current demands, Peking has not always been so principled. In the 1950s it was willing to deal first on other issues. Even then, however, it seemed not so much to want a better relationship with us as to undermine the GRC.* Recent attempts by us to work on other problems first—on grounds that a better atmosphere is needed or that we should solve whatever problems we can—have been rebuffed as an effort to create a status quo in which Taiwan is permanently estranged from Mainland China.

How firm Peking's position really is remains to be seen. Time may not be on China's side. Peking's leaders may feel the United States must eventually withdraw and leave Taiwan to its fate, but they also must have deep doubts about a resurgent Japan's growing interest in Taiwan. They have expressed fears that Taiwan would again enter a "Japanese sphere of influence" and about an independent Taiwanese republic protected by Japan. Concerned with reducing the likelihood of these eventualities, Peking might respond to partial solutions "in principle" that fell well short of actual

---

*See Documents 7-9 for an effort by Peking to bring about a U.S.-Chinese Communist foreign ministers' conference while leaving the issue of Taiwan blurred.

reversion of Taiwan to the mainland at an early date—or even any fixed date at all.

B. Possible compromises. There are several potential directions of accommodation: "two Chinas"; "one China, one Taiwan"; U.S. flexibility on other issues, unaccompanied by any change in our policy toward Taiwan; or "one China but not now."

"Two Chinas" and "one China, one Taiwan" arrangements have built up a considerable following in non-Chinese circles, especially the United States and Japan. Such solutions, it is argued, merely reflect current realities or, for "one China, one Taiwan," an emerging reality; Peking (but not we) will just have to adjust to reality. In the end, so it may be.

One difficulty to these solutions is that both Peking and the GRC oppose them. A more consequential problem is that they would commit the United States or Japan indefinitely to providing a military shield for Taiwan. Such flexibility as we have now would be dissipated.

Peking's present strategy focuses on obtaining recognition as the sole Chinese government and replacing the GRC in the UN. Peking is making progress and would actively oppose anything that encourages other governments toward either "two Chinas" or "one China, one Taiwan." The mere prospect of our moving toward either of these positions—however obliquely and whether intended by us or merely suspected by Peking—produces a response from Peking verging on paranoia. Peking's reactions no doubt reflect its preoccupation with the Taiwan issue and are consistent with its overall strategy focused on minimizing the future likelihood of permanent alienation of Taiwan from the mainland. Our commitment to either policy now would seriously aggravate relations with Peking, rather than improve them. It would take a bold man to predict that such a deterioration in relations now would lead to improvements later on. (See Chapter 7 for more on the problem of timing.)

U.S. flexibility unaccompanied by movement on the Taiwan issue would also run afoul of Peking's current strategy, but at least it would not in itself make our relations worse. If the recent past is any guide, though, this policy would defer the prospects for a fundamental improvement in relations—leaving them to the uncertainties of the future. The atmosphere might improve. Better communications might be established. But these things are subject to sudden tactical shifts. They could shortly be reversed or even used to our disadvantage, if Peking does indeed give the priority it proclaims to the Taiwan issue. For the United States to pursue the more basic objectives that might be obtained from a better relationship with Peking, therefore, it may well be necessary to show at least some willingness to address the Taiwan issue.

A policy of "one China but not now" might be viewed in Peking as a small step toward its preferred direction—especially if endorsed by Japan, because future Japanese governments would then find it more difficult to extend their protection to Taiwan. Later we set forth a specific proposal embodying the mechanics of a "one China but not now" policy. The essentials of this policy are simple enough: nominal recognition of the territorial integrity of China including Taiwan, but no de facto reversion at present. Would this have any meaning for Peking's leaders?

Peking's hopes for recovering Taiwan must rest on developments in the future. It is not in Peking's power to get what it wants now. Today's policies, therefore, must focus on increasing tomorrow's prospects. The GRC must live in the present, as must we. For now, actual reunification is neither feasible nor desirable, but the difference in time perspectives between Peking and us allows room for maneuver.

What happens between now and the future depends largely on U.S. policies. Some can increase the probability of future reunification; others (such as formal U.S. commitment to a "two Chinas" position) can greatly reduce it. Logically, Peking should have an interest in seeing the United States take successive steps that increase the probability of reunification, even though many more such steps may be needed before the probability even approaches certainty. Whether Peking is likely to view the matter this "logically" and act accordingly is unknown. Realistically, very small steps now are as much as Peking can expect. We can try a few small steps in this direction without committing ourselves to any final outcome. In this way, Peking's reactions could be tested.

Peking would be left to wonder whether our new position betokened anything more for the future than perpetual delay, given that our defense commitment to the GRC would initially remain valid. Our answer could only be that future movement hinged on Peking's future conduct—both with respect to *our* other interests and in making reunification more acceptable *to the people on Taiwan*. We would have to make credible our ability and our willingness to move further under the right circumstances. With Japanese cooperation, there is no reason why this should not be feasible.

We cannot anticipate accurately what Peking's response would be nor when it would come—if ever. That is why our first steps would have to be cautious and planned to permit retreat. Similarly, even if Peking is interested, its initial response is likely to be equally slight. The steps on both sides can only be small and often faltering. This is one reason that we should think of the whole process as requiring a long span of time. And there are other reasons of even greater importance for going slowly.

The most important is that we want the *future* prospect of recovering Taiwan to continue as an incentive for Peking during a long enough time to establish stable, peaceful relations elsewhere in Asia. We want to see a pattern emerge and take root with promise for the future as well as the here and now. (Ways in which that might happen are discussed in Chapters 2 and 3.)

The second reason for going slow is that it will take a great deal of time for all the accommodations of attitude and circumstance necessary to protect the welfare of the people on Taiwan. The prospects now may look bleak, but over a long enough interval much can happen. For example, a more flexible leadership in Peking could adopt a policy of "small steps" toward reconciliation, in the pattern now used by West Germany toward East Germany. If the United States (and Japan) gave both positive encouragement and reassurances, a future regime on Taiwan might ultimately find the confidence and the motivation to respond—cautiously, selectively, and guardedly, to be sure. The next few decades seem likely to witness some important innovations in the relations between such divided states as the two Germanys—perhaps modes of federation that do not rigidly impose either side's social or political peculiarities on the other.

With a long enough time horizon, it need not exceed the ingenuity of man to devise arrangements that can be accepted as reunification by Peking but adequately protect the welfare of the people on Taiwan.

Finally, there is the matter of our Mutual Security Treaty with the GRC. The treaty provides for cancellation by either party on one year's notice, but even the narrowest calculation of our self-interest warns us against an abrupt termination of any such commitment. Too many of our hopes for world peace depend on maintaining our reliability in such matters. But that does not mean that a commitment once made can never be altered. A foreign policy based on that principle would be rigid to the point of recklessness. Still, changes in our commitments must occur only under reasonable and honorable conditions and only as our reasons for change are understood and accepted by others. That takes time—time well spent. But if our other allies in Asia see their security improving, if Peking really tries to create suitable conditions for the people on Taiwan, and if the latter gradually realize that they too must accommodate, our military commitment to the GRC might no longer be necessary.

Peking has often stressed its ability to wait for its desired outcomes. We should put its patience to the test.

But any willingness to compromise with Peking incurs costs, and these must be weighed, not necessarily before some exploration of Peking's attitude but before we commit ourselves to any long-term course.

C. Problems on Taiwan. The resolution of Taiwan's relation to the mainland is necessarily a long-term problem. The possible dangers in the short run could only come from the GRC's developing suicidal tendencies (notably lacking in the past) or the growth of political instability on Taiwan. Both are unlikely, although either in large doses could be damaging to our prestige and posture.

The GRC will be alarmed by any U.S. movement on Taiwan's status. It will fear for its international position. It will look for signs that U.S. movement marks the beginning of the end. While it is looking, it will gradually perceive that nothing concrete has changed. Daily life on Taiwan goes on much as before. The future appears more uncertain, but the present remains preferable to any available alternative.

The GRC might attempt to embroil the United States by conducting provocative attacks on the mainland or pressure us by acts against our people and property on Taiwan. Such actions, particularly the former, seem unlikely, however, since we have made clear that we would not consider ourselves bound by our Mutual Defense Treaty if the GRC provoked a Chinese Communist attack.

While President Chiang lives, a GRC-Peking "deal" is quite unlikely. One conceivably might develop later, but that will be largely contingent on what happens between now and then—U.S. policy being a major determinant. We can stand fast, leaving Taiwan's status unchanged in actuality; or we can allow or even encourage Peking-Taipei accommodation, should circumstances merit.

There is another important prospect. The GRC is already militarily strong. Its existing forces could make an attack on Taiwan extremely costly. Given access to sources of military equipment, it might soon be able to defend itself against all but nuclear attack. This development will occur (or not) independently of our official position on Taiwan's status. Whether it happens or not, therefore, we still want a position on Taiwan's status that is most likely to permit us better relations with Peking. If Taiwan becomes militarily self-sufficient, we would not be needed and we should therefore act to remove the Taiwan issue as an obstacle to better U.S.-China relations.

The problem of political stability also centers on the Taiwanese. They, at least the more sophisticated, recognize that GRC rule gives them protection against the mainland because it provides the rationale for a U.S. shield. Should the United States appear to move toward accommodation with Peking over Taiwan, the Taiwanese would be torn in several directions. Taiwanese hopes of inheriting the U.S. commitment from the GRC through an independence movement would be reduced, making continued GRC rule all the more indispensable. At the same time, the GRC would lose face, exacerbating anti-GRC sentiment. Some Taiwanese would try to turn to Japan. Finally, some Taiwanese would wonder if they should not seek accommodation with the mainland on their own, because of uncertainties about the future.

Much would depend on how well the GRC handles itself, particularly on the state of the Taiwan economy and developments that may follow President Chiang's death. The former would still offer profits and security competitive with Hong Kong, given proper GRC economic policies. The process by which we move toward accommodation with Peking, the consultations and advance notice we give the GRC, our rhetoric, and any countervailing moves will be important.

Many Americans are concerned over a moral commitment they feel has been built up over the years to Taiwanese welfare and to the general principle of self-rule. Problems such as Taiwan are difficult because they are laced with opposing principles and values, for example the principle of self-determination as opposed to the principle of upholding the territorial integrity of other countries. GRC policies and political realities on Taiwan virtually preclude the evolution of self-government for the people on Taiwan. Peking, like the GRC, insists that Taiwan is part of China, and prior to the Korean war we were prepared to accept this. Even assuming the United States were in a position to bring about a resolution of this problem, are we prepared and able to carry through the military responsibilities this would involve for the future? Clearly there is no way to unravel this problem—except over time, as changing circumstances allow.

D. Japan's role. Even the beginning of U.S. movement on the Taiwan issue will raise questions about the durability of U.S. commitments. Thailand, South Vietnam, and South

Korea will worry, but their attitudes hinge mainly on their bilateral relations with us. Our greatest concern will be with the reaction of the Japanese, whose interest in Taiwan is much more direct and whose foreign and defense policies could be seriously affected.

The Japanese would view any "solution to the Taiwan question" with mixed feelings. Many would be relieved over the reduced likelihood of conflict in Asia. Many would be pleased to see some "movement" on the China issue, especially if the Japanese government participates. However, most Japanese would be very uneasy over an accommodation that threatened to turn Taiwan over to the mainland at any early date. Japanese feelings derive mainly from a large and growing economic stake and emotional ties from their occupation of Taiwan. Strategic considerations may be invested with importance as the Japanese reoccupy Okinawa, nationalism increases, and the U.S. presence in Asia declines. Feelings about Taiwan, the GRC, and Chiang personally run deep in important segments of the Liberal Democratic Party and the business community.

Japanese reaction to any U.S. try at accommodating with Peking on the Taiwan issue may turn on timing. A U.S.-Chinese accommodation may or may not be welcomed by the present Japanese leadership. Undertaking almost any process of adjustment, however, will grow more difficult as Japanese interests in Taiwan increase, as Japan becomes economically and militarily stronger, and as Japanese attitudes and political leaders change. Indeed as time passes, the problem of Taiwan will become less one to be dealt with between the United States and China alone and more a triangular problem with declining freedom of action for all of the parties.

E. Taiwan as a U.S. base? The reversion of Okinawa,

including the removal of nuclear weapons and the uncertainties about U.S. bases elsewhere in the Pacific, suggests the use of Taiwan basing, particularly for a Southeast Asia contingency. Taiwan at present offers a hospitable political climate for constructing such bases. Preliminary studies indicate cost advantages—an important consideration. An increased reliance on Taiwan, however, would also make the United States vulnerable to GRC intransigence. And if we make Taiwan a vital military base, either piecemeal or as part of a larger plan, our general military posture in the Pacific will be at stake or stand in the way of any accommodation with Peking over the Taiwan issue.

It may be possible to relocate some military functions to Taiwan without upsetting Peking—we do not know. There is little doubt that putting a large U.S. military presence on Taiwan would have to be read in Peking as a forceful, negative response to the two "principles" we have been asked to accept. This would certainly increase the difficulties of compromising with Peking over Taiwan. It might rule out all negotiations.

The issue has many ramifications. Two are worth noting:

• The *implicit* threat (as opposed to the actuality) of increasing our military presence on Taiwan may make Peking less unyielding.

• Peking might react with violence to a large U.S. military build-up on Taiwan, for example, by precipitating a crisis over Quemoy and Matsu. Even if the islands were successfully defended, the political fallout in the United States and throughout the world could be unpleasant to experience. Or Peking might react with a larger, more overt role in the insurgencies of Southeast Asia. A Southeast Asian contingency (guerrilla war) for which we are ill-prepared could be triggered by our preparing Taiwan for a

Southeast Asia contingency (conventional attack) that does not occur.

F. CHIREP. After 20 years of heavy wear, a U.S. policy seemed to reach a dead end when the UN General Assembly majority voted in November 1970 to seat Peking in place of the GRC.* A crisis in a long-standing policy tends to rivet bureaucratic attention on the need for repairs. This could propel us to treat CHIREP as primarily a UN issue, giving inadequate weight to its broader consequences. The closeness of New York will reinforce this tendency. Trying to protect our national and even Presidential prestige in the UN context alone, however, could well expose it to much greater damage elsewhere.

More is involved than who represents China in the UN. Peking's entrance into the UN, whether or not the GRC remains, will not immediately affect the fundamental power situation in Asia, but it will stimulate a process of change for the United States and the whole world. The issues go to the heart of China policy and beyond. Involved are:

• The possibilities of better U.S. relations with Peking. How should we relate (or decouple) CHIREP and the status of Taiwan—or, as Peking and Taipei claim, the "territorial integrity of China"?

• U.S.-GRC relations. How do we minimize frictions with Taipei, without closing options for approaching Peking?

• U.S.-Japanese relations. UN movement toward accept-

---

*Because the General Assembly had earlier voted this an "important question," the simple majority received by Peking was insufficient to transfer the seat to it from the GRC; the necessary two-thirds was not obtained. However, 1970 was the first year with even a simple majority for Peking and therefore a harbinger that the policy planning premises of the past were losing their reliability.

ing Peking will lead to increased political pressures on the Japanese government to bring its policy into line with world public opinion. It will want to accommodate to these pressures without straining its ties to the GRC. Is there a position that fills both our needs and theirs?

- Universality of UN membership. This theme is very much in the air. But do we want our handling of CHIREP to be a decisive factor in our ability to deal with the future status of Germany and Berlin and our relations with South Korea? Do we want to adopt the "two Chinas" overtones of universality? Universality implies the simultaneous admission of divided states, which in turn makes the permanence of their division that much more likely. It would be a big step toward "two Chinas."

- Public criticism of the UN in the United States. How do we minimize the present erosion of support for the UN in the United States, given the momentum now developing for Peking's entry?

There are many issues of policy and intent to be solved. The key operational ones are how hard and long do we fight to keep the GRC in the UN and on what grounds?

- **We should fight hard enough to show our heart is in the right place.** But we should not expect to find an ingenious route to victory. It is clear that Peking will not cooperate. Its strategy is to force the UN to choose between it and the GRC. Faced with this simple choice, the UN members are all too likely to choose Peking no matter what we do or how good our arguments are in principle. Therefore, we should not stake too much prestige nor arouse the U.S. public on a matter this risky. Indeed the long history of the issue and the expectation of change has already taken much of the sting out of developments contrary to our preference. In the long run, the intensity with which we push our position may have a greater effect on our larger interests than the details of the position itself. Peking is likely to gauge the seriousness of our opposition (and the U.S. public the seriousness of any defeat we risk) mainly from the magnitude of our efforts. Besides, the GRC cause may not be furthered by too much U.S. arm twisting. (Peking may itself stumble badly enough to stave off the issue for us, but this possibility does not require us to take a vulnerable posture on our own.) Our policy stance should also enable us to avoid unseemly parliamentary gyrations in the UN.

• **Our grounds should be consistent with those preferred by the GRC,** which means they cannot challenge GRC legitimacy by violating its basic governmental writ. The GRC will have to judge how much flexibility it can accept. We should not coerce or bribe it to adopt a formulation of ours. Should Taipei insist, we should even consider staying with our previous position. But Taipei would then have to accept responsibility for the outcome and our publicly playing down the importance of the issue, given the possibility of losing. There would, of course, be serious public relations problems involved with maintaining the previous position. The Administration might find it difficult to stand firm against press and Congressional charges of immobilism and bowing to the whims of the GRC. Working out an acceptable public posture would be a prerequisite to going this route.

The specifics of our CHIREP position, then, have to be developed as we go along in close consultation with both Taipei and Tokyo, and therefore this study proposes no details. However they evolve, though, they would automatically turn out to be consistent with a U.S. policy of "one China but not now" so far as Taiwan's status is concerned. This will happen because the GRC's rationale must contain some form of reaffirmation of China's territorial integrity. It will also be in keeping with the official Japanese position favoring peace-

ful unification of divided states, stated by Prime Minister
Sato in his October 1970 UN address.

G. Substantive Study Proposals

1. We should and could know more about how the Japanese regard the Taiwan issue and our potential handling of
it. We need to understand not only the views of present
government leaders but the attitudes of others in positions
of public responsibility—political rivals of the present leadership (both within and without the Liberal Democratic
Party), non-governmental opinion makers, and the like. We
need to understand how their views are changing and how
they would weigh the pluses and minuses of alternative U.S.
policies, in terms of the consequences for Japan and for their
personal objectives. This could be done through informal as
well as formal contacts and also through research. It might
be wise to do some of the research first. But the issue is of
great importance to both countries. We each know the kinds
(if not the details) of questions and policy options that must
be under review by the other. We would gain little and could
lose much by being coy instead of candid in communicating
on the matter. Illustrations of the issues to be explored include:

• In what ways, if at all, is Taiwan considered important
to Japanese security? By whom? For what reasons? How is
this changing?

• What might be Japanese reactions to our relocating
military facilities from Japan and Okinawa to Taiwan?

• What are probable Japanese reactions to a U.S. move
toward some form of "one China but not now" policy? Would
the Japanese government be likely to follow suit? What
might be the domestic political reactions in Japan? Who
might approve? Who disapprove? For what reasons?

- What is the range of Japanese attitudes toward a role for their government in Taiwan's defense?

2. Mainland China. We would like to know more about the real feelings of Peking's leaders on the Taiwan issue, but this kind of information is unlikely to be obtained by research and intelligence alone. We can perhaps strengthen the basis for our efforts to explore their attitudes via policy moves, however, by looking at such questions as:

- Is there any evidence to suggest that Taiwan may not in fact have the primary importance accorded it in Peking's public statements?

- Is there evidence of differences of view among Chinese leaders on the Taiwan issue?

- Are there any significant differences between Peking's position on the disposition of Taiwan, as expressed to the U.S. government and to others, in private or official capacities?

- Have there been any differences in Peking's discussions, either public or private, of the U.S. military presence in Taiwan or changes in that presence?

H. Policy Planning Proposal: "One China but not now"

Efforts to improve relations with Peking by putting aside the Taiwan issue may or may not succeed. Peking keeps saying they won't. We keep trying. But we should have another string to our bow. If we are to explore a "solution to the Taiwan issue in principle" with Peking, we need an approach that meets demanding standards. It must be consistent with our contractual obligation to the GRC to defend Taiwan and the Pescadores. It must be at least tolerable to the Japanese government, though preferably it would have their support. The problems it may raise in certain other countries must be manageable. It must contain something Peking might view as of substantive interest.

More specifically, the United States might clarify its current position (as stated in Document 3 in the Appendix) that the "future status" of Taiwan awaits determination, which now carries the implication that it will be settled through *international* negotiations. The clarification would indicate that our position is based on unresolved differences between the authorities in Peking and the GRC. Taiwan's status is therefore a matter to be decided between them. Our understanding is that both regard Taiwan as a part of China, though in practical terms this appears to have different implications for each of them. We accept their views on Taiwan being a part of China and indeed would agree to any peaceful resolution between them of remaining differences, however distant the prospect now seems. (No international negotiations are required.) Meanwhile, though, we will honor our contractual obligation to the GRC to defend Taiwan and the Pescadores. While modest enough in practical consequence, this "clarification" would mark a significant nominal change over the position reflected in the peace treaty with Japan, which does not accept Taiwan as part of China and holds open the possibility of an independent Taiwan with U.S. or Japanese protection.

Further elucidation of this position would depend on reactions in Peking, Taipei, and elsewhere. If these reactions merited further movement on our part, there are any number of small additional steps we could take. The process is open-ended. For example, we could add that the permanent alienation of Taiwan from the mainland "is not U.S. policy"; or later, if warranted, "is contrary to U.S. policy"; and so on. We could reduce the U.S. military presence on Taiwan, eventually even eliminate it. In each case, the step would require Japanese government concurrence and have greatly increased weight with its overt support.

Such a policy stance raises a number of collateral questions:

- What do we want from Peking in response? How much would Peking have to do for us to go further? What is the best way to first broach our proposal to Peking? How might we convey that further evolution on the Taiwan issue could be forthcoming if Peking's conduct led to reduced tensions in Southeast Asia and Northeast Asia?

- How do we indicate to our allies in Southeast Asia and Northeast Asia that a first step by us on the Taiwan issue does not imply the inevitability of additional steps? How do we make clear that further steps by us are contingent upon *increased* security for them?

- What do we say and when in Tokyo? In Taipei? In Bangkok? In other places?

- What countermeasures should we have in store to offset adverse reactions in non-Communist Asia? How might these look to Peking?

2 | Japan and Korea

The Japanese expect their GNP to approach that of Russia by 1980. They can soon afford the finest weapons money can buy, and their neighbors, especially China (to say nothing of North Korea), are coming to view them with corresponding apprehension. Recent Japanese visitors to Peking have expressed shock at the intensity of Chinese feeling.* The Russians, too, have begun to express their concern with rising frequency. Both Russia and China will be looking toward this future prospect as they shape their current political and military positions. What are the options for Japan as she feels herself becoming the target of their policies and weapons? And what is our role in moving her toward options acceptable to us?

In contrast to the situation in the 1950s and 1960s, in the coming years East Asia will be more and more shaped by the interaction of four powers. In practical terms U.S. policymakers will have difficulties coming to grips with this new situation. Complexity multiplies. Long-term factors become

*See Documents 11-12 on Peking's fears of a rearmed Japan.

particularly important, and these are inherently difficult for policy formulation.

A. Preserving the U.S.-Japanese relationship. Our principal concern in Asia is to maintain our present friendly relationship with Japan as long as possible. This will not be easy. Rapid economic growth and rising nationalism are bound to change the low profile of Japan's international role. Our main concern here is with the extent to which Japan will play a military role in world affairs. This can be decided only by Japanese political forces. And these in turn will be driven by what happens inside Japan and by how the Japanese look at the rest of the world, especially the United States and its policies in Asia.

Some deterioration in the Japanese-U.S. relationship has begun. The potential for friction between the two countries is great. Anti-Americanism has some roots in every part of Japanese society—rightist, leftist, and neutralist. The business community objects strongly to our trend toward protectionism and fears domination by U.S. investment in Japan. Leftists and pacifists resent our attitude toward Peking and the encouragement they think we give to Japanese "militarism." For reasons of national pride, opposition is growing to bases under the U.S. flag. As they pass inevitably under Japanese control or even joint tenure, our use of them will be increasingly controlled by the Japanese government according to its views of Japanese interests, which may conflict with our preferences.

Any or all of these frictions can gather momentum, reinforcing each other in the process. Any or all of them can weaken the less formal but more binding cement that ties the alliance. They involve difficult domestic issues. And despite an increasing familiarity with each other's political system, each of us is easily lulled into believing we cannot manage our own domestic political problem, but the other side can.

B. Japan has begun to rearm. So far, the Japanese public has accepted as a goal only the defense of its own homeland. There are influential groups that would like to do more. There is a natural momentum toward nuclear acquisition generated by the perceived security needs, great-power ambitions of many Japanese, and industrial interests now expanding peaceful nuclear production. There are also numerous constraints on an increase in Japan's military power, particularly nuclear power. Many Japanese emphasize painful recollections of World War II, constitutional restrictions, the lack of fear of a conventional Chinese attack because of their island position, and their dread of falling again under military rule. Requirements for domestic spending are also going up and may accelerate.

It might lighten our burden if Japan took more responsibility for its own security and perhaps that of South Korea and Taiwan. Whether it would help us or not, the Japanese may not care to do so. Even if we persuaded Japan, the political processes that led the Japanese public to accept these goals are likely to stimulate other political forces and aspirations, too. It would be quite unrealistic to expect Japan to significantly expand its military establishment but limit it to conventional weapons only. Once the Japanese political system has accepted the need and accompanying rationale for military goals, sharpening the hostility of China and no doubt Russia in the process, will not the Japanese public follow those leaders who argue that Japan's safety requires a complete arsenal, nuclear weapons, and full great-power status? Will not present confidence in the U.S. nuclear shield be undermined?

A large expansion of Japanese military power, particularly with nuclear weapons, would profoundly change the current power balance in Asia. Certainly the now latent fears of a militarist Japan would reappear in full bloom. New alignments could emerge, some perhaps quite disadvantageous to us. We cannot foresee Japan's course under those circumstances, but certainly the main element of our posture in the Pacific (friendship and alliance with Japan) would turn into a management problem—perhaps of unmanageable dimensions.

The United States does not face a watershed decision but a continuing process of policy evolution. As we go along, we must take full account of factors that will influence Japanese domestic politics. We must be especially responsive to those friends among rival Japanese leaders who have bound their political fate to alliance and military interdependence with the United States. They have the greatest common interest with us in maintaining the present relationship. To the extent that we create political problems for them, we may contribute to changing their attitude toward us or to their being replaced by others supporting different policies.

We will have to work with our friends on a whole range of difficult issues. Some are military, some economic. The latter, in fact, are now the most pressing and may even prove most decisive in the relationship. This situation will require an unusual degree of candor, which neither side should avoid out of human weakness or the temptation to leave unpleasant matters for the future. Dealing with China will be one of these issues, because Japan's concern about our relations with China (as well as her own) will weigh heavily in Japan's politics and, therefore, in determining her foreign and defense policies. Two additional requirements in considering the U.S.-China relationship are generated: better information and analysis of Japanese attitudes and motivation, and the most careful evaluation of the costs and benefits for Japan of our efforts to reduce the dangers in U.S.-China hostility.

C. U.S.-China relations and their consequences for Japan. The credibility of our commitment to defend Japan—and hence the durability of the present satisfactory U.S.-Japanese relationship—is strengthened both by our displaying firmness toward China and, paradoxically, by reducing Chinese motives for conflict with us or Japan. Performing to these standards will not be easy. Their contradictory requirements could make our intentions misunderstood by the Chinese or the Japanese or both.

If we appear less opposed to an enlarged role for Peking with respect to the governments of Southeast Asia, reduce our presence in Korea, and soften our stand on the Taiwan issue, the Japanese will wonder where it will all end. Are they seeing the beginning of U.S. withdrawal from Asia willy-nilly? Or do developments in U.S.-China relations warrant this change of position? What conclusions should they draw for their own defense needs? Measures we might take to reassure them could easily be viewed by the Chinese as menacing. While perhaps seeming to reassure the Japanese in the short term, they could arouse U.S.-China tensions and serve to strengthen Japanese fears in the long run.

Quite possibly the confluence of Japanese nationalism, affluence, and doubts about the United States will leave us little we can do. But Japan's course will be greatly influenced by Peking, and Peking too may misread our intentions. For example, what if we try to adjust to Japanese nationalism by shifting certain military functions from Japan and Okinawa to South Korea? (There is little doubt of how the Chinese would view the move of such functions to Taiwan.) A move to South Korea would increase our presence on the Asian mainland and could signal our intention to stay there indefinitely. China might take it as a further U.S. threat. But it yields to Japanese nationalism without generating additional pressure for Japanese rearmament by undermining our security guarantee. Could Peking conceivably view this as tolerable? This in part depends on a reading of our general intentions in the area. Even in the unlikely event that the Chinese saw benefits in it, would they convey their recognition to us?

But whatever Peking's response to our posture and explanations, Japan will face a China with a growing nuclear arsenal. Peking has already hinted at the possible use of nuclear weapons against Japan if the Japanese allow their soil to be used for "war against China" and will soon be able to target many of Japan's major industrial cities. What are Japan's choices? There are at least three.

Conceivably, Japan could choose neutralism (perhaps decorated with concessions to China) without its own nuclear arms. But this is quite unlikely.

It can build nuclear weapons, with or without retaining its alliance with us. Obviously, we would prefer to retain our friendship with a nuclear Japan. But Japan could become not just another nuclear power, it could be a major one. And that would produce very serious consequences indeed. It would not only sink the NPT,* but it would change the world's balance of terror in ways we have scarcely explored analytically, let alone evaluated. We should do the analysis, but probably no evaluation can be reached because of the great inherent uncertainties. In any event three successive

---

*The Non-Proliferation Treaty, intended to build a world consensus that would halt the spread of nuclear weapons. To take effect, the treaty must be both signed and ratified by adhering nations. Many have signed, but few have ratified (Japan has not yet ratified, for example). Potential adherents are waiting to see what others will do and what else may happen in the world.

presidents have adopted non-proliferation as a major and a general U.S. policy objective. If our government is serious about halting the spread of nuclear weapons, this goal must find a serious mode of expression in our policies. Unless we mean to abandon non-proliferation, we should make good use of the period in which nuclear weapons are still anathema in Japan. The last thing we want is a policy rift between Washington and Tokyo on Japanese nuclear acquisition. To avoid this, we need an Asian environment that does not force the issue.

If we want Japan to forgo nuclear weapons, we must try to reduce the Japanese risk of relying exclusively on our nuclear shield. Relying on U.S. protection involves some risk of Japan's being left at China's mercy. Japanese fears will increase when China finally deploys ICBMs and has its own deterrent against the United States. Will the United States put an American city at risk to protect Japan?

U.S. firmness and détente with respect to China are the needed ingredients to reassure Japan. Firmness, to underline the durability of our commitment; détente, to minimize the strains imposed upon it as Chinese nuclear strength grows. This combination will be easier to achieve if we start to seek détente before the Chinese have ICBMs.

Thus Peking, Tokyo, and Washington may have a common interest in reducing tensions in Asia. Properly perceived, this could be the most important incentive of all for Peking to want better relations with us *and* Japan. All this may be true, but it should not be taken as self-evident to all parties. Even less should it be taken as self-evident that every step *we* take in pursuit of that goal will be properly understood and hence productive. There is the danger, for example, that once we set our sights on a goal (such as non-proliferation) the bureaucracy will pursue it with an intensity that raises Japanese tempers rather than lowers Asian tensions. We do not want to relive with the Japanese government our unhappy experience with de Gaulle.

How we discourse with Peking and the degree to which we take the Japanese government into our confidence in our dealings with China will profoundly affect Japanese thinking about the reliability of the United States. China is more and more becoming a political issue in Japan, and the Japanese government is vulnerable on both its right and its left in appearing too constrained by U.S. policy toward China. The Japanese government could be extremely embarrassed by excessive U.S.-Chinese hostility, or if we jumped far ahead of Japan in coming to terms with Peking, or if it became known that we were merely discussing important questions with China without keeping Japan informed. All of these concerns are likely to increase in the future.

D. Korea. The division of Korea has evolved into a situation acceptable if not satisfactory to the four powers concerned, but none of them are actively seeking to legitimatize the split, as in the case of Germany. The two Koreas have the capacity for a sizable degree of independent military action, perhaps increasing the risks of a war the major powers themselves might not want. A further reduction in U.S. control in South Korea is a concomitant of the Nixon Doctrine.

Our knowledge of North Korea compares unfavorably even with our knowledge of China. The applicability of usual standards of deterrence is uncertain. Kim Il-sung has obvious pretentions and a formidable war machine to back them up. He has not shown any reluctance to carry out serious provocations against the South or even the United States. The Sino-Soviet split, moreover, has enhanced his independence. All we know about his future behavior is that we cannot forecast it reliably beyond expecting it to be troublesome.

We know from bitter experience the importance China attaches to North Korea. (She maintains more troops and jet fighters in the Shenyang Military Region adjoining Korea than in any other single military region, although these forces may also be needed as a defense against possible Soviet attack.) She may see Communist gains in South Korea as leading to political benefits in Japan. Conceivably, the way the war ends in Vietnam may induce Peking to undertake greater risks in support of Kim.

Our problem is managing the continuation of the present balance in Korea. If experience is any guide, the U.S. deterrent and military presence and South Korean political cohesion and military force make a North Korean attack unlikely. In giving military aid to Seoul we need to avoid generating fears of ROK* offensive action in both Pyongyang and Peking. Similarly we should manage our military reductions in Korea without offering inducements to the Communists.

Lowering our Korean force levels must be balanced against the possibilities of alarming the Japanese. Conversely, we must be concerned with the Japanese presence in Korea. Despite unhappy Korean memories of the Japanese occupation, Japanese influence will inevitably rise in South Korea. This could adversely affect Chinese and North Korean perceptions and lead them to more militant conduct. Finally, unlikely as it may now seem, we should scout the opportunities for interesting the Chinese in defusing tensions in this area, a development which would also have salutary effects on the Japanese domestic scene.

Reunification of the two Koreas has recently become a

*The Republic of Korea (South Korea).

political issue in both halves of the peninsula. It is not a current U.S. objective. We clearly do not want reunification of Korea by force. But we should be interested in some process of gradual movement toward peaceful unification, however protracted, if that would reduce or eliminate the possibility of open conflict on the peninsula.

So far, only the Russians (but not the Chinese) have indicated any interest in normalizing relations between the two Koreas. In any case, it is the Koreans who will control the pace and nature of relations between them. Nevertheless, U.S. policymakers must play their role. We and the Japanese cannot leave the Koreans alone in facing the Chinese and Russians in diplomatic maneuverings on the Korean question. Sooner or later, we may also have to revise our position on Korea and the UN.

E. Substantive Study Proposals

Chinese-Japanese relations are an underdeveloped area in U.S. research and analysis, to say nothing of the question of the impact of U.S.-Chinese relations on Japan. Hard information is needed, but at this early stage speculative studies would also be valuable in helping to structure the problems.

- What views have the Chinese expressed about Japanese conventional rearmament and in particular about the prospects for avoiding it? About Japanese nuclear acquisition? What role does Japan play in Peking's own nuclear doctrine? Can we say anything about Peking's view of the U.S. role in determining the pace and nature of Japanese rearmament? About our motives on this question? Can we say anything about Peking's view of Japan's relation to the NPT? Are there signs of modification in Peking's hostility toward the NPT? Any changes toward the question of proliferation generally?

• How do the Japanese envision Peking as a threat to their security? What are the concerns current in Japan about a U.S.-China rapprochement? About U.S.-China hostility? About a Soviet threat? About U.S.-Soviet hostility?

• Does Peking distinguish between a U.S. threat as opposed to a Japanese threat to China's security? Do they have a strategy for dealing with the Japanese threat? Is there a material difference between an American threat only as opposed to a joint U.S.-Japanese threat? How does Peking view possibilities for a U.S.-Japan falling out?

• How does Peking interpret the forthcoming partial U.S. troop withdrawal from Korea? How does Peking interpret the current Japanese role in Korea and how does it see this role evolving? How do the Japanese view Korea with respect to their own security? How do they view U.S. force reductions in Korea? What are Japanese and Chinese reactions to maneuvering between the two Koreas on peaceful unification?

• What is the likelihood of Japan's rearming conventionally in substantial degree without going on to nuclear weapons? What domestic political forces would be set in motion? What braking forces would remain?

F. Policy Planning Proposals

1. **Working with the Japanese government.** We want to employ an unusual degree of candor and cooperation with the Japanese in developing China policy. What is the array of channels of communication we could use for this purpose? What are the subjects that should be taken up? In what order should they arise? Which subjects are best handled through which channels?

2. **Approaching Peking.** Could we approach Peking directly or through a third party—such as Canada—with the

ostensible purpose of explaining our position on the NPT and seeking Chinese adherence? Even if no positive Chinese response were expected, we would have a context in which to spell out our general position on non-proliferation and therefore to discuss, however obliquely, our position on Japanese non-acquisition and the other conditions in Asia we think might be required for Japan to go along. Initially, Peking might show little interest, but we have listened to plenty of talk, too, of little interest to us. If Peking is concerned, it should be able to get our message sooner or later, without our saying anything that had not already been said publicly or given to the Japanese beforehand as background on our talks with the Chinese. What would be the nature of our prior consultations with the Japanese government? How would we handle an adverse reaction? How would this effort mesh with our current situation in SALT?

3 | Southeast Asia

The war in Indochina apart, our most pressing current problem in Southeast Asia centers on the future of Thailand. There (and elsewhere) China can challenge the Nixon Doctrine, primarily by supporting local insurgencies. No doubt the ultimate success of the insurgents will depend mainly on indigenous factors, but a heavy dose of Chinese support might tip the balance in their favor.

Even if it did not, increased Chinese involvement could transform what would otherwise be an internal conflict into a China-U.S. confrontation. A Chinese policy decision to move further in this direction would pose a dilemma for us. One choice would be accepting the costs and risks of contesting the outcome with the Chinese. The other would be to remain uninvolved, facing erosion in the credibility of our commitments if the Communists succeeded. Obviously, we would prefer not to face these alternatives. An objective for better U.S.-Chinese relations would be to reduce the likelihood of such a choice.

Past Chinese involvement has been very limited. Perhaps it will continue to be so. Certainly a conventional invasion southward by Chinese forces is unlikely. But there are other, less risky courses of action that may be available to Peking. It could increase training and material assistance to the insurgents. It might be willing to supply advisers or cadre. It might use Chinese military units to support or spearhead insurgent attacks in ways similar to North Vietnamese practice in support of the Pathet Lao. Should the Chinese take such actions in, say, Northern Burma, the risks to Peking would be small indeed, but the problems for policymakers in Washington and Bangkok might be large. The same sort of adventure in North Thailand would be riskier for China but also more trying for us.

Most U.S. specialists think that Chinese military policies will be much more cautious than this, being largely limited to assuring China's territorial security and probably that of adjacent Communist states. The sizable Chinese force introduced into North Vietnam after 1965 is usually explained on this basis. But this view is not without its inconsistencies. After all, Chinese anti-aircraft batteries in North Vietnam were shooting at our planes and our planes were shooting at the Chinese in return. The war was still escalating then, with the attendant risks of out-and-out U.S.-Chinese conflict. Yet Peking was exerting heavy pressures on Hanoi *not* to end the war through negotiations. If the security of China's borders (and *North* Vietnam's) was the dominant concern, Peking should have been less opposed to a compromise in *South* Vietnam.*

Apparently, Peking's leaders had broader motives. Among these may have been the desire to score points against the Soviet Union or a moral commitment to revolutionary war (perhaps sharpened by ideological disputes among the leaders in Peking). These motives fit well with another Peking objective, that of inflicting political and mili-

*See Document 10 for some of Peking's views on this subject.

tary pressures on the United States. Together these factors outweighed the risks of continuing a war then in the process of escalation. At that time, too, Peking drew public attention to its analysis of the Korean war. It stressed that its Korean role was managed so as to be both militarily effective *and* successful in avoiding a U.S. attack on China. This raises questions about how Peking views both risks and offensive payoffs (political as well as military) in its dealings with us.

Mao has been talking for years about a revolutionary situation developing in the United States, stoked by the Vietnam war and our domestic racial and economic problems. This may sound like empty rhetoric to us, but he may think his analysis is proving true. It charts a way of using limited military force to contribute to a political upheaval in the United States severe enough to bring total U.S. withdrawal from the Western Pacific.

The simultaneous removal of our forces and our commitments from China's sphere of ambition would finally end the U.S. military threat to China. It would also open up not only Southeast Asia but Taiwan and other areas of greater importance to China in a way that Chinese military strength alone cannot achieve. To Peking, all of this may seem defensive, though it would hardly appear that way to us and the rest of Asia. Such differences of view are the stuff from which conflicts are made.

For China, therefore, the stakes in Southeast Asia may be greater than—in fact distinct from—the value of the real estate directly involved. How much Peking can actually do toward attaining such larger objectives is unclear. Since 1967, the Chinese have been placing new emphasis on programs of support and sanctuary for ethnic minority insurgents in northern Burma and Thailand. So far, their efforts and their accomplishments have remained modest, and most U.S. specialists think they will continue to be.

It should be the work of U.S. policy to help make these reassuring estimates come true. However, the estimates rest on certain assumptions about Chinese behavior. And the grounds for these assumptions could change for the worse, gradually or even abruptly through any of several developments: The insurgents might start to perform better, meriting more Chinese help. The non-Communist governments might perform worse. U.S. public attitudes might move toward isolationism, leading Peking to reduce its estimate of the risk of more direct intervention. Or Peking might decide to accept a greater risk, to react against other U.S. policies it opposes (for example, Taiwan basing or CHIREP), or to replace the pressures of a dwindling Vietnam war as a means of moving the United States out of Asia.

Perhaps none of these things will come to pass, but we cannot be sure. If events go badly instead of well, we will need some countervailing factors. The deterrent effect of the U.S. military commitment to defend Thailand will no doubt continue to be one. Given the uncertainties, we would prefer not to rely on deterrence alone.

Avoiding problems in Southeast Asia, then, is one goal we might seek through better relations with China. It is unlikely, however, that the United States and Peking can soon reach any accommodation, explicit or tacit, in a context confined to Southeast Asia. It is an area of built-in conflict between the two countries because of its proximity to China, because each country rejects the legitimacy of the other's role there, and because the risks for Chinese efforts are less there than elsewhere.

On the other hand, there are ameliorations of attitude and action each country could make at no great sacrifice, if other considerations made it worthwhile. For example, China's pre-1967 relation with Burma (cordial government-to-government relations, virtually no Chinese support to the

Communist insurgency) would not threaten us, any more than our relations with Burma then posed a challenge to Peking. Can Peking-Rangoon relations be encouraged back toward that easier condition? Would a mutual abatement of U.S. and Chinese involvement in Thailand be feasible?

Getting China to move her Southeast Asia policy in such directions on a reliable long-term basis might require playing upon her broader interests, outside Southeast Asia itself. These extra-regional interests are discussed in other chapters. However, it is also important to focus on China's relations with the region, to know more about what she might threaten and what possible compromises she might be willing to accept there. This is a tall order, but, as will be suggested next, there appear to be feasible research and intelligence studies that could fill in part of such a picture.

A. Substantive Study Proposals

Except for Indochina, Thailand is the only Southeast Asian country that is both immediately vulnerable to Chinese pressures and protected by a U.S. defense commitment. The foremost issue for our policy toward China, so far as Southeast Asia is concerned, therefore, is whether Thai-Chinese relations can assume a basis acceptable to us after the Indochina war is over. This is not a question that can be answered by research and intelligence alone, or in a context confined to Southeast Asia. But we can gain some inputs with policy relevance by looking at what goes on between China and the countries of the region.

1. Is there a geographic sphere in Southeast Asia in which Peking, not Hanoi, clearly calls the tune for the local insurgents? Some specialists believe Thailand to be such an area. The North Vietnamese role there, in this view, is one of cooperation and facilitation of Chinese interests but does not reflect an independent ambition on the part of

Hanoi; China's claim is preclusive so far as Hanoi is concerned. This view discounts the likelihood of an important degree of autonomy on the part of the Thai insurgents from either Peking or Hanoi. The available evidence is consistent with this view, but not conclusive. This theory has not passed such tests as rigorous examinations of counterevidence. Yet if true, it is of great policy relevance, because it tells us with whom we must deal if the Thai insurgency is to be handled by means other than counterforce.

This is not to underestimate the potential consequences for Thailand of a Hanoi-dominated Communist presence on its borders in Laos. But would Hanoi's role there be less that of a predator than of an auxiliary party accepting policy guidance from Peking?

Given the secrecy normally maintained about relations among Communist movements, is it really feasible to address a question of this nature? There are some grounds for optimism. Similar questions have been answered in the case of Laos, for which we now have relatively concrete information about the relations and working arrangements between both the military and the political organizations of Hanoi (clearly the senior party) and Laos (the junior).* Obtaining this information required a relatively modest (two man) but unusual research effort in the field and in Washington, including substantial cooperation from U.S. agencies and extensive interviews with defectors and other former participants in the movements. Both the U.S. and Thai governments have a deep interest in this question. It should be possible to organize an effort along similar lines for Thailand, even though the findings may not be so rich.

2. What is the range of potentially acceptable rela-

*See, for example, P. Langer and J. Zasloff, *North Vietnam and the Pathet Lao* (Cambridge, Harvard University Press, 1970); and same authors, *The Pathet Lao,* forthcoming.

**tionships for Peking with the non-Communist govern-
ments of mainland Southeast Asia?** In particular, is the
pre-Cultural Revolution Peking-Rangoon relationship within that range? There is no way of knowing what will be
accepted in Peking, because the Chinese leaders then in
power will make their policy decisions in the light of many
prevailing circumstances, domestic as well as international.
But the likely possibilities could be illuminated by looking
at variations in Peking's past policies and at policy disputes
among Chinese leaders.

More concretely, late in 1964 "some people" within the
Chinese leadership came under very high level attack for
advocating a "revisionist" foreign policy with four characteristics: accommodation with imperialism (the United
States); accommodation with revisionism (the Soviet Union);
accommodation with reactionaries (for example, India); and
reduction in Chinese support to revolutionary movements
abroad. During the Cultural Revolution, the charges were
sharpened and leveled specifically at the head of state, Liu
Shao-ch'i. Earlier Chinese policies toward Burma were singled out as reflecting this policy, with Liu primarily responsible. Liu's decline was accompanied by harshness in Peking's policy toward Rangoon and increased support for the
insurgents.

We need to know with more reliability whether there
really was such a policy position (or just a charge to attack
Liu). If it existed, what was its content and who were its real
advocates? This search may prove unrewarding, but its potential value merits a serious effort. If it was actually advanced at the indicated level in Peking's leadership, it is
important that U.S. policymakers be aware of it and that it
be considered in the range of possibilities for the future. The
Red Guard materials attacking Liu claim the policy was
advanced in 1962, a time of severe internal problems for

China. Similar policies might be proposed in a new period of internal preoccupation—such as the succession period. As far as is known some of the original advocates are still alive and some may be in a position to make their views felt.* With luck, work on this subject might further illuminate other Peking disputes on military policy known to have occurred at the same time.

Clearly, this problem should not be approached solely from an internal Chinese point of view. It needs a Burmese perspective too. This could come by our investigating Peking's relationship to the Burmese insurgency, done—to the extent feasible—with comparable depth and in comparative terms as a companion to the study of the Thai insurgency proposed above.

3. **What indications are there of Peking-Hanoi disagreements about Cambodia, past and future?** It has been widely assumed among U.S. specialists that all former French Indochina, including Cambodia, has been accepted by Peking as Hanoi's domain. It is not clear, however, that Sihanouk, at least, ever accepted such a division. A starting point for this study, therefore, would be an examination of his views, publicly and privately expressed over time. This should be related to Peking's and Hanoi's responses. When Sihanouk tried to use China as a counterweight to Hanoi, was he encouraged or rebuffed by Peking? How did Peking and Hanoi treat his statements? His actions? How does this compare with the relative treatment they are giving him now? Soviet materials should be consulted, too. Obviously,

---

*The total "revisionist" package proposed accommodation going well beyond Peking-Rangoon relations. Most of its implications sound welcome to us. But accommodation with the Soviet Union is a much more troublesome matter. This would produce problems for us, especially if the Russians were prepared to respond to it—and even more if we were unprepared. They have contacts and experience that make response far easier for them than for us.

this is a matter of near-term as well as long-term interest, because of its potential usefulness during peace negotiations on the Indochina war.

B. Policy Planning Proposals

Relationships in Southeast Asia are characteristically ambiguous—ours with our friends in Bangkok, Saigon, Vientiane, and Phnom Penh; Peking's, no doubt, with Hanoi, Sam Neua, and the insurgents of Thailand and Burma. All the more ambiguity stands between us and an accurate picture of the doings of our adversaries. It is necessary, even so, to do business there when our interests require, knowing all the time that we will be lied to by our friends, lied to by our enemies, and often misled by our own intelligence. This means operating by feel and indirection, showing patience and caution in discerning results.

On the Taiwan issue (see Chapter 1) the United States can make small, successive concessions to Peking's views if events merit our doing so. In Southeast Asia, Peking can take positive steps we desire, or refrain from taking negative ones, with similar gradations and timing.

On the positive side, Peking could improve relations with Rangoon and Bangkok. On the negative side, it could limit its involvement with local insurgents. Both aspects go together, in that Rangoon and Bangkok could and should balk at trade or diplomatic advances from Peking accompanied by Chinese augmentation of military pressures via the insurgencies.

The United States could have two roles. We could quietly but explicitly indicate to Bangkok, Rangoon, and Peking that we do not oppose—indeed that we even favor—a genuine improvement in their relations. It will be difficult, but we would have to show both Bangkok and Peking that this was a complement to our defense commitment to Thailand, not a way out of it. In particular, care will be needed in relating our military presence in the region to any efforts along these lines.

Our other role will also be difficult. We want to convey to Peking that further progress on the Taiwan issue (and other matters that may be pending at the time) will depend in part on their activities in Southeast Asia. This may not work, especially in the short run. Therefore, we want our initial movements on this question to be very slight. To avoid any misunderstandings, it is important that both Peking and Bangkok know something of our dialogue with the other, so that what occurs between them is seen as an *objective* of U.S. policy and not a deal done behind their back or precipitated by our weakness.

Among the questions requiring further study are:

1. What specific improvements in relations between Peking and Bangkok are possible and agreeable to us? Private ambassadorial talks? Trade? Cultural exchanges? Recognition? A friendship treaty? Does one lead to another? Do we want them to? Which should come first? Will a modest change in U.S. attitudes toward Peking (for example, over CHIREP) be enough to move Bangkok in this direction?

2. Have we a role and an interest in improving Rangoon-Peking relations? How might this relationship serve to break ground for an improvement in relations between Bangkok and Peking?

3. How should we convey our views about Southeast Asia to Peking? For example, in discussing the "Five Principles of Peaceful Coexistence," should we contrast Peking's past relations with Rangoon to the present? Should we indicate a change in U.S. acceptance of the earlier relationship, were it restored with Rangoon? Established with Bangkok? How could we relate all this to U.S. policies elsewhere in Asia? Should we relate it to the level of the U.S.

military presence and our bases in mainland Southeast Asia?

4. How do we handle the above questions with Bangkok? With Rangoon and the other non-Communist governments of Asia? What collateral steps should we be prepared to take to reassure Bangkok that we are not abandoning them?

5. What if any Hanoi-Bangkok understandings might advance U.S. interests? How might Peking be affected?

4 | The United States and the Sino-Soviet Dispute

The major interest of the United States is that the Sino-Soviet controversy continue to limit the challenges either Russia or China poses to U.S. security interests, without its reaching an intensity that might erupt into nuclear war. A highly restrictive SALT agreement, plus Chinese nuclear weapons development, plus some real Sino-Soviet rapprochement would make a major increase in military, political, and budgetary problems for us.

The prevailing wisdom is that we need worry little about rapprochement. However, our forecasts of Sino-Soviet developments have hardly been precise. Initially, we were unaware of our role in hastening it (for example, in exacerbating differences over nuclear sharing). Long after the specialists were sure the split was real and large, it was still vague or absent from the working knowledge of the policymaker. Even for the specialist, the intensity of the rift has produced frequent surprises, from the pullout of Soviet advisers from China in 1960 until the border brinkmanship of 1969. If nothing else, this history tells us, as does the abysmal record before 1966 of *all* China experts on understanding Peking's leadership, that we know little about the participants and

44

our role in their calculations. Little wonder—their doings are as difficult to predict as political developments in our own country.

In the end, our shared apprehensions and rivalry toward the Soviet Union may turn out to be the most important elements in U.S.-Chinese relations. The potential Soviet threat to each of us is great. Circumstances not now foreseen might bring it to the fore in ways that would overshadow all else. Yet, we are exceedingly ill-equipped to plan or even think with much depth about how best to handle this fearsome triangular relationship. (We are even less prepared to analyze the circumstances under which a more stable Sino-Soviet relationship might work to U.S. advantage.) This will probably continue to be the case unless a more rounded U.S.-China relationship evolves. The policy proposals we make in this area are correspondingly slender. Nothing more seems available at this stage—which may be the most powerful argument for proceeding in as many other areas as possible.

A. Sino-Soviet hostilities. Fighting could erupt through miscalculations by either side or by deliberate resort to force. It could range from localized border clashes to Soviet strikes against Chinese nuclear facilities. Once started it could escalate.

Conceivably we might take measures that would inhibit (or unintentionally encourage) Sino-Soviet fighting. It is not easy to think in concrete terms about what these measures might be. It is even harder to estimate with any reliability whether they would in the end move matters in the direction we intended.

However, certain aspects of the hostile relationship deserve consideration. One is the nuclear policies and postures of the two countries toward each other. As she develops nuclear delivery means, China will be forced to examine and

re-examine the adequacy of her deterrent against Soviet attacks. At the same time, the Russians will experiment with
maintaining a counterforce capability against China. The
Chinese will have to ask themselves if their own nuclear
force is a deterrent or a tempting target system. The strategic postures China and Russia assume toward each other
may well have implications for our own defense posture and
for disarmament negotiations with both powers. In any
event the mutual targeting and accompanying doctrine and
strategy will give the Sino-Soviet dispute roots in both the
Chinese and the Russian military establishments, and thus
a lease on the post-Mao future.

The second aspect is that the dispute constrains the two
parties differently in their military freedom of action. The
military preponderance of the Russians is so great that in
spite of their apparent emotionalism they can scarcely
worry about their ability to handle a major Chinese attack.
Their problem with China will not fade to zero. For internal
reasons alone, they probably do not want it to. But no doubt
they can reduce their distraction with the subject, if their
own priorities warrant. Not so for China. The Soviet Union
can threaten China's very existence, and, as long as the
Russians choose, the Chinese will have the Soviet threat as
a major concern, limiting their freedom of action elsewhere.
A residue of animosity and mistrust would remain even if
Soviet policy softened. How could the Chinese be sure that
the attacks and hostility of the past would not be resumed?

B. Sino-Soviet rapprochement. Any significant degree of
Sino-Soviet rapprochement would have repercussions all
over Asia, particularly on Japan. Although the Japanese
may not see clearly how a joint Sino-Russian threat would
manifest itself, the psychological effects could be sufficiently
great for Japan to step up rearmament and perhaps turn in
a neutralist direction.

Our policy appears to be one of taking the dispute for granted and letting events unfold. We are reluctant to proceed in uncharted areas. We have clearly indicated our desire to improve relations with both parties. We will not let the Chinese determine our Soviet policy nor the Soviets our policy toward China. This gives us the flexibility and rationale for any steps we might take to create continued uncertainty for the Chinese and the Russians.

Our constant negotiations with the Russians, for example, on the Middle East and particularly SALT, serve to keep differences between the two to the front. And perhaps our greatest opportunities for keeping China and Russia apart are precisely our variegated dealings with the Soviets. Nevertheless, we need to think more concretely about opportunities on the Chinese side that could also serve this purpose.

China has a hole card in playing with the Soviets—improved relations with the United States—and we do not know when and if she will be willing to play it. This is more likely to open opportunities for constructive movement in matters of substance between the United States and China if preliminary contacts and explorations have prepared the way.

C. Can we consciously make use of the split? Perhaps, though precise measurement of results may be neither feasible nor necessary. We should be looking in the first instance toward generating a greater awareness on the part of each adversary of our position and potential in the triangle.

But to do this we must ultimately define our aims with enough specificity to be able to talk seriously with either or both parties about problems of substantive interest. We may have a reasonably good idea of what business we are willing to transact with the Russians, but the same scarcely holds true in regard to China.

The Chinese assume American hostility and U.S.-Russian collusion. Nevertheless, they are sensitive to their interests, and their reactions will depend in large part upon what is proposed, under what circumstances, in what forum, and in what terms.

There are ample indications that the Russians would be seriously upset by our playing up to the Chinese. Russian efforts to tidy up certain problems elsewhere in the world may indicate a sense of vulnerability on the China issue. (This may also explain their currently playing down their dispute with China.) Disarmament proposals on both sides relate intimately to the problem of pressure on third parties, such as China. We have only recently begun to sort out this set of issues, in spite of their great importance.

D. Offshoots of the hostility. The Sino-Soviet dispute has spilled over in such diverse places as Indochina, Eastern Europe, and Outer Mongolia. A recent outcropping is Soviet talk about a collective security arrangement for Asia. The fact that a figure as authoritative as Brezhnev first floated this trial balloon must indicate a serious, if still undefined, interest in the Soviet Politburo. The Soviets face a degree of internal contradiction in their policy in Asia. Efforts to erode the U.S. presence in Asia collide with the desire to engage the United States in checking China. Brezhnev's motivation was certainly anti-Chinese. His talk tells us little about what the Soviets might do in the non-Communist parts of Asia, but it does tell us they are looking for ways to do something. Stalinist policy encouraged U.S.-Chinese hostility. At present the Soviets may look to the United States as the main —temporary but necessary—counterbalance to increasing Chinese influence in the Far East. Both Soviet motivations (short-term anti-Chinese, long-term anti-U.S.) mean that an active Russian role in Southeast Asia* is likely to be mainly

---

*South Asia, especially India, falls into a different category of considerations not treated here.

a source of mischief for us—except insofar as the prospect of it can be used to pressure or induce the Chinese into arrangements that make us both prefer to see the Russians kept out.

E. Substantive Study Proposals

1. In reviewing National Intelligence Estimates of Sino-Soviet behavior over the past twenty years, what factors did we miss or evaluate incorrectly? Which were evaluated well but inadequately reflected in current policies?

2. What plausible steps or series of steps might be taken by either China or Russia to begin a process of rapprochement?

3. How have the Chinese responded to Japanese overtures to improve relations? Have they perceived the use of improved relations with Japan as a means for raising Soviet concern? What factors inhibit them?

4. What are the likely Sino-Soviet strategic interactions and force postures as China attempts to acquire a nuclear deterrent against the Soviet Union? What do the Chinese think would be needed to deter the Russians? What do the Russians need to keep the Chinese from obtaining a deterrent? What implications may be drawn for the United States from the nuclear postures of each country?

5. What are the strategic implications for China of alternative SALT outcomes?

F. Policy Planning Proposals

Our understanding of the Sino-Soviet dispute is all too thin. We do know that both parties take it very seriously. We know too that they are seriously concerned about how U.S. policies might affect their positions in it. The dynamics of the triangle are new to all three powers. This is one reason it is so difficult for us to shape policies for it. We will inevitably learn more about the Soviet-U.S. leg as our dealings with the Russians evolve. We have little to balance this on the Chinese side. We should have more.

1. Chinese apprehensions about SALT. How can we learn more about Chinese sensitivities on this score? Should we consider countermeasures to keep the Russians from exaggerating SALT implications for China? To counterbalance Russian pressure on us in SALT and other forums? To alleviate any side effects of SALT that block better U.S.-Chinese relations? More specifically, should we explore Peking's interest in talking with us about questions such as the exchange of information in the event of a surprise attack on either nation? What should we say publicly and privately, directly to the Chinese and to third parties, about the implications of SALT for China? How do we deal with the Russians on this score?

2. An indirect approach. What measures might we take toward Communist countries, such as Albania, Outer Mongolia, or Romania, where the Sino-Soviet dispute rages? How would we minimize risks of adverse Soviet reactions affecting other issues in which the United States is interested? More specifically, we might (quite tentatively) consult the Yugoslavs about our attempting to ameliorate relations with Albania. We could solicit their opinion about its desirability from Belgrade's point of view and its helpfulness, if any, in our bettering relations with Peking. In some way, we should see that the content of these consultations becomes known to Peking and Moscow. Even if the Yugoslavs quickly turned us off, we would have generated an awareness in several capitals of a potential U.S. role that might prove important elsewhere for the Sino-Soviet dispute.

5 | Some Special Problems of Interacting with Peking

A. The need for a broad approach. A central problem of seeking better relations with China is finding steps we might take with enough substance to evoke a meaningful response from Peking—without paying a high price only to learn that Peking's attitude is unacceptable. There is no general solution to the problem. Perhaps a single issue, such as Taiwan, will prove insurmountable. Our initial explorations should be carefully hedged, but we should also be prepared to explore several subjects more or less concurrently. If one produces no results, perhaps another will. Of greater importance, we would gradually sketch for Peking a more precise picture of our attitudes on the set of issues between the two countries and receive back some clearer notion than we now have of Peking's attitudes on the same set. In this way, we may discover usable relationships between those interests more important to us and those more important to Peking.

A broad approach like this is difficult because it would require us to canvas our own thinking on many issues now unresolved. It has value for the same reason. Besides, no real progress may be possible until the two sides see more clearly how individual measures fit into a larger picture. For exam-

51

ple, how would Peking interpret a U.S. declaration that we no longer intended to help defend the off-shore islands? As a sign of U.S. weakness or of conciliation? As an attempt to improve relations or to make permanent the separation of Taiwan from the mainland? The answer could depend on what else was happening and what else we were saying to each other.

B. Principles versus specifics. The main problem facing the Chinese leadership now is governing China (as opposed to foreign affairs). The ability to govern, however, depends to no small extent on legitimacy, and legitimacy is very much a matter of ideology in Peking these days. In this way, foreign affairs get re-injected into the problems of domestic government, because Maoist ideology is universal in scope and has a large foreign affairs component.

Better relations between the United States and China would require compromising differences. But Peking (even if interested) may be adamant about compromising its principles, one of which is hostility to "U.S. imperialism." This can make for awkward going, though the consequences may be ameliorated if we are forewarned and forearmed.

In the past, Peking has shown extraordinary elasticity in interpreting Maoism to fit its international needs. Chinese economic aid to the feudal kingdom of Yemen was a case in point. Profitable co-existence with the British Crown Colony of Hong Kong is another. Where a specific mode of behavior fits Peking's needs, it can be accommodated without embarrassment or the overt renunciation of principle. On the other hand, principles are unlikely to be disavowed. And even elasticity may be lacking where there is no specific benefit in view. Thus an invitation to Peking to join Big Four (or Five or Six) talks on some very general topic might be rejected because it would symbolize participation in great power "collusion"—and because no concrete payoff for Peking was clearly in view. A private proposal on a specific issue might get serious consideration, if Peking saw its interests served.

C. Invective and double-talk. Interest by Peking in our point of view, concessions to us even if made in fact, may be accompanied by denunciations of the United States and denials that any understanding or concession is intended. To the extent we can, we must distinguish between what Peking says and what it does (or refrains from doing).

D. Reciprocity and unilateral moves. For reasons of both ideological purism and craftiness, Peking may be reluctant to deal explicitly in quid pro quo terms. If so, we should also try to explore the prospects for mutual accommodation through ostensibly unilateral moves. This might take the form, say, of sketching for Peking some steps it could take that we would regard as accommodating, of identifying some we might take of interest to Peking, of watching to see if Peking does the sort of thing we have proposed, or of making moves on our own while looking for responses in kind from Peking. The Chinese have employed such patterns in the past. The release of Bishop Walsh may have been a case in point. It means, however, that we should be careful not to give them the wrong impression of the kind of "unilateral" move *we* might respond to.

E. Time and strategy. One prominent Sinologist has argued that the Chinese think of using time strategically in the way that Russia has used geographic space—to absorb and smother an opponent's efforts. However this may be, Peking's sense of timing may differ from ours. In some cases this could produce intransigence, with Peking rejecting accommodations in the thought that time works in its favor.

But this way of thinking need not always be disadvantageous to us—if, for example, Peking could be reliably committed to applying indefinite patience in the matter of using force to "liberate" Taiwan. Without looking only for this large a simplification of our problems, we should stay alert to positive opportunities and try to learn what Peking's time perspectives are. On Taiwan in particular, a long Chinese time perspective (greater perhaps than we would normally anticipate) may be our best hope for dealing with a sticky problem.

6 | Where Are We Heading?

What follows are some broad brush strokes suggesting where U.S.-Chinese relations might stand some time hence. Where we will be in actuality would depend in part on the lines of exploration pursued by the U.S. government, even more on Peking's responses, but most of all on events and forces external to our purely bilateral dealings.

The picture sketched below is therefore not intended as a prediction nor even painted in much detail. Its purpose, rather, is to illustrate how different parts of a complex picture might fit together as the relationship evolves. It also depicts how adversarial relationships, without shedding their underlying hostility, might develop along lines that reduce the dangers of conflict to both sides. It is about as good as could be realistically expected, if circumstances favored the lines of policy exploration previously suggested. Needless to say, much worse outcomes are possible (and may be likely if we make no effort to try such policies). Even progress, if it comes, will be interrupted and threatened by crises and trials of will.

Suppose, by degrees, we evoke interest in Peking by taking the following approach: A general relaxation of tensions throughout Asia would serve both governments. The United States could contribute by showing concern for Peking's worries, for example, Taiwan and Soviet-U.S. "collusion"; Peking by showing restraint in Southeast Asia; both of us by working toward an environment that does not push Japan toward nuclear acquisition. Major achievements will take much time and can only be attained gradually by small steps.

A. In Southeast Asia, Peking (with some explicit cooperation from us) improves government-to-government relations with Rangoon and feels out Bangkok about trade (but not diplomatic) relations. It neither reduces nor increases the present modest flow of assistance to insurgents in Burma and Thailand. It continues to call on revolutionary forces everywhere to defeat "U.S. imperialism," linking the liberation of Taiwan, South Korea, and so on to the effort. But it ceases personal invective against Thai and Burmese government leaders. Peking maintains its capability to threaten Southeast Asia by continuing to train potential insurgents but holds them in China.

B. Taiwan's status is declared by the United States to be a subject for peaceful resolution between Peking and the GRC. We stand by our contractual obligation to defend the GRC, but recognize that ultimately Taiwan should be part of China (as both Taipei and Peking insist). In effect, we reduce the likelihood of Taiwanese independence or a future Japanese defense commitment to the GRC, without foreclosing either. We can move further in the same direction if we wish —or not. Peking declares that this is insufficient to resolve the Taiwan issue "in principle," but improves atmospherics by facilitating cultural exchanges, admitting more U.S. visitors, buying goods from U.S. firms, and agreeing to discuss other outstanding issues with us.

C. Japan remains an object of criticism by Peking, but the annual trade agreements get easier to negotiate, and there is growth in "friendly" trade.* Peking demands that Tokyo adopt the Canadian formula on recognition** as a political precondition for a major expansion in official trade. However, Japan-China ambassadorials*** begin in a neutral capital. The Mutual Security Treaty is maintained by a moderate Liberal Democratic regime in Tokyo, which is "committed to" and "working toward" NPT ratification. The Japanese government praises U.S. movement on the Taiwan issue but does not specifically endorse the U.S. formulation.

D. Sino-Soviet hostility remains high. The United States demonstrates its neutrality by proposing separate talks with Peking about informational exchanges and other possible measures in the event of a surprise attack against either.

E. Would such modest results be worth the effort? That would largely depend on what followed. The gains sketched above are slender, but they are gains. A not improb-

---

*The bulk of Sino-Japanese trade is carried on by firms that are designated by Peking as "friendly" to China. In actuality these firms are largely ones set up specifically for the China trade by the major Japanese companies.

**Under the "Canadian formula," Peking accepted Ottawa's recognition only when Canada officially declared Peking the "sole legitimate government of China" but did nothing more than "take note" of Peking's claim to Taiwan. Thus Canada withdrew recognition from the GRC as the "government of China" but took no position on the territorial issue.

***The Japanese government has repeatedly proposed ambassadorial level talks with Peking, without establishing formal diplomatic relations, on the pattern of U.S.-Chinese talks in Warsaw. Peking has thus far refused.

able but much more pessimistic picture of events could be traced in the absence of such moves. They show an ability of both governments (if not necessarily the further desire) for *give-and-take* as opposed to pure hostility. More important, they establish a basis for a more substantial improvement in relations. This might ultimately produce a very large payoff.

7 | At What Pace Should We Move?

A. Conclusions: Going slow but starting fast. It may take a long time to make much progress with Peking, if indeed progress is possible at all. This is a reason (among others detailed below) not only for starting as soon as circumstances permit, but also for starting cautiously. Caution means risking little, and risking little means offering little —though not offering nothing. If our openers are to be appropriately small, they also should at least touch on the substance of a broad range of interests important to both parties. That is why the policy proposals of the earlier sections are so timid but embrace so many subject areas. To the extent possible, they are meant to be tried concurrently, not seriatim.

Once a menu of possibilities like this is laid before Peking, we should not add to it materially until Chinese reactions merit. Instead, we should use the time that passes to reiterate our views, to keep them alive in Peking's thinking, and to get them conveyed to a broad circle of Peking's leadership.

B. As a practical matter there is slight danger of haste.

The reasons for starting slowly will receive full weight in policy deliberations. And their weight will be reinforced by the natural proclivities of the bureaucratic system. Essentially these are:

- Reluctance to incur any present risk for an uncertain future benefit.
- Reluctance to take difficult policy decisions when events do not force them.
- Reluctance to act now when the future might turn up something more attractive.

C. Accidental diversions. Starting slowly has its own risks. Some unanticipated future event might make Peking easier to deal with. But it is too easy for unplanned or unrelated developments to derail a process with as little momentum as our current contacts with the Chinese. Peking's cancellation of the May 1970 Warsaw meeting over the Cambodian issue is a case in point. Presumably that episode did not have lasting effects, but it left time for additional unexpected events to intervene. Future diversions could be stickier. Some might even lead to more or less direct U.S.-Chinese conflict, indefinitely deferring the search for better relations that might otherwise have helped us avoid such a confrontation altogether.

D. Signals with little substance can be helpful and are all the easier to make when they have side benefits. They are not, however, a substitute for policy. Taken in isolation, they can waste time and permit opportunities to be lost.

Our conciliatory moves toward China so far have on balance been beneficial to the United States—entirely apart from the response or lack of response from Peking. They have been welcomed by most other countries, reduced frictions with many friendly countries, given us additional flexibility in China policy for the future, and brought support from most of the U.S. public and Congress. There may well be additional steps with similar benefits or at least minimal net cost.

Constructive policy moves should certainly not be disparaged *because* they bring mainly side benefits. But it should be realized that this aspect of them is not usually lost on Peking—or Moscow, or other interested capitals. Peking, like Hanoi, has developed a stereotyped analysis of certain U.S. policy moves, tagging them with the ungenerous title of "peace hoax." Conciliatory U.S. initiatives that win world or domestic public support but do not satisfy Communist demands are often so branded in their public statements and to some extent no doubt in their internal analysis as well. Their argument is that seeming to be conciliatory wins the public support that allows the U.S. government to persist in its "stubbornness."

Peking's reactions to our moves thus far suggest that they have not been dismissed as pure "peace hoax." At the least, we have indicated our policy is not governed by sheer hostility to Chinese communism. At this stage, it may be hard for Peking to read much more than that into them. There may be interest, nonetheless, as a means of needling the Soviet Union. This can be useful from our point of view too. But should all parties come to view the triangle in this light—a game of meetings and cancellations, atmospherics with little content—the usefulness of contacts alone will wear thin. Without some prospect of the emergence of a more *substantive* U.S.-Chinese relationship, even the motivation of needling the third member of the triangle will dissipate.

E. Diversion through self-deception. Looking back, it is clear that economic relations were not important in bringing the United States and Russia into a more substantive relationship. In spite of much talk from both sides about trade serving this purpose, military and political considerations are what counted.

This will probably hold true for China, too.* Our time will be more productively spent if we are realistic about this from the outset. Attitudes toward economic relations, such as our recent trade measures, may serve the two sides for signaling changes in mood or atmosphere. Movement on this front can be useful. But we should not let a concentration on economic matters displace our attention from the areas that really matter. We should not generate expectations (that could later turn into pressures) on the part of the U.S. public. We will not wring major concessions out of Peking using economic benefits as bait. We should not emphasize them to the point that Peking thinks that economic issues can be so used with us.

F. Mao and the succession in Peking. Mao's frequently voiced hostility toward the United States does not make him a promising partner in a search for mutual understanding. One might doubt that much will be discovered while he rules China. But we have not always understood him very well. And we clearly do not understand his manner of exercising authority at all. We do not know what will happen should his authority wane through physical or political weakness. For these reasons it seems unwarranted to conclude that nothing of importance can be done during his tenure in Peking.

1. While Mao lives. We know now there have been major disputes about policy within Peking's leadership and that

---

*The relative unimportance of mutual economic relations to both China and the United States is set forth in detail in Jerome A. Cohen, Robert F. Dernberger, and John R. Garson, *China Trade Prospects and United States Policy*, Alexander Eckstein, ed. (New York, National Committee on United States-China Relations, 1970).

there has been an ebb and flow in the policy lines actually implemented, both before and since the Cultural Revolution. Most of the differences have been about domestic affairs, but official Peking statements of policy toward the United States, the Soviet Union, and other international matters have varied too. These variations may have been directed by, concurred in, or imposed upon Mao. However that may be, they do suggest that Chinese behavior is not necessarily set in concrete simply because Mao is alive and well. The reverse may even be true—major changes in policy may be easier for an authoritative figure such as Mao than for a successor or successor collegium. Without expecting too much, we should not conclude in advance that all explorations will prove barren.

2. The succession. There is no reliable way to forecast the leadership that will succeed Mao, but one of its most probable characteristics is worth noting: No single leader will soon command Mao's authority. Lin Piao is designated in writing as the successor, but even if he gets the office he will not soon have comparable popular standing in China. Each of his potential rivals will have an interest in limiting the authority accrued by him and other possible leaders. If so, Mao's death or decline will evoke a period of internal maneuvering, during which individual leaders will try to bolster their own authority, using policy positions as one instrument in their search for support. Promises, deals, and personal and organizational loyalties will all be involved, but policy questions will be among the means used too.

The succession period is also likely to be a period of great internal preoccupation for the leaders. They will be intent on their relations with each other, which will make it a difficult time for them to get new messages from us. If, in spite of this, one leader perceived new opportunities opening in U.S.-Chinese relations, he would evoke disagreement or suspicion from his rivals. And that, in turn, would make it hard for Peking to agree on a response that might be understandable to us.

Surely we would like to see some policy of "better" relations with the United States among the policy positions advocated in Peking during the succession debates and maneuvers. If so, it would be better to establish our ideas on the matter in the inventory of Chinese leadership thinking as early as possible. In other words, our interest in better relations and the shape they might take should be conveyed to Mao's potential successors *before* they face the succession decisions. They would then have the time to consider the prospects and find areas of agreement or coalition among those so inclined. And it would clue them in to the policy directions likely to evoke a positive response from the United States.

The Cultural Revolution revealed to us how widespread and high in level the opponents of Mao's policies were in the past. Similar hidden opposition may still exist or develop in the future. Our policies should be prepared for the possibility that views quite contrary to Mao's will predominate after his authority is removed.

It is highly speculative but interesting to reflect on developments just after Stalin's death. Apparently Beria-Malenkov-Molotov at least flirted with far-reaching new arrangements for Germany, but mutual suspicion and lack of communication made it impracticable for us even to probe them effectively for possible concessions. Bulganin and Khrushchev may also have been interested in dealing on the German question and on arms levels, but here, too, both sides were ill prepared to discover if there was anything of mutual benefit.

G. The succession on Taiwan. Although President

Chiang K'ai-shek is well into his eighties, his authority and fixedness of purpose are strong, to say the least. His leadership therefore minimizes the likelihood that changes in U.S. policy would produce either an unmanageable situation on Taiwan or a detrimental shift in GRC determination to maintain its independence and claim to governmental legitimacy. Things might look different in his absence. This, too, is a reason for the United States to start soon to seek better relations with Peking. Later, we may find ourselves paralyzed by our own fears about the repercussions on Taiwan of any of the needed U.S. policy moves.

H. The war in Southeast Asia. Without attempting to predict either the *future development* of this war or the *ways it might end,* we do know:

• Peking is interested in both aspects of the war and can influence both should it try to do so. The Chinese road and presence in North Laos is one indicator of their interest and capability. The probable inclusion of China, should there be an international peace conference, is another. Others could be cited.

• Peking has referred to the Taiwan issue as the "only" obstacle to improved relations with the United States. Significantly, the Vietnam war has not been specified as such an obstacle. How receptive Peking will be to our approaches, how rapidly U.S.-China relations can improve (if at all), and what shape they may take—all may be influenced by the future course of the war in ways we cannot begin to predict. But none of this negates the rationale for at least starting our efforts to improve relations with China now.

On the contrary, it suggests the value of trying to move toward better relations with China at an early date. We might be better able to continue our efforts in spite of potential disruptions caused by some unexpected development in the war. We might learn something useful about Peking's attitude toward the war (for example, toward the fighting in Laos or the current role of Sihanouk). Finally, if we found grounds for a *mutual* interest in better U.S.-Chinese relations, we might find Peking easier to deal with at an international peace conference.

I. U.S.-Japan relations. The probable continuation of the present Japanese governmental leadership for the next two years or so is an important opportunity for the United States. It is a group with whom we have explicitly identified many basic objectives in common. It is one, therefore, with whom we could work closely and with unusual candor in deciding what we should and should not contemplate in any further explorations with regard to Peking. We may not be able to have the same degree of intimacy with Japanese governments of the future. The U.S.-Japanese relationship is far more important to us than any probable bettering of relations with China. This is a valid constraint on our freedom of action on the China front, but not an absolute one. Besides, the two things are not necessarily in conflict. A primary goal is finding China policies that benefit both ourselves and the Japanese government. Life might be easier for the Japanese government if the United States took leadership on certain issues. We should use our present relationship to work out such policies—or to reduce or neutralize the side effects for Japan, if a unilateral U.S. interest is to be pursued. Either way, this appears to be an optimum time to work out new directions in China policy with the Japanese. The going may be stickier by far later on.

Part II | Some Problems of Governmental Decisionmaking

8 | Problems in Developing Policy-Relevant Information About China

The U.S. government has many kinds of problems in dealing with China policy. Some have to do with the intractability of the subject matter. Some have to do with the attitudes of Congress and the public. Some are legacies of ideological positions and missteps of previous administrations. Some are built into the bureaucratic process, especially the generation of information for the use of policymakers. The last is the problem addressed below.

A. Much that we feel we "know" about China is not really usable for policy purposes. The number of China specialists in the U.S. government—and their output—is large. Some recent Defense Department seminars on China were attended by over 200 specialists, almost all employees or consultants of U.S. agencies. But how much of their output really influences policy? Too little of it is used, but also too little is "usable" for this purpose. In a sense, therefore, we seem to know more about China than can be put to practical use. The reason is neither sloth nor indifference but inadequate interaction between specialists and the policy-making side of the government.

B. In government policymaking, what kinds of information are "usable"? The following are the main characteristics:

1. The information must be relevant to a policy or operational decision that might be made. Some decisions are forced by world events. Where there is at least some time for reflection and the issue is not too sensitive, the area specialists will be consulted and the information they have developed will be used, even if it is not entirely appropriate to address the problem at hand. In a crisis, the specialists are often cut out because the issues have become "sensitive." Policymakers take exclusive control and rely on information (or impressions) stored up in advance. On the other hand, the policymaker will not welcome *advance* education unless the specialists' information meets his skeptical tests of credibility and clearly relates to the kinds of policy issues that are his daily work. In times of quiet, therefore, when he could take the policy initiative, the policymaker's contact with the specialists will be slight—unless their information is well tailored to his concepts of policy relevance. Thus, the policymaker's receptivity to information when things are calm is small; as events press him, it increases; during a crisis he flies alone, by the seat of his pants. The problem for the specialist is producing information with enough policy relevance and persuasiveness to establish itself (and its authors) with the policymaker when there is time to think.

2. Alternatively, the information must relate to resource allocations such as force levels and deployments. These decisions are part of a budgetary cycle and hence must be made with or without a fully satisfactory informational base. The inertia of conservatism and bureaucratic protectiveness in such decisionmaking can scarcely be overestimated. Changes in budget shares among services or important programs are unlikely unless there is extraordinary informational support for them.

This situation produces imbalance in the weight accorded different kinds of information. Hard information (usually numbers) tends to prevail over soft (usually political). More important, information that eases the budget share problem tends to prevail over information that does not. Often the two tendencies push in the same direction. For example, we might ascertain that Taiwan would be cost-effective as a military base, lessening budget pressures on each individual service as well as the government as a whole. But it is much harder to measure the political advantages and disadvantages of using Taiwan. This difference in the availability of information could—but obviously should not—decide the issue, if it arose. The problem is to make political information "harder."

3. **Usable information usually requires some degree of agreement among (and within) agencies.** Where specialists differ on the facts or analysis, policymakers may properly hesitate to act. Or they may act on the specialist whose advice they prefer. Or they may cease to take the specialists seriously at all. None of these courses need yield good policy.

4. **But lowest-common-denominator agreements are not the only basis for information usability.** Where specialists disagree, they could still provide usable information by agreeing on a policy-relevant description of their differences. This would mark out an area of uncertainty, which prudent policy would take into account.

5. **Finally, usable information should be communicable and persuasive to decisionmakers.** Chinoiserie has its uses. But to influence policy, the decisionmaker must find the information intelligible enough and firm enough to pass

his own tests. In important matters it must also be suitable for him to use with other officials and with the public.

C. Why is more usable information on China not produced? The fault cannot be entirely attributed to the China specialists, because usability is uniquely the product of interaction between substantive specialists and policymakers. This must take place at different levels in the hierarchy. But in every case, their mode of interaction is different for China than for other important countries and is a fundamental weakness on both the information generating and policy development sides of the government.

1. **We have no bilateral relations with China.** The policymaker must usually deal with China as part, but not the center, of the problem. Hence China as a whole is rarely brought into focus for him. Current efforts, such as the Warsaw talks, are too immature to integrate our now fragmented views and conjectures. Furthermore, for the talks to reach that stage may depend on our developing more usable information about China—rather than their automatically producing it for us. The talks now lack self-sustaining momentum, and policy-relevant information may be needed to supply it.

2. **Few senior policymakers have a personal background of familiarity with China as a country,** nor are they forced to acquire one by their routine in office. They may already have or be forced to adopt policy views on China, but these are less apt than in the case of, say, Russia or Western Europe to be based on a relatively concrete picture corrected over time by experience with the Chinese.

3. **When China does come up at the policymaking level, some other country or consideration is almost always of central concern.** The responsibility for action lies primarily with those in the bureaucracy who are in-

volved with problems or relations focused on countries other than China. The China aspect will be commented on, but the problem is structured for the policymaker from an origin and orientation other than China. This happens at times with other countries, too, but in important cases not as consistently as with China.

4. **National intelligence estimates or NSC policy studies can and do view China as a nation,** but they are not part of a self-sustaining process of interaction between specialists and policymakers.* There is little feedback to these efforts from the policymaking level. More important, they do not move with time and opportunities and are quickly overtaken by events.

5. **The value of information about China has been recognized within the government**—as an abstract proposition. The result is a substantial expenditure of resources, but too much of the effort starts and ends within the specialist community. Without clearer guidance from the policy side, there is a tendency to prefer "hard" (military) rather than "soft" (political) intelligence, even though a lot of the "hard" data are of modest practical value. This can result not only in misallocation of resources but in unbalanced conclusions, in missed opportunities for policy, and in intelligence collection becoming a goal in itself. The costs of the last may not be limited to money. Peking can mistakenly ascribe hostile intent—for example, to reconnaissance efforts—where in fact no U.S. *policy* is reflected at all.

6. **The policymaking process does not often compel the policymaker to picture China for himself** or ask

---

*Within the NSC (National Security Council) system, interagency studies of issues such as China policy are conducted from time to time on a one-shot basis. Once the study is completed, the members of the working group responsible for drafting it return to the ongoing business of the participating agencies.

questions about China as a country. This means some usable information goes unused, because the policymaker does not recognize its value. Much more important, it means that the policymaking process does too little to propel the information-generating parts of the government in the direction of usability. For such countries as Russia or Germany, the policymaker must constantly ask questions he needs answered, reject answers he finds irrelevant or unpersuasive, demand interagency agreement or explanations of agency disputes. His demands orient the substantive specialists to the needs of policy, just as their responses (when successful) permit more sophisticated policies to be developed and more sophisticated demands for information to be levied by the policymaker.

9 | Explorations via Policy: Another Source of Information

A. Better information and communications alone may not be enough.

    1. The paucity of business between the United States and Peking is not only a major source of weakness for us in the interaction between our policymakers and area specialists, it must produce a similar weakness in Peking. This is one reason neither country has more usable information about the other.

    2. Furthermore, communications for their own sake are inhibited by present tensions. Peking wants concessions from us—for example, on the Taiwan issue. Even if Peking also wants better communication with us, it must try to bolster its bargaining position by generating pressures on us, posing maximum demands and concealing areas of "give." We have similar concerns. More generally, the present noise level that surrounds communications between us and Peking is extraordinarily high, the signal level all but inaudible. There are many acts and declarations made by both countries for purposes other than communicating with each other. (If we relocate a fighter wing from Japan to Taiwan or Korea to accommodate Japanese complaints, Peking may misinterpret our motive completely.) A real signal from either side can easily be overcome by the noise.

3. Ideological and bureaucratic considerations both in Peking and in Washington make it hard for either government to decide how it is willing to act toward the other or what picture of itself it is willing to convey. Difficult decisions—what attitude the U.S. government might adopt about the future status of Taiwan, what Peking might do in return—are not taken unless there is some reason to think them worth the effort. For this reason, some of the most crucial usable information will not even come into existence in the absence of a more substantive U.S.-Chinese relationship.

B. The intent behind a policy move can be divided into two parts, material and informational. To some extent policy moves may affect the relations among countries—they may change the world a bit (or a lot). Second, they may produce feedback—information. The mix between the two results should be variable, depending on the design of the policy move. The problem is to find steps with enough substance to evoke usable information about China and potential movement toward better relations without paying a high price in terms of our other international concerns. We want moves that produce lots of information, including positive reactions from Peking, but initially at least with minimal impact on the rest of the world. These might be taken in any of several ways:

- Direct U.S.-Chinese interactions (diplomatic or other).
- The interaction of a third country with China (perhaps stimulated by us).
- Our interaction with a third country of special interest to China.

There will always be costs to such moves, which will be exaggerated in our calculations because of the third country focus of our foreign policy bureaucracy. "Now" is never the time to risk a near-term flap with some friendly country (or adversary agency) just to explore a possible long-term benefit to our China policy. These concerns should be taken seriously but also carefully analyzed. In appraising them, the embassies and bureaus responsible for the countries concerned should describe the costs in concrete terms, spell out their implications, and suggest possible ways of ameliorating them. This is now rarely done.

Possible side benefits should not be overlooked. A move that disturbs country X may be helpful in dealing with country Y. Those with responsibility for country Y should appraise these benefits and make proposals, if possible, to increase such offsetting benefits.

For the results of policy explorations to be useful, we must listen as well as talk. Official Chinese approaches to the United States have gone through broad swings in the past without evoking a material response from the United States or changing our official interpretation of what Peking was about. To this day, we have left the meaning of these swings largely unexplored by our most powerful means, policy. Whether or not these were lost opportunities is therefore still a matter of conjecture. Should opportunities occur now or in the future, we would not want to miss them through lack of awareness or inadequate preparation.

10 | Changes in Policy Development Procedures

A. Conclusions. Within quite modest time constraints, policymakers could materially improve the development of China policy—in terms of their own contributions and those of the specialists. The key lies in getting maximum mileage out of staff work. Needed are:

1. **A China Group with membership at the policy-making level** that meets periodically to discuss China policy and make recommendations.

2. **Staff for the group** that responds to *its* interests and needs and therefore reflects them in the requirements transmitted to the specialist community.

3. **A staff director** with enough stature and quality to command the confidence of the group's principals and get the required performance out of both his staff and the specialist community.

4. **An agenda of projects** for the staff to start on.

5. **A working style** that promotes better (rather than flagging) performance with time and experience.

B. The China Group. Its major problem is time—policymakers do not have enough to go around. However, without *some* of their time, little can be accomplished. Even an hour of thoughtful discussion at the policymaking level could make a material difference, if it were supported by (which also means if it provided adequate incentives for) really good staff work.

The group could be interagency and form part of the NSC system. In that case, its principals would be at the under-secretarial level. Permanent members would include the Under Secretary of State, the Deputy Secretary of Defense, the Chairman of the Joint Chiefs, the Director of Central Intelligence, and the President's Assistant for National Security Affairs, who would probably chair it. (When appropriate, others could participate from Treasury, Commerce, or non-cabinet agencies.) Ultimately, this would be the best arrangement, but it may be biting off too much at the start, with disappointing results.

A better place to begin might be to form a group within the State Department. State has exceptional responsibilities for China policy anyway. Strengthening its in-house capability to support the Secretary on these issues could permit it to weigh in more effectively with other agencies as part of the interagency NSC system. If State's group were successful, other individual agencies might follow suit, leading in the end to NSC adoption of the principle. Meanwhile the functioning of State's group should build morale within the Department.

If limited to State, the group's principals would be at the Assistant Secretary level. The Secretary or Under Secretary could head it, or it could be chaired by the Assistant Secretary for East Asia. The former is preferable because it would give the group more clout, enable its educational function to take place at a higher policy level, and broaden the group's policy perspective and, hence, the guidance for its staff and the specialist community. Its creation within State need not forgo participation—perhaps informal and occasional—of officials from other agencies. As its core membership, it should include the following Assistant Secretaries or bureau directors: East Asia, Europe, International Organizations, Political-Military Affairs, Intelligence and Research, Planning and Coordination, and Congressional Relations. Other bureaus might be represented when appropriate, such as Economics, the Legal Advisor, or Public Affairs.

Wherever located, the group should not have a narrow base. The issues go beyond our relations with China or even the rest of Asia. Although the government now lacks a China focus, it cannot focus on China alone. The group would need the viewpoint of other regions and functional concerns.

Organized as an NSC body, the group's market would be the President. Within State the market would be the Secretary, its objective the enhancement of his policymaking capabilities.

C. Staff for the group should include at least some full-time people, with others drawn into projects from appropriate parts of the government as needed. There are tradeoffs between the extent of permanent staffing and the role of the staff director, so these aspects of the staffing arrangements should be decided together. For the staff work to be good enough, someone of energy and ability must have the successful functioning of the group as his sole preoccupation. He should feel rewarded if it works, deeply chagrined (with no way to pass the buck) if it flickers and goes out. Given the usual half-life of such governmental efforts, this will pose a real challenge for someone.

D.   The staff director should be full-time and report to the chairman of the group. It will be easier to get someone with the needed stature on a part-time basis, but that passes the life-or-death responsibility for the group's success down to a lower level. A part-time director would need either a good full-time deputy or a couple of very good full-time staff members. The total size of the full-time staff is of less importance than the quality of these few

E. The functions of the staff and its director are procedural and tactical, as well as substantive. Their prime task may be structuring agendas for the group with enough relevance and motive power to summon that minimum of higher level attention needed to make the enterprise work. If they succeed in this, it will not only mean that their work is good enough to improve the quality of our China policy, but also that they are fulfilling the main role of staff—getting the specialist community to respond effectively to their principals' needs as policymakers.

Substantively, the staff must identify important issues and generate policy-relevant papers about them. They can do some (or much) of the work themselves, but their viewpoint must be that of their principals, not of the area specialist.

The ordinary workings of the government are action-oriented. Getting the longer-term, contemplative perspective required for good China policy will need staffing innovations such as this. But to avoid the neglect ordinarily accorded by the government to pure policy planning, the staff must also have an operational role. This would keep it in touch with the daily flow of decisionmaking that produces most government policy, permit it to earn its spurs with the group's principals by helping them with their normal and more pressing operational concerns, and thereby inhibit other bureaucrats of coordinate rank from ignoring it and its work. In addition to generating relevant information and long-term policy development, therefore, the staff should

provide ordinary operational support to the group's principals when issues with a China aspect come up. For example,
the staff director could function as a special assistant for
China policy to the group's chairman. When China policy
was at the heart of the issue to be decided, he would have the
central role in staffing it for his boss. But even when China
policy was peripheral, he would contribute to the staffing to
assure that the China aspect was adequately considered.
Other staff members might act in the same capacity for other
group principals, depending on the makeup of the group and
its staff.

Some projects the staff could begin on were proposed in
Part I of this study. A proposal aimed at working style is
made in the next chapter.

11 | A "Chinese Objectives" Paper As a Device for Bureaucratic Self-Improvement

As Part I of this study shows, the facets of China policy are numerous and interrelated, and our understanding of them is often shallow and unreliable. Underlying the recommendations on policy in Part I are assumptions about how Peking views its objectives and their relative priority. Any purposive effort to elicit reactions from Peking must rest on such assumptions. But are they any good? If not, can we learn enough to draw a more accurate picture from our initial explorations and disappointments? A task of the staff of the China Group could be to examine these assumptions.

One way to test the validity of the assumptions (perhaps before any explorations are even begun) would be to pull them together into a single paper and attempt to depict Chinese objectives as seen from Peking *in terms of specific issues that have policy relevance for us.* Such a paper should allow for the fact that there may be differences among Chinese leaders and governmental institutions. Because of the uncertainties on our side, it should also reflect differences in estimates by differing U.S. specialists and among agencies. Without this, it would have little value for policymaking. It would focus on potential U.S. policy directions, but it could be reviewed both for internal consistency and for consistency with what else is known about Chinese doctrine and behavior.

As more information becomes available and as events occur, whether or not connected with our attempt to establish better relations with China, the paper would also be confronted with reality. Were Chinese reactions consistent with the premises of the paper? If not, what have we learned? What use can we make of this for further explorations? The subject could be readdressed periodically, with new papers drafted to make use of what we have learned and to suggest new modes of exploration via policy.

For this effort to produce anything more functional than chinoiserie, however, it is essential that it be part of the bureaucratic processes through which operational decisions are made. This means that the paper must be drafted by people who also have operational responsibilities and therefore will be concerned to see that their papers have well specified implications for the issues that policymakers will have to decide.

Should this effort succeed, it would produce a bureaucratic context in which it is possible to make practical use of many quite fundamental things about China that specialists take seriously but that the policymaking process too often slights. These are matters of great importance in the behavior of nations and hence may affect our vital interests. They include such things as Chinese pride and concomitant bitterness about past "unequal" treatment at the hands of the west; the Sinocentrism that generates time horizons so different from ours where dealings with other countries are concerned; Chinese concepts of governmental legitimacy and their consequences for how Peking may feel compelled to comport itself in international relations; the implications for the conduct of both soldiers and civilians of the fact that

Chinese attitudes toward equity and the proper relationship between the individual and the state have their roots in Confucianism and Buddhism rather than Christianity and pragmatism. Such considerations are not ignored in present policy papers. But for reasons already given they too often act more as flavoring for the dish than as the basic ingredients from which policy is made. Because our understanding of them is still immature and because of the inherent difficulties of working them into the policymaking process, giving them greater weight will be a slow process at best. Yet it is clearly the direction in which we should try to move.

Appendix | Selected Documents on U.S.-China Relations

The twelve documents that follow were chosen to provide additional background for points made earlier in this book. Most are little known or forgotten by the general public. They were picked for their intrinsic interest and pertinence, not as a balanced cross-section of the multitude of documents on this subject.

Documents 1-2: Misunderstandings about the Korean War

The story of how the United States and Communist China went to war against each other in Korea is far too complicated even to summarize, let alone pass judgment on, in this brief space. These short extracts illustrate the role played on both sides by miscalculation and mutual suspicion.

Document 1 is part of an "eyes-only" Joint Chiefs of Staff instruction sent to General MacArthur in September 1950, reflective of official Washington's determination to avoid fighting the Chinese. Among other things, it specifically enjoins MacArthur against sending U.S. forces into "the area along the Manchurian border." Although the authority and intent of this message are clear enough, it was only one of many messages and many events taken into account by MacArthur at the time. On October 24, he ordered both U.S. and South Korean forces to march on the Yalu. Large Chinese forces suddenly appeared inside Korea and attacked both South Korean and U.S. units on October 26 and 27.

Among the efforts made to cope with this new situation was the invitation to the UN of a special representative from Communist China. Peking sent Wu Hsiu-chuan. Document 2 illustrates the kind of argumentation he presented. Immediately after the North Korean surprise attack on South Korea, President Truman had ordered the U.S. Seventh Fleet to prevent the Chinese Communists from occupying Taiwan, still held by the Chinese Nationalists. With U.S. forces fighting the Communists in Korea, Truman felt it unacceptable to permit a Communist takeover of Taiwan. (See Document 4, below.) Wu also links the Taiwan and Korean issues, claiming that our actions there together reflect a U.S. "overall design of attack against the mainland of China," thus justifying Chinese intervention in Korea and rejection of assurances that the fighting there would not be extended to China. (For a later and more detailed Peking explanation of Chinese intervention, see Document 10.)

Document 1
Joint Chiefs of Staff Instructions to General MacArthur, September 27, 1950

Your military objective is the destruction of the North Korean Armed Forces. In attaining this objective you are

authorized to conduct military operations, including am-
phibious and airborne landings or ground operations north
of the 38th parallel in Korea, provided that at the time of
such operations there has been no entry into North Korea
by major Soviet or Chinese Communist Forces, no announcement of intended entry, nor a threat to counter our operations militarily in North Korea. Under no circumstances,
however, will your forces cross the Manchurian or USSR
borders of Korea and, as a matter of policy, no non-Korean
Ground Forces will be used in the northeast provinces bordering the Soviet Union or in the area along the Manchurian
border. Furthermore support of your operations north or
south of the 38th parallel will not include Air or Naval
action against Manchuria or against USSR territory.

In the event of the open or covert employment of major
Soviet units south of the 38th parallel, you will assume the
defense, make no move to aggravate the situation and report
to Washington. You should take the same action in the event
your forces are operating north of the 38th parallel, and
major Soviet units are openly employed. You will not discon-
tinue Air and Naval operations north of the 38th parallel
merely because the presence of Soviet or Chinese Communist troops is detected in a target area, but if the Soviet
Union or Chinese Communists should announce in advance
their intention to reoccupy North Korea and give warning,
either explicitly or implicitly, that their forces should not be
attacked you should refer the matter to Washington.

Source: RAD JCS 92801, JCS Personal to MacArthur, 27 September
1950. As cited in Dean Acheson, *Present at the Creation: My Years in the
State Department* (New York, Norton, 1969, pp. 452-453).

Document 2
Extract from the Text of a Speech by Wu
Hsiu-chuan, December 16, 1950

There is indeed a close relationship between the United States aggression on Taiwan and its aggression on Korea. But the relationship is not that the armed intervention in Korea by the United States Government may be used as a justification of its aggression against Taiwan. The true relationship is that the aggressions of the United States Government against both Taiwan and Korea are part of its overall design of attack against the mainland of China. The Chinese people view those who are waging an aggressive war against the Korean people in Korea as the same aggressors who are guilty of the same crime against Taiwan. As the United States Government has simultaneously launched aggression against the territory of China, Taiwan, and against its close neighbour, Korea, there is no reason why the Chinese people should not support the Korean people, on a voluntary basis, against the United States armed aggression on Korea—at the same time as they are resisting the United States armed aggression on Taiwan.

I have heard much empty talk in the Security Council to the effect that the troops now fighting in Korea have no intention of committing aggression against the northeastern territory of China. Moreover, it is said that the majority of the members of the Security Council are ready to put such assurances into a resolution. It seems that the Chinese people should now rest assured. This is taking the Chinese people for idiots.

It is to be noted that those countries which wish to assure us that the United States troops in Korea would not violate the territory of China are precisely those which maintain that the United States Seventh Fleet should remain in the Taiwan Straits and continue its aggression against China.

Suppose a detachment of the armed forces of a country hostile to the United States had occupied Hawaii, while another detachment of this same country was attacking the neighbour of the United States, Mexico. And suppose the aggressor then assured the American people: "You have nothing to fear. Our troops in Mexico will not commit any aggression against the United States." Is it conceivable that the American people would believe in the assurances given by such an aggressor and its accomplices? Just so, the United States Government has invaded the territory of China, Taiwan, while its armed forces threaten to approach the border of China from another direction. Yet the United States Government and its accomplices are demanding that the Chinese people believe in their assurances that the armed forces which are approaching China's border would not invade China's territory.

SOURCE: *Important Documents Concerning the Question of Taiwan* (Peking, Foreign Languages Press, October 1955).

Documents 3-6: U.S. Policy on the Status of Taiwan

These documents reflect the main points in the evolution of the official U.S. position on the status of Taiwan.

Document 3 was issued in January 1950 by President Truman in response to the domestic controversy then brewing over the "loss of China." It countered proposals by critics of the administration that the United States prevent the Chinese Communists from extending their 1949 takeover of the mainland to include Taiwan. In essence, it stated that Taiwan had already become Chinese territory in keeping with the Cairo and Potsdam declarations, and that the fighting between the Chinese Communists and Nationalists was a civil war in which U.S. forces would not be used. This document has been cited endlessly (and understandably) by Peking, in demanding that we return to these principles.

Document 4, another Presidential statement, shows how our position changed when the Korean war broke out. The "future" status of Taiwan was to "await the restoration of security in the Pacific, a peace settlement with Japan, or consideration by the United Nations." This was not only a major change in content but also a large increase in the ambiguity of our position. When the peace treaty with Japan was finally signed in September 1951, it left the future status of Taiwan all the more ambiguous by stating only that Japan renounced all territorial claims to Taiwan—without specifying whose territory it had become.

Documents 5 and 6, our Mutual Defense Treaty with the GRC and the Understandings by the U.S. Senate upon ratification of that treaty, deepen the ambiguity still further. The treaty (Article VI) limits the territory covered by our defense commitment to Taiwan and the Pescadores.

The Understanding of the Senate is that the treaty does nothing "affecting or modifying the legal status" of the territories to which it applies. Thus we incurred an obligation to the GRC to defend those territories, but we did not thereby recognize them as part of China.

The introduction and retention of these ambiguities in our position were undoubtedly intentional. They left our options open for the future, and to some extent these options are open still. At a minimum, we retain the option of making small clarifications of our policies (such as the ones proposed in Chapter 1) without feeling compelled to remove all ambiguity from our position at one fell swoop.

Document 3

United States Policy toward Formosa
Statement by President Truman (Released to the
Press by the White House January 5)

The United States Government has always stood for good faith in international relations. Traditional United States policy toward China, as exemplified in the open-door policy, called for international respect for the territorial integrity of China. This principle was recently reaffirmed in the United Nations General Assembly resolution of December 8, 1949, which, in part, calls on all states—

To refrain from (a) seeking to acquire spheres of influence or to create foreign controlled regimes within the territory of China; (b) seeking to obtain special rights or privileges within the territory of China.

A specific application of the foregoing principles is seen in the present situation with respect to Formosa. In the joint declaration at Cairo on December 1, 1943, the President of the United States, the British Prime Minister, and the President of China stated that it was their purpose that territories Japan had stolen from China, such as Formosa, should be restored to the Republic of China. The United States was a signatory to the Potsdam declaration of July 26, 1945, which declared that the terms of the Cairo declaration should be carried out. The provisions of this declaration were accepted by Japan at the time of its surrender. In keeping with these declarations, Formosa was surrendered to Generalissimo Chiang Kai-shek, and for the past 4 years, the United States and the other Allied Powers have accepted the exercise of Chinese authority over the Island.

The United States has no predatory designs on Formosa or on any other Chinese territory. The United States has no desire to obtain special rights or privileges or to establish military bases on Formosa at this time. Nor does it have any intention of utilizing its armed forces to interfere in the present situation. The United States Government will not pursue a course which will lead to involvement in the civil conflict in China.

Similarly, the United States Government will not provide military aid or advice to Chinese forces on Formosa. In the view of the United States Government, the resources on Formosa are adequate to enable them to obtain the items which they might consider necessary for the defense of the Island. The United States Government proposes to continue under existing legislative authority the present ECA program of economic assistance.

Source: *Department of State Bulletin,* January 16, 1950, Vol. 22.

Document 4
U.S. Air and Sea Forces Ordered into Supporting Action, Statement by President Truman
(Released to the Press June 27)

In Korea, the Government forces, which were armed to prevent border raids and to preserve internal security, were attacked by invading forces from North Korea. The Security Council of the United Nations called upon the invading troops to cease hostilities and to withdraw to the 38th Parallel. This they have not done but, on the contrary, have pressed the attack. The Security Council called upon all members of the United Nations to render every assistance to the United Nations in the execution of this resolution. In these circumstances, I have ordered United States air and sea forces to give the Korean Government troops cover and support.

The attack upon Korea makes it plain beyond all doubt that communism has passed beyond the use of subversion to conquer independent nations and will now use armed invasion and war. It has defied the orders of the Security Council of the United Nations issued to preserve international peace and security. In these circumstances, the occupation of Formosa by Communist forces would be a direct threat to the security of the Pacific area and to United States forces performing their lawful and necessary functions in that area.

Accordingly, I have ordered the Seventh Fleet to prevent any attack on Formosa. As a corollary of this action, I am calling upon the Chinese Government on Formosa to cease all air and sea operations against the mainland. The Seventh Fleet will see that this is done. The determination of the future status of Formosa must await the restoration of security in the Pacific, a peace settlement with Japan, or consideration by the United Nations.

I have also directed that United States forces in the Philippines be strengthened and that military assistance to the Philippine Government be accelerated.

I have similarly directed acceleration in the furnishing of military assistance to the forces of France and the Associated States in Indochina and the dispatch of a military mission to provide close working relations with those forces.

I know that all members of the United Nations will consider carefully the consequences of this latest aggression in Korea in defiance of the Charter of the United Nations. A return to the rule of force in international affairs would have far-reaching effects. The United States will continue to uphold the rule of law.

I have instructed Ambassador Austin, as the representative of the United States to the Security Council, to report these steps to the Council.

SOURCE: *Department of State Bulletin,* July 3, 1950, Vol. 23.

Document 5

Mutual Defense Treaty between the United States and the Republic of China, Signed at Washington, December 2, 1954

The Parties to this Treaty,

Reaffirming their faith in the purposes and principles of the Charter of the United Nations and their desire to live in peace with all peoples and all Governments, and desiring to strengthen the fabric of peace in the West Pacific Area,

Recalling with mutual pride the relationship which brought their two peoples together in a common bond of sympathy and mutual ideals to fight side by side against imperialist aggression during the last war,

Desiring to declare publicly and formally their sense of unity and their common determination to defend themselves against external armed attack, so that no potential aggressor could be under the illusion that either of them stands alone in the West Pacific Area, and

Desiring further to strengthen their present efforts for collective defense for the preservation of peace and security pending the development of a more comprehensive system of regional security in the West Pacific Area,

Have agreed as follows:

ARTICLE I

The Parties undertake, as set forth in the Charter of the United Nations, to settle any international dispute in which they may be involved by peaceful means in such a manner that international peace, security and justice are not endangered and to refrain in their international relations from the threat or use of force in any manner inconsistent with the purposes of the United Nations.

ARTICLE II

In order more effectively to achieve the objective to this Treaty, the Parties separately and jointly by self-help and mutual aid will maintain and develop their individual and collective capacity to resist armed attack and communist subversive activities directed from without against their territorial integrity and political stability.

ARTICLE III

The Parties undertake to strengthen their free institutions and to cooperate with each other in the development of economic progress and social well-being and to further their individual and collective efforts toward these ends.

ARTICLE IV

The Parties, through their Foreign Ministers or their deputies, will consult together from time to time regarding the implementation of this Treaty.

ARTICLE V

Each Party recognizes that an armed attack in the West Pacific Area directed against the territories of either of the

Parties would be dangerous to its own peace and safety and declares that it would act to meet the common danger in accordance with its constitutional processes.

Any such armed attack and all measures taken as a result thereof shall be immediately reported to the Security Council of the United Nations. Such measures shall be terminated when the Security Council has taken the measures necessary to restore and maintain international peace and security.

ARTICLE VI

For the purpose of Articles II and V, the terms "territorial" and "territories" shall mean in respect of the Republic of China, Taiwan and the Pescadores; and in respect of the United States of America the island territories in the West Pacific under its jurisdiction. The provisions of Articles II and V will be applicable to such other territories as may be determined by mutual agreement.

ARTICLE VII

The Government of the Republic of China grants, and the Government of the United States of America accepts, the right to dispose such United States land, air and sea forces in and about Taiwan and the Pescadores as may be required for their defense, as determined by mutual agreement.

ARTICLE VIII

This Treaty does not affect and shall not be interpreted as affecting in any way the rights and obligations of the Parties under the Charter of the United Nations or the responsibility of the United Nations for the maintenance of international peace and security.

ARTICLE IX

This Treaty shall be ratified by the United States of America and the Republic of China in accordance with their respective constitutional processes and will come into force when instruments of ratification thereof have been exchanged by them at Taipei.

ARTICLE X

This Treaty shall remain in force indefinitely. Either Party may terminate it one year after notice has been given to the other Party.

In witness whereof the undersigned Plenipotentiaries have signed this Treaty.

Done in duplicate, in the English and Chinese languages, at Washington on this second day of December of the Year One Thousand Nine Hundred and Fifty-four, corresponding to the second day of the twelfth month of the Forty-third Year of the Republic of China.

For the United States of America: John Foster Dulles
For the Republic of China: George K. C. Yeh

SOURCE: *Documents on American Foreign Relations, 1955,* Paul E. Zinner, ed. (New York, Harper, 1956).

Document 6

Understandings by the United States Senate in Giving Its Advice and Consent to Ratification, February 9, 1955

(With reference to Article V of the Treaty:)

It is the understanding of the Senate that the obligations of the parties under Article V apply only in the event of external armed attack; and that military operations by either party from the territories held by the Republic of China, shall not be undertaken except by joint agreement.

(With reference to Article VI:)

It is the understanding of the Senate that the "mutual agreement" referred to in Article VI, under which the provisions of Articles II and V may be made applicable to other territories, shall be construed as requiring the advice and consent of the Senate of the United States.

(With reference to the status of Formosa and the Pescadores:)

It is the understanding of the Senate that nothing in the treaty shall be construed as affecting or modifying the legal status or sovereignty of the territories to which it applies.

Documents 7-9: Washington-Peking Negotiations about Taiwan

This set of documents reflects a U.S.-Chinese effort to deal with the Taiwan issue through negotiations. During the fall and winter of 1954-1955, the Chinese Communists shelled and seemed poised to invade the Nationalist occupied off-shore islands of Quemoy and Matsu. As the tensions grew, the United States reacted. In December, we signed the Mutual Security Treaty with the GRC. (See Document 5, above.) In March, President Eisenhower publicly indicated that the United States might resort to nuclear weapons.*

The shelling subsided in April 1955 as the Afro-Asian nations gathered to discuss peaceful coexistence at Bandung. While there, Chou En-lai first proposed direct U.S.-Chinese negotiations about Taiwan (Document 7). He elaborated on this the following July (Document 8) in two ways. On one hand, he limited the issue to be settled between the United States and China to "the United States' occupation of China's territory Taiwan and its interference with the liberation of China's coastal islands." On the other, he raised the "possibility," if the United States stood aside, that Peking's efforts to regain Taiwan would employ "peaceful means," including "negotiations with the responsible local authorities of Taiwan." He left no role for the United States in the latter negotiations, nor did he explicitly bind Peking to use *only* peaceful means. As with so many official Peking formulations, the studied ambiguity of his statement created questions rather than resolving them, but clearly invited further exploration.

*See Dwight D. Eisenhower, *Mandate for Change* (New York, Signet, 1965, p. 570).

The matter was passed on to the U.S.-Chinese ambassadorial talks that October when the United States proposed that the two sides agree to renounce the use of force in the Taiwan area except for purposes of defense. There followed a battle of draft resolutions (Document 9) in which the language of the two sides came closer and closer together, without ever arriving at a point acceptable to both sides. The main sticking point was that all the U.S. drafts explicitly reaffirmed the right of "individual and collective self-defense" (which could imply the validity of the U.S.-GRC Mutual Security Treaty), whereas the Chinese drafts all omitted this but asserted the principle of "mutual respect for territorial integrity" (which could imply the legitimacy of Peking's claim to Taiwan).

Given the depth of animosity and mutual distrust between the two countries then, it is little wonder no agreement was reached. An interesting aspect of the episode, however, is that the objectionable features of the drafts for the respective sides were there by implication only. Our drafts did not require Peking to renounce Taiwan. Peking's drafts did not require us to renounce the Mutual Security Treaty. Had both sides felt their interests would be served, they could have signed one or another of the drafts—reserving the right to differ about what was only implicit therein. Under the circumstances of the day, it is possible that no useful purpose would have been served. But the drafts show an ability bordering on scholasticism by both sides to play with language and tailor it to blur or elude irreconcilable differences. It is interesting that Peking spent as much time and ingenuity as it did in trying to find language it might get us to accept. The moral, if any, is not to dismiss too lightly what might be accomplished through the careful wording of official formulations and statements.

Document 7
Premier Chou En-lai's Statement on the Situation
in the Taiwan Area*
April 23, 1955

"The Chinese people are friendly to the American people.

"The Chinese people do not want a war with the United States of America. The Chinese Government is willing to sit down and enter into negotiations with the United States Government to discuss the question of relaxing tension in the Far East, and especially the question of relaxing tension in the Taiwan area."

SOURCE: *Important Documents Concerning the Question of Taiwan* (Peking, Foreign Languages Press, October 1955).

Document 8
Excerpts from the Speech on the Present
International Situation and China's Foreign Policy
Delivered by Chou En-lai, Premier and Foreign
Minister, to the First National People's
Congress of the People's Republic of China
at its Second Session, July 30, 1955

After the Korean armistice and the restoration of peace in Indo-China, the situation in the Taiwan area has become the most tense in the Far East. It must be pointed out that this tension has been caused by the United States' occupa-

*Premier Chou En-lai of the People's Republic of China made this statement at a meeting of the heads of the delegations of Burma, Ceylon, China, India, Indonesia, Pakistan, the Philippines and Thailand to the Asian-African Conference in the afternoon of April 23, discussing the question of reducing tension in the Far East and especially in the Taiwan area.

tion of China's territory Taiwan and its interference with the liberation of China's coastal islands. This is an international issue between China and the United States. The exercise by the Chinese people of their sovereign rights in liberating Taiwan is a matter of China's internal affairs. These two questions cannot be mixed up. During the Asian-African Conference, the Chinese Government already proposed that China and the United States should sit down and enter into negotiations to discuss the question of easing and eliminating the tension in the Taiwan area. There is no war between China and the United States; the peoples of China and the United States are friendly towards each other; the Chinese people want no war with the United States, so the question of cease-fire between China and the United States does not arise. After the Asian-African Conference, the Chinese Government has further stated that there are two possible ways for the Chinese people to liberate Taiwan, namely, by war or by peaceful means. Conditions permitting, the Chinese people are ready to seek the liberation of Taiwan by peaceful means. In the course of the liberation by the Chinese people of the mainland and the coastal islands, there was no lack of precedents for peaceful liberation. Provided that the United States does not interfere with China's internal affairs, the possibility of peaceful liberation of Taiwan will continue to increase. If possible, the Chinese Government is willing to enter into negotiations with the responsible local authorities of Taiwan to map out concrete steps for Taiwan's peaceful liberation. It should be made clear that these would be negotiations between the central government and local authorities. The Chinese people are firmly opposed to any ideas or plots of the so-called "two Chinas."

In conformity with the principle of easing international tensions and settling international disputes through negotiation, the Chinese Government has taken a series of steps to relax the tension between China and the United States. These efforts of the Chinese Government have received warm welcome and support from world public opinion. Many countries have expressed their willingness to offer good offices between China and the United States. The Chinese Government welcomes the efforts of these countries and expresses its thanks.

SOURCE: Same as Document 7.

Document 9

Chinese Communist and U.S. Draft Resolutions on the Renunciation of Force in the Taiwan Area

Chinese Communist Draft Declaration on Renunciation of Force, October 27, 1955

1. Ambassador Wang Ping-nan on behalf of the Government of the People's Republic of China and Ambassador U. Alexis Johnson on behalf of the Government of the United States of America jointly declare that,

2. In accordance with Article 2, Paragraph 3, of the Charter of the United Nations, "All members shall settle their international disputes by peaceful means in such a manner that international peace and security, and justice, are not endangered"; and

3. In accordance with Article 2, Paragraph 4 of the Charter of the United Nations, "All members shall refrain in their international relations from the threat or use of force against the territorial integrity or political independence of any state, or in any other manner inconsistent with the purposes of the United Nations";

4. The People's Republic of China and the United States of America agree that they should settle disputes between

their two countries by peaceful means without resorting to the threat or use of force.

5. In order to realize their common desire, the People's Republic of China and the United States of America decide to hold a conference of Foreign Ministers to settle through negotiations the questions of relaxing and eliminating tension in the Taiwan area.

United States Draft Declaration on Renunciation of Force, November 10, 1955

1. The Ambassador of the United States of America and the Ambassador of the People's Republic of China during the course of the discussions of practical matters at issue have expressed the determination that the differences between the two sides shall not lead to armed conflict.

2. They recognize that the use of force to achieve national objectives does not accord with the principles and purposes of the United Nations Charter or with generally accepted standards of international conduct.

3. They furthermore recognize that the renunciation of the threat or use of force is essential to the just settlement of disputes or situations which might lead to a breach of the peace.

4. Therefore, without prejudice to the pursuit by each side of its policies by peaceful means they have agreed to announce the following declarations:

5. Ambassador Wang Ping-nan informed Ambassador U. Alexis Johnson that:

6. In general, and with particular reference to the Taiwan area, the People's Republic of China renounces the use of force, except in individual and collective self-defense.

7. Ambassador U. Alexis Johnson informed Ambassador Wang Ping-nan that:

8. In general, and with particular reference to the Taiwan area, the United States renounces the use of force, except in individual and collective self-defense.

Chinese Communist Draft Counterproposal for an Agreed Announcement, December 1, 1955

1. Ambassador Wang Ping-nan, on behalf of the Government of the People's Republic of China, and Ambassador Alexis Johnson, on behalf of the Government of the United States of America, agree to announce:

2. The People's Republic of China and the United States of America are determined that they should settle disputes between their two countries through peaceful negotiations without resorting to the threat or use of force;

3. The two Ambassadors should continue their talks to seek practical and feasible means for the realization of this common desire.

United States Revision of Chinese Communist December 1 Counter-proposal, January 12, 1956

1. Ambassador Wang Ping-nan, on behalf of the Government of the People's Republic of China, and Ambassador U. Alexis Johnson, on behalf of the Government of the United States of America, agree to announce:

2. The People's Republic of China and the United States of America are determined that they will settle disputes between them through peaceful means and that, without prejudice to the inherent right of individual and collective self-defense, they will not resort to the threat or use of force in the Taiwan area or elsewhere.

3. The two Ambassadors should continue their talks to seek practical and feasible means for the realization of this common desire.

United States Draft Proposal for Announcement of April 19, 1956

1.   Ambassador U. Alexis Johnson, on behalf of the Government of the United States of America, and Ambassador Wang Ping-nan, on behalf of the Government of the People's Republic of China, agree, without prejudice to the pursuit by each side of its policies by peaceful means or its inherent right of individual or collective self-defense, to announce:

2.   The United States of America and the People's Republic of China are determined that they should settle disputes between their two countries through peaceful negotiations without resorting to the threat or use of force in the Taiwan area or elsewhere.

3.   The two Ambassadors should continue their talks to seek practical and feasible means for the realization of this common desire.

Chinese Communist Draft Counterproposal for an Agreed Announcement, May 11, 1956

1.   Ambassador Wang Ping-nan, on behalf of the Government of the People's Republic of China, and the Ambassador U. Alexis Johnson, on behalf of the Government of the United States of America, agree, without prejudice to the principles of mutual respect for territorial integrity and sovereignty and non-interference in each other's internal affairs, to announce:

2.   The People's Republic of China and the United States of America are determined that they should settle disputes between their two countries in the Taiwan area through peaceful negotiations without resorting to the threat or use of force against each other;

3.   The two ambassadors should continue their talks to seek and to ascertain within two months practical and feasi-

ble means for the realization of this common desire, including the holding of a Sino-American conference of the foreign ministers, and to make specific arrangements.

Document 10: Peking's Views on War with the United States

This piece is unofficial but undoubtedly authoritative. Nominally, it is a personal appraisal written in April 1966 by an aging American Communist newspaper woman in Peking. It is certain that these views, specified by her as those of "China's leaders," would not have been packaged with this content and sent to the west from Peking as the war in Southeast Asia was escalating except under the most authoritative auspices. Despite the polemical style, it is carefully argued and worth a close reading.

The main message is a threat to send Chinese to fight in Vietnam if the United States "continues to escalate" and if "the Vietnamese people need them." It is noteworthy that this threat would be issued at the same time Peking was placing heavy pressures on Hanoi *not* to end the war through negotiations. The article acknowledges several times that a war between the United States and China might ensue. But it also introduces countervailing considerations. For example, it characterizes Chinese intervention in the Korean war as having been handled in a way that was both militarily effective and "successful in keeping the war from spreading." It cites the reluctance of the U.S. public to engage in a major land war against China. This is followed with arguments intended to show that U.S. reliance on bombing China would be ineffective or counterproductive—ineffective because the dispersal and self-sufficiency of China's communes could withstand a small attack; counterproductive because a nuclear attack big enough to "wreck China" would produce fallout levels that would "wreck" Japan, Korea, Southeast Asia, the Philippines, and parts of the Soviet Union.

Document 10
When and How Will China Go to War?
by Anna Louise Strong
Peking, April 1966

The subject most debated just now by guessing-game of Washington's "experts" is "when and how will China go to war." This has been answered many times by China's leaders but the experts misinterpret or refuse to believe. A campaign is on by part of the U.S. administration to assure the American people that China "never will come in." Other campaigns contradict this by claiming that China is "bellicose."

General Matthew B. Ridgway, who commanded the U.S. forces in the Korean war, warns that the U.S. must limit the Vietnam war "or risk an upward-spiraling course that may approach annihilation" and adds that "easy conquest through air power" is a delusion. Senator J. William Fulbright says the danger of war between the U.S. and China is "real" and blames it on China's "abnormal and agitated state of mind." His solution goes only as far as the "two-China policy" which the U.S. State Department favored long ago. And when some claim that a "shift of U.S. policy" may induce "later generations of leaders in Peking ... to turn away from conquest" *(Ch. Science Monitor,* March 16, 1966) this seems the ultimate in insolent ignorance. "Conquest?" It is Washington, not Peking, that sends troops to all continents to invade and dominate other lands.

As seen from Peking, China does not intend to go to war but expects that war may come to China. China has not a single soldier outside her borders and has never attacked another nation despite the Western myths of her "aggression" in Korea, Tibet and India. She is, however, prepared to defend her country and its socialist achievements if attacked. She also supports the Vietnamese people "in their heroic and just struggle against U.S. aggression." The U.S., now escalating war in Vietnam, is thus on a collision course with China. If China's support of the Vietnamese people's resistance leads to a U.S. attack on China, the Chinese are prepared to make this a war that the U.S. cannot win.

Korea, Tibet, India. That China is non-aggressive is easy to prove to anyone who looks at facts instead of myths. The myths spread abroad against China list Korea, Tibet and India. But Tibet has been recognized as part of China for centuries. "It was Kublai Khan who took Tibet into China about 1250 A.D. in your Western calendar," they told me in Lhasa in 1959. No foreign government in all these centuries ever recognized Tibet as independent by sending an ambassador there, though Britain, the U.S.A. and now India, have played with the idea.

Few deceptions are more brazen than the claim that China invaded India, which is widely believed in the West but easily disproved by careful reading of even American news reports. The border was never defined; India refused to negotiate it. India began the fighting, seizing areas that Britain never held and building military roads and air-bases for years to intrude into new territory, despite repeated diplomatic protests by China. Finally on October 20, 1962, India launched all-out offensive along the border and China counter-attacked and broke the Indian army all down the slopes of the Himalayas. Even then Chinese troops never went beyond the disputed area but withdrew back up the mountains to lines they had held for years, returning all prisoners and even all captured weapons. China then again proposed to negotiate a "friendly border"; India has always made conditions.

It is instructive to consider the Korean war which the West commonly cites as one of China's "aggressions." China had no part in this war until four months after the U.S. troops had invaded North Korea; China did not enter until the U.S. troops reached China's own border, dropped bombs on Manchurian cities and threatened to march into China. Peking sent warning to President Truman through the Indian ambassador as to the point at which China would be forced to enter the war. The big scandal of U.S. intelligence in that war was General MacArthur's assurance to Truman that China's warnings were only bluff. Greater disaster may now attend disregard of China's warnings about Vietnam.

Note that China had three reasons for entering the Korean war and that all these were widely discussed in China: (1) a friendly neighbor, overrun by aggressors, asked aid; (b) China's own border was threatened and some areas in China had been bombed; (c) MacArthur's obvious intent was to drive as far as he could through Manchuria, against both the USSR and the new Chinese government in Peking, which would have threatened a third world war. China's unofficial volunteers caused no such peril. They helped drive the U.S. troops back to the Parallel and brought the war to an end. Both China's actions and the method she chose were successful in keeping the war from spreading. Yet the United Nations, under U.S. pressure, declared China an aggressor, a fact which has disqualified the U.N. in Chinese eyes ever since. China's volunteers, after helping the Koreans repair the devastation made by the U.S.A., returned home in 1958, while U.S. armed forces made a permanent base in South Korea. Who is the aggressor in all this?

Who Threatens Whom? The U.S. automatically repeating

that China is "bellicose," takes as proof a much publicized press conference by Foreign Minister Chen Yi last September in which he said: "For sixteen years we have been waiting for U.S. imperialism to attack us. My hair has grown grey in waiting. If the U.S. imperialists are determined to launch a war of aggression against us, they are welcome to come tomorrow."

Note that Chen Yi never said: "I have waited sixteen years to attack the U.S.A." His expectation of attack by the U.S. is quite rational and not, as Senator Fulbright thinks, an indication of China's "agitated and abnormal state of mind." For twenty years the U.S. has been attacking the Chinese Communists in many ways. When I visited Yenan in 1946, Washington had already spent billions to help Chiang Kai-shek fight the Chinese Communists, even though General Joseph Stilwell, chief of the U.S. Military Mission, reported that the Communists, not Chiang, had been the main Chinese force in defeating Japan. Stilwell was recalled; the U.S. kept on helping Chiang after he lost China. Washington thus put class lines higher than national interests.

Washington not only waged the Korean war to reverse China's revolution but used it as excuse to seize Taiwan (which had been restored to China by agreement) and financed French action in Indo-China. When none of this halted the new China's progress, Washington put embargo on China's trade and encouraged the bombing of Shanghai with many civilian casualties and the seizing of off-shore islands to block the ports of Amoy and Foochow. China today trades with more than a hundred nations but her coastal navigation is still harassed by the U.S. Seventh Fleet and Chiang's protected gunboats. Recently U.S. planes have directly bombed and strafed Chinese fishing boats on the high seas.

China has sent some 400 "serious warnings" of violations of China's air and waters in recent years by the U.S. Seventh Fleet. Washington ignores them but China puts them down for the record. What would the U.S. have done if any nation had similarly violated her air and waters 400 times in seven years? Unlike the U.S., China is patient. Mao's strategy is to let the aggressor reveal himself to the world by many aggressions so that, if war comes, world opinion will know where to fix the blame.

Washington announces that an aim of the present Vietnam war is "to contain China." But it is Washington, not China, that sends soldiers to make war in Southeast Asia and all over the world. U.S. aggressions against China have steadily increased. A year ago the U.S. sent submarines with Polaris missiles of 1,800 mile range to cruise the continental shelf of China, "taking positions to lob nuclear fire over China," as the U.S. press openly bragged. Eight U.S. planes made the first U.S. probe over south Hainan Island on April 9, 1965; they flew over four countries and shot off two missiles, one of which in the confusion brought down a U.S. plane. Washington denied this but China published photographs of parts of the missile and a jettisoned fuel tank on two adjacent commune fields. Later a U.S. plane flew over north Hainan September 20; the Chinese shot it down. Still later, a U.S. plane was shot down over Kwangsi Province. Many spy-planes both manned and "drone" have been shot down over China; I saw three of these "drones" exhibited in Peking in April 1965, with 40,000 people walking past them daily to see them.

The latest incident was the intrusion of a U.S. A-3b heavy-attack plane which made extended flight over Kwangtung Province on April 12, 1966. Intruding over Hainan Island from the southeast at 1:30 p.m., it crossed the big island and the Hainan Straits and proceeded up the Leichow

Peninsula—a total distance of several hundred miles. Chinese aircraft rose to meet it and accompanied it for some time, closing in and giving warnings. When the U.S. plane continued on its flight, they shot it down. What happened to the pilot was not revealed.

All this provocation is sound reason for China's belief that the U.S. intends war. In a sense the U.S. has waged against China for twenty years, a cold war and at times a shooting war in which Washington never made peace. But when the West speaks of war, it means big war, possibly nuclear war. Will such a big war develop? The answer is that if the U.S. keeps on its present collision course, it probably will.

China's Position on Vietnam. China's leaders have given their position, both in general terms and concrete terms with respect to Vietnam for more than a year. Support to the Vietnamese people in their resistance to U.S. aggression has been repeatedly stated: in the *People's Daily,* March 23, 1965; by Foreign Minister Chen Yi March 28; by Premier Chou En-lai March 29 and on April 20, 1965 by the resolution of the National People's Congress, the body which, like the U.S. Congress, has power to declare peace or war.

This response to an appeal on April 10 by the National Assembly of the D.R.V. in Hanoi to the "parliamentary bodies of the world," declared that as signatory to the 1954 Geneva Agreements, and also as a member of the socialist camp of which the D.R.V. is also a member, China solemnly states that "aggression by the U.S. against the D.R.V. means aggression against China," that "the Chinese people have done and will continue to do their utmost to assist the Vietnamese people to defeat the U.S. aggressors completely."

The resolution then calls on the Chinese people to do two things: to join with the peoples throughout the world in a "mighty mass movement to compel the U.S. aggressors to get out of Vietnam," and specifically in China "to make full preparation to send our own people to fight together with the Vietnamese people and drive out the U.S. aggressors in the event that U.S. imperialism continues to escalate its war of aggression and the Vietnamese people need them." These two things were deliberately confused in the Western press. Secretary Rusk said "more threats," sensation writers said "mobilization for war." What Rusk called "more threats" will be seen by history as a clear promise of utmost support to the Vietnamese people and a warning to Washington.

For reasons of mutual security China does not publicize what help she gives to Vietnam or how much. Premier Pham Van Dong thanked China a year ago on April 25 for "the most powerful, most resolute, most effective assistance." The Vietnamese leader whom I interviewed last November for the *Guardian* said: "China gives us all that we ask and considers us as her own front."

None of this help makes China a belligerent as yet. To those Western experts who one day say "China won't fight" and the next day China "is bellicose" and the third day that "Ho Chi Minh doesn't want Chinese troops anyway," one replies: "No nation wants its allies' troops on its territory unless it needs them to repel its enemies." Both North and South Vietnam have effective armed forces for present needs. If the U.S. continues to pour in troops until the Vietnamese feel a need, the Chinese will be there. China's guarantee thus makes the Vietnam war what the West called "open-ended," i.e., the Vietnamese resistance will continue to be able to match the U.S. aggression.

The further the U.S. escalates the more it will be entangled. Even now it is hard to tell whether the U.S. ruling class really want the long war which the experts say it will take to subdue South Vietnam, or whether they are on a tiger and cannot dismount. This past month they have greatly in-creased the bombing in Laos and the threats against Cam-bodia and settled deep into Thailand. They have moved troops and weapons and ships from Europe to Southeast Asia. Hence one must face the fact that a big war with China is possible, either as gradual escalation or by sudden attack. Opinion on this is confused in America. A prevalent view is that such a war can be won by bombing, without the entan-glement of a big land war. This delusion is promoted to calm the American people, already disturbed by the casualties and defeats in South Vietnam with its fourteen million peo-ple and unwilling to take on China, whose 700 million people equal 50 South Vietnams!

Can Nuclear War Win? The American people's instinct in this is very sound. The dream of winning a war by bombing is a myth. Conventional bombs were found powerless in World War II to win final victories; they are failing now against North Vietnam. Some people think nuclear bombs might wreck China with little damage to the U.S.A. Chinese are aware of what American scientists also begin to admit, that nuclear bombing sufficient to wreck China would also wreck by fall-out several nearby countries, Japan, Korea, Southeast Asia and the Philippines, as well as nearby areas of the USSR. The 10,000 megaton bombardment, estimated in *Life* magazine, May 28, 1965 as adequate to kill half of China's population, would raise the radio-activity of the world's atmosphere by 20 times, making a world health haz-ard even in the United States. It is delusion to think the U.S.A. can thus ruin China without danger to itself.

Chinese know from experience, as Hanoi knows, that they can survive and win without cities, railroads or bridges. They did it once and can do it again. When I saw the people's communes in 1958 I said at once: "This is the country that can best survive even nuclear war." Every commune, which is a township, is a local unit combining state power, economic resources and home defense. It produces food and often textiles. The great steel drive of 1953, at which the West laughed, taught 60,000,000 Chinese people how to make steel in their own backyards, and also where the nearest iron ore and coal was found. If China was split into its 75,000 communes, each of them would be able to raise food, make clothing and housing, and even tools and ammunition from home-made steel. The county level would be even more self-sufficient than the township and the provinces more self-sufficient still. Even the splitting of China by wide zones of radio-active waste would not prevent the Chinese people in all these isolated areas from organizing life and defense in a fairly efficient manner, communicating by radio as in Yenan days.

At some stage in the bombing the U.S. would realize that nothing had been won except the scorn and hatred of an outraged world. If U.S. imperialism was then driven, as in Vietnam, to try to occupy territory, it would really encounter the deadly wrath of the Chinese.

What China may have in advanced weapons is not known to me. I take it for granted that some such surprises may exist; it is known, of course, that China has detonated two nuclear bombs and also brought down high-flying U-2s and drones. But I also take for granted that those foreign experts who judge China weak in long-range offensive weapons may be right; China's military strength is built to defend China, not to attack other lands. It is primarily based on the quality of man-power.

Quality of Man-Power. From open sources, known by many friends and by myself, I can testify that the People's Liberation Army is composed of men of exceptionally high quality, physically, mentally and morally. Every soldier is trained to understand strategy, for the tradition of the PLA is to discuss battle plans with the rank and file. Physically, they seem all to be acrobats. They can walk swiftly and silently right up the side of a many-storied building either by raising a bamboo pole and climbing it, or by climbing in couples from window to window, each man swinging the other to the window ledge above him.

Their small arms are considered better than the American. "And why not?" said a friend. "Does the U.S.A. ever ask the soldiers what kind of weapons they need? We develop ours by the 'mass line' so that every soldier has a chance to suggest 'innovations' and we get precisely the weapon the soldiers want." An American former G.I. who tested a Chinese rifle told me it was light, easy handling, with little recoil and in general the best he had ever seen.

As for the militia, they are countless. In every town and village you see them drilling and marching; they include practically all energetic able-bodied youth and are under local control. Whenever Chiang Kai-shek drops agents by parachute into remote areas or sends them by boat, the militia of the nearest commune is usually the first to capture them. If U.S. forces invade China, they will have no "front" to fight on; they will be encircled by militia like a sea.

China's youth is patriotic and revolutionary; friends who are teaching in the universities convince me of this. A teacher who interviewed sixty individual students gave me some of their remarks: "If the U.S. gets into war with China, then DeGaulles will spring up all over the world," said one. "Our generation is given by history the task of eliminating imperialism from the world," said another. "For this the American people must overthrow U.S. imperialism and thus make possible world peace. We Chinese cannot export revolution. But a movement already begins in America because of the

Vietnam war. If the Americans invade China, we shall help make the revolution in America by the way we handle their troops." These comments are from youth of college age.

Official Statements. On the background of these comments, the official statements by Chinese leaders on the subject may be better understood. One of the earliest was that by Lo Jui-ching, Chief of Staff of the People's Liberation Army, published in *Peking Review,* May 14, 1965 celebrating the anniversary of the anti-Nazi victory over Hitler. "Our principle is: We will not attack unless we are attacked; if we are attacked, we will certainly counter-attack. On whatever scale the U.S. attacks us, we shall reply on that scale." The author sees no contradiction in stating in the same article: "We are prepared to send our men to fight together with the Vietnamese people when they need us."

A longer statement was that by Lin Piao, Minister of Defense, in his famous pamphlet on "People's War." "Chinese people definitely have ways of their own for coping with the U.S. imperialist war of aggression ... the most important is still the mobilization of the people, reliance on the people, making everyone a soldier and waging a people's war. We want to tell the U.S. imperialists that the vast ocean of several hundred million Chinese people in arms will be more than enough to submerge your few million aggressor troops. If you dare to impose war on us, we shall gain freedom of action. It will then not be up to you to decide how the war shall be fought.... The naval and air superiority you boast cannot intimidate us and neither can the atom bomb you brandish. We have the courage to shoulder the heavy burden of combating U.S. imperialism and to contribute our share in the struggle for final victory over the most ferocious enemy of the people of the world."

Vice-Premier Chen Yi said in that press conference last

September: "Should the U.S. imperialists invade China's mainland, we will take all necessary measures to defeat them. By then the war will have no boundaries. . . . With the defeat of U.S. imperialism the time will come when imperialism and neo-colonialism will be really liquidated throughout the world. . . . China is ready to make all necessary sacrifices for this noble ideal."

Mao Tse-tung said it in essence nearly ten years ago in a speech on "Correct Handling of Contradictions Among the People," February 27, 1957, "People all over the world are discussing whether a third world war will break out. . . . We stand firmly for peace and against war. But if the imperialists insist on unleashing another war, we should not be afraid of it. . . . Our attitude is: First, we are against it; second, we are not afraid of it." He goes on to state that in such a war "the whole structure of imperialism" might collapse.

SOURCE: Supplement to *Letter from China*, No. 38, April 25, 1966; also contains material from Letters Nos. 28 and 35.

Documents 11-12: Japanese Rearmament

These documents bear on Peking's fears of a rearmed Japan. Document 11 is an extract from the Sato-Nixon Communiqué of November 1969. Its fourth paragraph reflects a modification of Japan's inward looking foreign policies by officially specifying that the security of South Korea was "essential to Japan's own security" and that "peace and security in the Taiwan area was also a most important factor for the security of Japan." These nuanced phrases immediately came under fierce attack from Peking as marking Japanese ambitions to reestablish a military sphere of influence. With time, the intensity of the attacks rose, as did Peking's projections of the future extent of Japanese "militarism." Document 12 epitomizes this trend. Although florid and venomous in tone, its point of departure is not without logic. With matter-of-fact realism, it recognizes Japan's rapid economic growth, noting that this would permit a large increase in military strength, which in turn could be used for purposes highly objectionable from Peking's point of view.

Document 11

Text of Joint Communiqué
(White House Press Release Dated November 21, 1969)

1. President Nixon and Prime Minister Sato met in Washington on November 19, 20 and 21, 1969, to exchange views on the present international situation and on other matters of mutual interest to the United States and Japan.

2. The President and the Prime Minister recognized that both the United States and Japan have greatly benefited from their close association in a variety of fields, and they declared that guided by their common principles of democra-

cy and liberty, the two countries would maintain and strengthen their fruitful cooperation in the continuing search for world peace and prosperity and in particular for the relaxation of international tensions. The President expressed his and his government's deep interest in Asia and stated his belief that the United States and Japan should cooperate in contributing to the peace and prosperity of the region. The Prime Minister stated that Japan would make further active contributions to the peace and prosperity of Asia.

3. The President and the Prime Minister exchanged frank views on the current international situation, with particular attention to developments in the Far East. The President, while emphasizing that the countries in the area were expected to make their own efforts for the stability of the area, gave assurance that the United States would continue to contribute to the maintenance of international peace and security in the Far East by honoring its defense treaty obligations in the area. The Prime Minister, appreciating the determination of the United States, stressed that it was important for the peace and security of the Far East that the United States should be in a position to carry out fully its obligations referred to by the President. He further expressed his recognition that, in the light of the present situation, the presence of United States forces in the Far East constituted a mainstay for the stability of the area.

4. The President and the Prime Minister specifically noted the continuing tension over the Korean peninsula. The Prime Minister deeply appreciated the peacekeeping efforts of the United Nations in the area and stated that the security of the Republic of Korea was essential to Japan's own security. The President and the Prime Minister shared hope that Communist China would adopt a more cooperative and constructive attitude in its external relations. The Presi-

dent referred to the treaty obligations of his country to the Republic of China which the United States would uphold. The Prime Minister said that the maintenance of peace and security in the Taiwan area was also a most important factor for the security of Japan. The President described the earnest efforts made by the United States for a peaceful and just settlement of the Viet-Nam problem. The President and the Prime Minister expressed the strong hope that the war in Viet-Nam would be concluded before return of the administrative rights over Okinawa to Japan. In this connection, they agreed that, should peace in Viet-Nam not have been realized by the time reversion of Okinawa is scheduled to take place, the two governments would fully consult with each other in the light of the situation at the time so that reversion would be accomplished without affecting the United States efforts to assure the South Vietnamese people the opportunity to determine their own political future without outside interference. The Prime Minister stated that Japan was exploring what role she could play in bringing about stability in the Indo-china area.

Source: *Department of State Bulletin,* December 15, 1969, Vol. 61.

Document 12
Wild Ambition Completely Exposed
by "Renmin Ribao" Commentator

Soon after his "visit" to the United States, Yasuhiro Nakasone, a Japanese militarist and the so-called "Director General of the Defense Agency" of the Sato government, was very pleased with himself when he made a speech on the "future course" of Japan. This speech is worth reading as a piece of negative material. Nakasone resorted to various sophistries to cover up the revival of Japanese militarism.

But the more he tried to conceal, the more he revealed Japanese militarism's rabid designs.

In his speech, Nakasone made a great effort to deny that Japanese militarism has been revived. What was his argument? U.S. Defense Secretary Laird and Assistant to the U.S. President Kissinger, it was said, had told him: "Japan is not a militarist state." How ridiculous! It is precisely under the aegis of U.S. imperialism that Japanese militarism has been revived. Since it was his masters that Nakasone consulted, he naturally got the expected answer—Japanese militarism has not been revived. It is not surprising that both the U.S. and Japanese reactionaries find it necessary to hide the fact that Japanese militarism has already been revived.

Referring to Japan's "future course," Nakasone dwelt on three points: First, Japan "will not do things beyond its national strength"; second, Japan "will not seek adventures in foreign affairs"; and third, Japan "must keep up with the world current."

What on earth is Nakasone driving at?

Japan "will not do things beyond its national strength." In other words, Japan will do things commensurate with its present "national strength." Japan's economic strength has swollen enormously while its military strength, in the eyes of the Japanese ruling clique, does not yet "correspond" to its economic strength. Therefore, their aim now is to turn Japan, a so-called "economic power," into a so-called "military power." So, when Nakasone implied that Japan would do things commensurate with its present "national strength," this actually meant arms expansion and war preparations on a larger scale to meet the demand of Japan's monopoly capital for expansion abroad.

Nakasone's speech also gave away the ambitious attempt of the Japanese reactionaries to carry out nuclear armament. During his visit to the United States, he proposed setting up a U.S.-Japan "joint organization for the production of enriched uranium." The Japanese reactionaries have long been supplied with enriched uranium by the United States and now they seek U.S. permission for producing enriched uranium themselves. In this way, with the enriched uranium produced under the cloak of "peaceful purpose" Japanese militarism can easily turn to manufacturing nuclear weapons. In fact, the Japanese ruling clique has been seeking nuclear armament all the time and by every means. In its "National Defence White Paper" made public recently, the Japanese Government, while advertising a so-called "policy of non-nuclear armament," asserted that, according to the constitution, it is "possible" for Japan to possess so-called "small-sized nuclear weapons of a pure defence character." Is not this a flagrant attempt to seek "legal ground" for the nuclear arming of Japan? Nuclear weapons are nuclear weapons no matter what they are called, "small-sized" or "of a defence character." In seeking nuclear armament so impatiently, Japanese militarism aims at carrying out nuclear threat and nuclear blackmail against the people of the Asian and Pacific region so as to perpetrate aggression and expansion even more unscrupulously.

Japan "will not seek adventures in foreign affairs." What does it mean by adventures? In the eyes of the Japanese reactionaries, Japan's attack on Pearl Harbour in 1941 was probably an adventure whereas all the other wars of aggression unleashed by Japanese militarism were not. For instance, the Sino-Japanese War of 1894 in which Japan occupied China's Liaotung Peninsula and annexed China's Taiwan and Penghu Islands was no adventure at all! The occupation by Japan of the whole of Korea and turning it into a colony at the beginning of the 20th century were no adventure! Japan's occupation of China's Northeast in 1931 and all-out aggression against China in 1937 were no adventure either! In the opinion of the Japanese militarists, the Pearl Harbour incident alone was an adventure while the rest was not. In saying that Japan "will not seek adventures," Nakasone actually meant that Japan, instead of embarking on adventures such as the Pearl Harbour incident against the United States, would gang up with U.S. imperialism in energetically carrying out aggression and expansion against other countries. Are not such reactionary films as *Isoroku Yamamoto* and *Gateway to Glory* turned out in Japan in recent years an undisguised propagation of Japanese militarist ideas?

Japan "must keep up with the world current." What "world current" do the Japanese reactionaries think of keeping up with? In the present era, there are two world currents. One is the revolutionary main current which the Japanese reactionaries certainly do not want to keep up with. The other is the counter-revolutionary adverse current which opposes communism, opposes China, opposes the people, opposes the national-liberation movement and opposes the revolutionary struggle of the people of various countries. In saying that Japan "must keep up with the world current," Nakasone meant that it should tail after U.S. imperialism's policies of aggression and war, suppress the people's revolutionary movements in Asia and expand its sphere of colonial influence.

Nakasone even had the impudence to state that the Japanese reactionaries cherish so-called "goodwill" towards China. He also advertised "a definite limit of what should not be done (by Japan) in its relations with Korea and Taiwan." He seemed to imply that Japanese militarism would not commit acts like helping the south Korean puppet clique to attack the Democratic People's Republic of Korea and helping the Chiang Kai-shek bandit gang to attack the Chinese mainland. This is sheer eyewash. The forces of Japanese militarism have already swarmed into south Korea and stretched their tentacles to China's territory Taiwan Province. What is this if not an-attack? Moreover, a first step will be followed by a second. How could Japanese militarism possibly have any "goodwill"? And how could there be any "limit" to its aggressive designs?

Nakasone tried his utmost to strike a pose of "peace" to dispel the "fears" of the peoples of the world of aggression by the Japanese reactionaries; but that is completely useless. The aggression and expansion by Japanese militarism in Asia and other regions are facts obvious to all. Japan's aggressive forces have already penetrated into vast areas of Asia, into the Philippines, Thailand, "Malaysia," Singapore, Indonesia, South Viet-Nam, Laos, India and other countries or regions, in addition to China's territory Taiwan Province and south Korea. According to the Japanese press, the accumulated total of Japan's export of capital from 1959 to 1968 reached 4,950 million U.S. dollars, more than half of which was concentrated in Asia. The export of Japanese commodities also shot up sharply. In 1969, Japan's exports to Southeast Asia accounted for 4,460 million U.S. dollars, or double that of 1965, with a favorable trade balance of 2,100 million U.S. dollars in a single year. Japan's economic influence has also extended to the Middle East, Africa and Latin America. Japanese monopoly capitalist groups clamoured wildly that "the possibility of redividing the world market has already emerged" and that "the time for a second redistribution of international resources" has come. Thus it can be seen that the Japanese militarists' "Greater East Asia Co-prosperity Sphere" has gone beyond the sphere of East Asia and become a "Greater Asia Co-prosperity Sphere." Their ambition today is greater than in the pre-war period.

Today, Japanese monopoly capital has swollen to such an extent that it can no longer halt itself. In order to grab resources and markets, it is bound to carry out expansion abroad to feverishly practice militarism with the backing of armed force.

To put it bluntly, what Nakasone called Japan's "future course" is the embarkation once again on the Japanese militarist road of aggression and expansion by relying on U.S. imperialism, the road of serving as U.S. imperialism's gendarme in Asia in an attempt to dominate Asia through military adventure, the dangerous road of plunging the Japanese nation once again into an abyss of misery.

Our great leader Chairman Mao has pointed out: "The U.S. imperialists and all other such vermin have already created their own grave-diggers; the day of their burial is not far off."

The present era is not the year of 1937 or 1931, still less the year of 1894. The days when the imperialists could ride roughshod over others are gone for ever. Particularly, earth-shaking changes have taken place in Asia. Standing rock-firm is the great socialist China. The Democratic People's Republic of Korea has become a powerful bulwark at the anti-U.S. forefront in the East. The war waged by the people of Viet-Nam, Cambodia and Laos against U.S. aggression and for national salvation is developing victoriously. The awakening of the Japanese people has never been as high as it is today, and their struggle against U.S. imperialist aggression and the revival of Japanese militarism by the U.S. and Japanese reactionaries is growing with each passing day. The Japanese people will absolutely not tolerate Japanese militarism to embark on an adventure of aggression in Asia in collaboration with U.S. imperialism. Neither will this be tolerated by the Chinese people, the Korean people and the people of other Asian countries. If it dares to unleash anoth-

er war of aggression, there can be no other outcome for
Japanese militarism but inevitable and complete destruction.

SOURCE: *Peking Review,* October 30, 1970, No. 44.

Index

Acheson, Dean, xxii, 89n
Albania, better U.S. relations with, 50

Burma
Chinese support for insurgency, 33, 35, 39, 40
relations with China, 41-42, 56
pre-1967, 36-37, 39-40

Cairo declaration, 94
Cambodia
Chinese-North Vietnamese attitudes, 40
Sihanouk, Prince Norodom, 40
Canadian formula for Chinese recognition, 57
Chen Yi, 114, 121-122
Chiang Kai-shek, 10, 64-65, 94. *See also* GRC and Taiwan.
Chinese involvement in Southeast Asia, 33-34. *See also* Strong, Anna Louise, Chinese views of war with the U.S.
support for insurgency, 33, 35-36, 37-38, 56
CHIREP (Chinese representation in the United Nations), xiii, 14-17. *See also* GRC.
definition, xxviiin
public and Congressional reaction, 15, 16
reduction in U.S.-Chinese tensions, xxix-xxx, xxxvi
replacement of GRC, 5, 14
universality of UN membership, 15
U.S. action on, xxviii, 69
and U.S.-Japanese relations, 14-15
U.S. position on GRC membership, 15-17
and Vietnam war, 36
Chou En-lai, negotiating with U.S. on Taiwan status, 101, 103n, 103-105
Cohen, Jerome A., 62n
Cultural Revolution, 63
Burma and Liu Shao-ch'i, 39-40
opposition to Mao, 64

Decisionmaking, governmental
analyzing foreign policy, xxiv
"hard" data vs. "soft" intelligence, 71, 73
historical study of China, need for, xiii-xiv
information and communication, xxxi, 75-76

133

Selected Rand Books

Becker, Abraham S., *Soviet National Income 1958-1964, National Accounts of the USSR in the Seven Year Plan Period,* Berkeley and Los Angeles, University of California Press, 1969.

Bergson, A., *The Real National Income of Soviet Russia Since 1928,* Cambridge, Harvard University Press, 1961.

Bergson, A., and Hans Heymann, Jr., *Soviet National Income and Product, 1940-48,* New York, Columbia University Press, 1954.

Chapman, Janet G., *Real Wages in Soviet Russia Since 1928,* Cambridge, Harvard University Press, 1963.

Clawson, Marion A., Hans H. Landsberg, and Lyle T. Alexander, *The Agricultural Potential of the Middle East,* New York, American Elsevier, 1971.

Cooper, Charles A., and Sidney S. Alexander (eds.), *Economic Development and Population Growth in the Middle East,* New York, American Elsevier, 1971.

Dorfman, Robert, Paul A. Samuelson, and Robert M. Solow, *Linear Programming and Economic Analysis,* New York, McGraw-Hill Book Company, Inc., 1958.

Downs, Anthony, *Inside Bureaucracy,* Boston, Little, Brown and Company, 1967.

Gurtov, Melvin, *Southeast Asia Tomorrow: Problems and Prospects for U.S. Policy,* Baltimore, The Johns Hopkins Press, 1970.

Halpern, Manfred, *The Politics of Social Change in the Middle East and North Africa,* Princeton, Princeton University Press, 1963.

Hammond, Paul Y., and Sidney S. Alexander (eds.), *Political Dynamics of the Middle East,* New York, American Elsevier, 1971.

Harman, Alvin, *The International Computer Industry: Innovation and Comparative Advantage,* Cambridge, Harvard University Press, 1971.

Hirshleifer, Jack, James C. DeHaven, and Jerome W. Milliman, *Water Supply: Economics, Technology, and Policy,* Chicago, The University of Chicago Press, 1960.

Hitch, Charles J., and Roland N. McKean, *The Economics of Defense in the Nuclear Age,* Cambridge, Harvard University Press, 1960.

Hoeffding, Oleg, *Soviet National Income and Product in 1928,* New York, Columbia University Press, 1954.

Hsieh, Alice L., *Communist China's Strategy in the Nuclear Era,* Englewood Cliffs, N.J., Prentice-Hall, Inc., 1962.

Johnson, John J. (ed.), *The Role of the Military in Underdeveloped Countries,* Princeton, Princeton University Press, 1962.

Johnson, William A., *The Steel Industry of India,* Cambridge, Harvard University Press, 1966.

Johnstone, William C., *Burma's Foreign Policy: A Study in Neutralism,* Cambridge, Harvard University Press, 1963.

W9-BYV-314

8/2019

What Are Biblical Values?

What the Bible Says on Key Ethical Issues

JOHN J. COLLINS

Yale

UNIVERSITY PRESS

New Haven and London

Yale University Press books may be purchased in quantity for educational, business, or promotional use. For information, please e-mail sales.press@yale.edu (U.S. office) or sales@yaleup.co.uk (U.K. office).

Set in Janson type by IDS Infotech Ltd., Chandigarh, India.
Printed in the United States of America.

Library of Congress Control Number: 2018968057.
ISBN 978-0-300-23193-9 (hardcover : alk. paper)

A catalogue record for this book is available from the British Library.

This paper meets the requirements of ANSI/NISO Z39.48-1992 (Permanence of Paper).

10 9 8 7 6 5 4 3 2 1

To the students of Yale Divinity School who took the course
"What Are Biblical Values?" in the years 2012–18

Contents

CONTENTS

Acknowledgments

Key chapters of this book were delivered as the Sprunt Lectures at Union Theological Seminary in Richmond, Virginia, in May 2018. My thanks are due to Brian Blount, president of Union Seminary, and Professor Sam Adams for the invitation to deliver those lectures. Thanks are also due to the Reverend Jeff Braun, Professor Rebecca Raphael, and Professor Robyn Whitaker for invitations to lecture on biblical values on other occasions, to Fred Appel of Princeton University Press for feedback on the manuscript, to T. J. Thames for assistance when he was my teaching assistant, and to Jennifer Banks, Heather Gold, and Mary Pasti for guiding the book to publication at Yale University Press.

What Are Biblical Values?

TALK of biblical values is ubiquitous in American political discourse. An advertisement in the *Wall Street Journal* by the Billy Graham Evangelistic Association, published in the run-up to the presidential election in 2012, provides a typical example. In it the popular preacher calls on his readers to vote for candidates who affirm biblical principles and support the nation of Israel. He continues: "I urge you to vote for those who protect the sanctity of life and support the biblical definition of marriage between a man and a woman."[1]

Values are principles that offer guidance for human conduct, rather than specific laws or commandments. So, for example, we might think of "love of God and one's neighbor" or "the pursuit of holiness" as broad values that might be espoused in a variety of ways. In practice, however, biblical values are often boiled down, as they are in the *Wall Street Journal* advertisement, to specific positions on a few hot-button issues, most frequently the rejection of homosexuality and abortion and the affirmation of traditional "family values." These positions stand as symbols for a way of life. They are seldom accompanied by any serious reflection on what the Bible actually says about them. Rather, people who accord high symbolic value to the Bible tend to assume that it conforms to their own traditional views. If they read the Bible with any care, they might be surprised by what they find.

My purpose in this book is to examine what the Bible actually says, what values the Bible actually affirms, on several key issues.[2] The number of relevant topics is vast, and my discussion is illustrative rather than comprehensive. I have chosen topics that are both important in the Bible and relevant to contemporary discussions. I am not attempting a descriptive account of the ethical world of the Bible or of the moral values of ancient Israel and early Christianity.[3] My interest is in the relevance of the ancient texts to modern situations.

Before we turn to specific issues, however, there are some preliminary problems that must be addressed. To speak of what the Bible actually says is at best a deceptively simple task, at worst a hopelessly naïve one. The task is complicated especially by three questions.

First, the Bible is a written text, not a speaking agent. As such, does it say anything at all? It is conventional, of course, to say that the Bible, or a specific book, "says" this or that, but this is only convenient shorthand. To extract meaning from the written text, we must subject it to a process of interpretation, in which our own presuppositions inevitably play a role. We are constantly reminded that texts can be manipulated to reflect the agenda of the interpreter. Is it still possible to ascribe any kind of objective meaning to the Bible?

Second, the Bible is a collection of texts, written over the course of more than a thousand years. It is neither systematic nor consistent, and it often espouses contradictory positions. Is it possible to generalize about biblical values in a way that has overarching validity?

Third, if we can speak of biblical values, as I believe we can, must we always affirm them? The Bible has traditionally provided support for many positions that we may now regard as reprehensible: slavery, genocide, subordination of women, legitimization of violence, and intolerance of diversity. Any discussion of biblical values must consider not only what these values are but also whether anyone in the modern world has any obligation to conform to them.

DOES THE BIBLE ACTUALLY SAY ANYTHING?

Perhaps the fundamental challenge to any attempt to speak of biblical values concerns the possibility of objective interpretation.[4] As one critic puts it, "Texts don't mean, people mean with texts."[5] A text doesn't mean anything until it is interpreted or construed in a particular way. Interpretation depends on context and on the tradition of the community in which it is taking place. The conventions and assumptions of the interpreting community are especially important.[6] We are not free to interpret texts any way we wish, as Humpty Dumpty claimed to do in *Through the Looking Glass:* " 'When *I* use a word,' Humpty Dumpty said in rather a scornful tone, 'it means just what I choose it to mean—neither more nor less.' " If we want to

communicate with other people, we must have commonly accepted ways of interpretation. This is not because words have
inherent meanings, but because meaning is the product of social
consensus. Texts have no independent agency. That is, a text like
the Bible as a source of doctrine or ethics cannot be considered
separately from the interpreting Christian (or Jewish) community. It is available to us for instrumental use, to reinforce the
doctrine and ethics we have imbibed from several different
sources.[7] We might make a similar argument about the use of
the US Constitution in legal decision making. There, too, the
supposedly authoritative text can be manipulated to support positions that the interpreter wishes to affirm for reasons quite independent of the Constitution itself. The way we interpret any
text depends on the presuppositions and agendas we bring to it.

The claim that texts such as the Bible do not speak independently of interpreters is true in the literal sense. Texts
in themselves do not convey meaning without the agency of
authors and readers. "What the Bible really says" is a way
of saying "what I take the Bible to really mean." This does not
mean that interpreters can make texts mean anything they
wish. Readers are constrained by the communities in which
they live. Jewish and Christian believers have always filtered
the Scripture through their respective traditions. For many
Christians, it seems obvious that Old Testament prophecies
such as Isaiah 7:14 ("the virgin shall conceive and bear a son")
and Isaiah 53 (the Suffering Servant) are prophecies of Jesus,
even though they were written many centuries before his
birth. For Jews looking at the Hebrew Bible (the same text
as the Old Testament), such interpretations are not credible
at all. The argument that interpretation is, and should be,

determined by the tradition in which we stand and the interpretive community to which we belong has obvious appeal to
people who are committed to a given tradition, since it ex-
empts the community from assessing it with external criteria.

But the constraints on interpretation do not come only
from communal tradition and social consensus. There are also
constraints of language and grammar. The biblical texts were
written long ago in languages that are no longer spoken in
their ancient form. A reader who wishes to read the Bible com-
petently needs to master those languages and their ancient
contexts or rely on others who have that mastery. In effect, the
reader needs to know not only his or her own interpretive tradition but the linguistic world in which the text was produced.[8]
Texts are products of human authors and editors and arise in
specific historical contexts. A text may take on new meanings
in new contexts, but the meaning as determined by its original
context remains an essential point of reference.[9] So, for example, Isaiah 7:14 had to make sense, first of all, in the eighth
century BCE, when a reference to Jesus would have been un-
intelligible, whatever other meanings were later attached to it.
Meaning is a negotiation between author and reader. Readers
inevitably bring new perspectives to a text and see it differently in different generations, a point that is readily obvious
from the history of interpretation.[10] But the validity of any new
interpretation must still be assessed by its ability to account for
the words on the page in a way that does not do violence to
their grammar and their ancient context.

In short, interpretation does not yield meanings that are
objective in the sense of being timelessly valid, but they are not
simply indeterminate either. In the words of the literary critic

Robert Alter, "The words of the text afford us at least a narrow strip of solid ground in the quagmire of indeterminacy, because the words a writer uses, despite the margin of ambiguity of some of them, have definite meanings, and no critic is free to invent meanings in order to sustain a reading."[11] A text, biblical or not, may have more than one meaning, but we can at least set limits to the range of acceptable interpretations.

ETHICAL INTERPRETATION

The argument is not just about objectivity but also about the ethics of reading. Those who appeal to what the Bible "says" can mask or deny their responsibility for their interpretations: "It is not I who am saying this, but the Bible," or even "It is God who says this." This kind of appeal to the authority of the text is called "textual foundationalism." The Bible is taken as a relatively firm foundation for certain kinds of knowledge, just as nature is thought to be for scientific knowledge. Critics of biblical foundationalism argue that the Bible, historically interpreted, "cannot be depended on to deliver secure, ethical interpretations of Scripture."[12] By this they mean that the Bible, historically interpreted, has provided support for unethical positions. The debate about slavery in nineteenth-century America provides obvious examples.[13] Defenders of slavery pointed out that neither Moses nor Jesus outlawed slavery or proposed that the institution should be abolished. In this they were indisputably right. The Bible, historically interpreted, condones slavery and many other practices of questionable morality besides. Consequently, it has often provided a cloak of respectability to bigots, racists, and despots.

But biblical foundationalism involves two issues that should be carefully distinguished. One, as we have already seen, is whether the Bible has a determinate meaning. The other is the issue of biblical authority. In fact, there can be no reasonable doubt that slavery was condoned in the Bible. The nineteenth-century polemicists who said that the Bible does not condemn slavery were right. But to say that the Bible is a secure basis for doctrine or morals on this issue is quite another matter. The problem here lies in the kind of authority we ascribe to the Bible, regardless of how we interpret it.

We shall return to the question of biblical authority shortly. For the present, it may suffice to note that the question of authority should not be confused with that of determinate meaning. There are many issues—slavery, genocide, patriarchy, to take only the less controversial examples—on which biblical texts are quite clear, and their meaning is not in dispute, but the positions they expound are not edifying, and are problematic from a modern viewpoint. Intellectual honesty demands that we acknowledge profound contradictions between biblical and modern sensibilities on many issues. We cannot produce ethical readings by distorting or denying what the text says when it conflicts with our modern moral values, even when those values have long-standing support in Christian or Jewish tradition.

MULTIPLE COMMUNITIES

Most people in the modern world belong to more than one community and participate in more than one tradition. No one is shaped exclusively by a church or synagogue; any educated person also learns to read texts in a secular context. Christians who have been exposed to the academic study of the Bible know that there are different ways of reading Scripture, and an informed reader must choose between them. To rely on the authority of interpreting communities is just as much an evasion of responsibility as the textual foundationalism of a fundamentalist.

If people of different faith communities want to work together and have meaningful conversations, they need to see the biblical texts in a broader perspective than that of their own tradition. One way of doing this is to ask what the texts would have meant in their original context. The historical focus is a way of getting distance from the text and achieving a measure of objectivity. It appeals to criteria of language and history that are not derived from or beholden to modern faith commitments and ideologies, and this gives it at least a qualified objectivity in assessing issues in dispute.

Whether the historical meaning so constructed is in any sense binding for people in modern society is quite another question, to which we will return repeatedly throughout this book. But if we are to speak of the Bible at all, it is important to respect its integrity and not reduce it to instrumental use in the service of either traditional dogma or modern ideology.

THE DIVERSITY OF THE BIBLICAL MATERIAL

The Bible is not a coherent, systematic treatise but a collection of writings that grew over a thousand years or so. It contains different theologies and different emphases. The theology of Deuteronomy is quite different from that of Leviticus, and both are called into question by the Book of Job. Similarly, in the New Testament, the Gospel of Matthew and the Epistle of

James are quite different from the theology of Paul. We cannot expect, then, to distill from the Bible one coherent set of values. As Shakespeare said, "The devil can cite Scripture for his purpose." Conversely, to say that a particular value has a scriptural basis is not enough to establish its validity, since it may be undercut by other biblical passages. Scripture is not a univocal document but often has the character of a running debate. To adopt one set of biblical values may, on occasion, require rejecting another set.

Since biblical support can be found for various conflicting values, it is necessary to establish some hierarchy of values within the biblical material. In fact, such a hierarchy was established in antiquity. The Gospel of Mark 12:28–34 recounts an exchange between Jesus and one of the scribes. The scribe asked him, "Which commandment is the first of all?" Jesus answered, "The first is 'Hear O Israel: The Lord our God, the Lord is one; you shall love the Lord your God with all your heart and with all your mind, and with all your strength.' The second is this: 'you shall love your neighbor as yourself.' There is no other commandment greater than these."[14] The Gospel of Matthew adds: "On these two commandments hang all the law and the prophets" (22:40). Here Jesus combined the Shema ("Hear O Israel") from Deuteronomy 6:4–5 and the command to love one's neighbor in Leviticus 19:18. In the parallel passage in Luke 10:25–28, Jesus turns the question back to the questioner, who runs the two passages from the Hebrew Bible together.

The formulation of the double love commandment in these Gospel passages is distinctive, but not without parallel in ancient Judaism.[15] The Jewish philosopher Philo of Alexandria, a contemporary of Jesus, wrote:

> But amongst the vast number of particular truths and princi-
> ples there studied, there stand out, so to speak, high above the
> others, two main heads: one of duty to God as shown by piety
> and holiness, one of duty to human beings as shown by *philan-
> thropia* and justice, each of them splitting up into multiform
> branches. (*Special Laws* 2.63)[16]

Unlike Jesus, Philo does not speak of love, but the net
effect is similar. The tendency to organize the commandments under two headings is especially typical of the Greek-
speaking Jewish Diaspora and reflects the systematizing
influence of Greek philosophy and rhetoric.[17] The rabbis, too,
tend to subsume some commandments under others, but
they do not speak of one commandment that summarizes all
the others.[18] Rabbi Akiba is said to have regarded Leviticus
19:18 as *a* great general rule, not necessarily *the* great general
rule.[19]

Prioritizing these two commandments does not resolve
all problems in biblical values. Neither love of God nor love
of neighbor is unambiguous, and there are many things in the
Bible that are not easily reconciled with love of God and love
of neighbor on any interpretation.

We shall have to ask what these two commandments entail in practice when applied to specific issues. But already the
focus on these two commandments provides a criterion that
will bring some order to the diversity of biblical values.

THE NATURE OF BIBLICAL LAW

In popular perception, the Bible is often regarded as a source
of divine commands, timeless and nonnegotiable. This perception calls for several qualifications.

To begin with, while the Bible certainly contains laws, they are the exception rather than the rule in the biblical corpus. Much of the material is narrative, exhortation, reflection, or the expression of human fears and hopes.[20] This material may inform our decisions in various ways, but it is not directly prescriptive.

When we find laws, mainly in the Pentateuch / Jewish Torah (the first five books of the Old Testament), they are of two kinds. On the one hand, there are laws, which are absolute unqualified commands or prohibitions: "thou shalt not kill; thou shalt not commit adultery," and so on. Such laws are called apodictic. The Ten Commandments (Exodus 20:1–17; Deuteronomy 5:6–21) are the paradigmatic, but not the only, examples of apodictic laws. Other biblical laws are tailored to particular circumstances. (These are called casuistic laws.) A good example, widely paralleled in the laws of the ancient Near East, is the case of the ox that gores:

> When an ox gores a man or a woman to death, the ox shall be stoned, and its flesh shall not be eaten; but the owner of the ox shall not be liable. If the ox has been accustomed to gore in the past, and its owner has been warned but has not restrained it, and it kills a man or a woman, the ox shall be stoned, and its owner also shall be put to death. If a ransom is imposed on the owner, then the owner shall pay whatever is imposed for the redemption of the victim's life . . . If the ox gores a male or female slave, the owner shall pay to the slaveowner thirty shekels of silver, and the ox shall be stoned. (Exodus 21:28–32)

If a slave owner strikes a male or female slave with a rod and the slave dies immediately, the owner is punished. But if the slave survives a day or two there is no punishment, "for the slave is the owner's property" (Exodus 21:20–21). Examples could be multiplied. It is clear from this that the Ten Commandments may formulate general principles, but their application depends on circumstances. As Qoheleth (Ecclesiastes) would say, there is a time to kill and a time to heal (3:3). Biblical law, then, is not as draconian as it is sometimes thought to be. Even the Ten Commandments are broad statements of principle whose application may be qualified in light of circumstances. The commandments, so to speak, are not set in stone.[21]

Even the Ten Commandments are transmitted by a human agent, Moses. A strand of Jewish tradition holds that the Torah we possess is already an interpretation of the divine revelation; the words that we have are the words of Moses.[22] The Bible, even in this foundational revelation, is part of the stream of tradition, shaped by the human beings who transmit it from one generation to the next.[23] Modern scholarship goes much further than this and argues that the entire story of revelation is a human composition, dating several hundred years later than the time of Moses.[24] It is undeniable that biblical laws are formulated in the language of their time. There were no goring oxen in the wilderness around Mount Sinai. Such a law presupposes a settled agricultural society. It has analogical significance for modern society, but the details are relics of a bygone age. The biblical laws as we have them evolved over centuries. One major formulation, that of Deuteronomy, is no older than the reign of King Josiah in the late seventh century BCE. The Pentateuch/ Torah as we have it was completed in the postexilic period, in the fifth or fourth century BCE, and scribes were still making changes in the biblical text down to the turn of the Common Era. Biblical law, whatever its ultimate source, is a product of tradition, subject to change by the human beings who transmitted it, at least in its details. The laws as we have them are never pristine divine revelations but always entail human authorship and human motivations and arose in particular historical circumstances that must be taken into account.

Moreover, what is presented as divine law in the Bible is demonstrably changeable.[25] The laws in Exodus 20–23 (the Book of the Covenant) on such matters as the observance of the Passover and the treatment of slaves are revised and changed in Deuteronomy. For example, in Exodus 21:2, male Hebrew slaves must be released after six years, but this law does not apply to female slaves, 21:7. In Deuteronomy 15:12, the same law applies to male and female. Again, in the New Testament, Jesus tells his followers in the Sermon on the Mount: "You have heard it was said to them of old . . . but I say to you."[26] Jesus claims special authority, but he was not the first person in the biblical tradition to presume to change laws that were ostensibly given to Moses on Mount Sinai. Hellenistic Jewish authors, such as Philo of Alexandria, had a different view of such matters, holding that divine law was unchangeable. In this they were influenced by Greek traditions. The Jewish tradition, however, has always had the character of a running argument. The changeability of divine law in the Hebrew Bible has important implications for the authority of that law in later times. If Deuteronomy could change the laws of Exodus in light of new circumstances, is it not possible to envision further changes in light of vastly changed circumstances between the biblical period and our own time?

The consensus of contemporary scholarship is that neither the great Mesopotamian law "codes," such as that of Hammurabi, nor the biblical law codes functioned as statutory law or were binding on judges.[27] Judges relied on their sense of the mores of a community rather than on written law. Written laws were never cited as decisive in trial scenes, and sometimes cases were decided in contradiction of what was written. Law collections were descriptive rather than prescriptive. Accordingly, some scholars refer to the laws of Exodus as wisdom laws, with the implication that they functioned in a way similar to Proverbs: they helped inform the wise person but did not determine right conduct automatically.[28] This view of biblical law may also be of service in the modern world.

No one regards all the laws of the Bible as applicable in the modern world. Think, for example, of the laws pertaining to slavery in the Old Testament. Who, except perhaps the ultra-Orthodox, now worries whether a garment is made of two different materials? (Leviticus 19:19).[29] The sacrificial laws of the Old Testament became moot when the Jerusalem temple was destroyed. For the past two thousand years neither Christians nor Jews have sought to please God by slaughtering bulls or sheep or sending a goat into the wilderness on the Day of Atonement (Leviticus 16). Saint Paul dispensed Christians from most ritual law, including the food laws that are still observed by Jews. There is still much in the Bible that is easily applicable to the modern world, but it is well to remember that it was not written with our situation in mind. Some process of translation, adaptation, and application by analogy is necessary.

For many Christians and Jews, it is important that values and principles be grounded in the Bible, but no one can live by Scripture alone. Many factors besides Scripture necessarily influence our moral judgments.[30]

This is so for several reasons. One is the diversity of the biblical material and the need to choose between conflicting positions. Should Christians exult in freedom from the Law, as Saint Paul proposes (Galatians 3–5), or should they accept the dictum of Jesus in the Gospel of Matthew that no jot or tittle of the Law will pass away? (5:18). Another reason is that we are heirs to a tradition of reflection on moral issues dating back at least to the time of the Bible, and we cannot simply expunge this material from our consciousness. Slavery was accepted as an inevitable part of life in the ancient world. In the modern world it is completely unacceptable. Similarly, we have become more sensitive to the rights of women. Another influence arises from the demands of our own experience and intuitions, which may themselves be formed to some degree by the biblical material but are never fully determined by it.[31] It is not that we should trust our modern instincts completely; these, too, are prone to corruption by lust and greed. We need the restraining influence of traditional wisdom. But the Bible needs to be placed in dialogue with everything we know about ethical living from other sources.

It is possible, moreover, to construe the Bible in ways other than as prescriptive law. The philosopher Paul Ricoeur has spoken of the appeal of the Bible as a "nonviolent appeal," one that asks not so much for a submission of will as for an opening of imagination.[32] We should also remember that we can learn from the Bible in ways other than by reading it literally. Much of the Bible is made up of stories that do not culminate in direct prescriptions. Rather, like the parables of Jesus, they invite those who have ears to hear. Some parts, such as the Book of Judges, relate stories that are shocking to modern ears and may even have been shocking in antiquity. Think, for example, of Judges 19, where the Levite's wife is raped until she expires, and then her body is cut up into twelve pieces and distributed to the tribes, with the question, "Has such a thing ever happened" in Israel?[33] Such stories can convey moral lessons that are more powerful than simple prescriptions precisely by dramatizing actions that are obviously wrong and immoral.

FAITH AND LAW

For many Christians the importance of biblical law and ethical demands has been relativized by the Christian emphasis on faith. "We know," writes Saint Paul to the Galatians, "that a person is not justified by works of the law but through faith of Jesus Christ."[34] The Pauline concept of faith is notoriously controversial.[35] It arguably refers both to the faithfulness of Christ as a model for his followers and to their trust in and fidelity toward Christ.[36] It is quite clear, however, that biblical faith never excuses anyone from the demands of ethical behavior. The same Paul insists to the Corinthians that "wrongdoers will not inherit the kingdom of God" and provides a list of wrongdoers to illustrate his point ("fornicators, idolators, adulterers," etc.).[37] Indeed, Paul's ethical admonitions are in accord with Jewish law and tradition to a remarkable degree, apart from the matter of circumcision and the food laws.[38]

All of the Bible presupposes belief in a God who created the world and chose Israel as his special people. Since this belief was integral to the identity of biblical Israel, the assumption did not require confessions of faith in ancient Israel and Judah. The belief that Jesus Christ was the Son of God, raised from the dead and enthroned in heaven, was novel in the first century CE. It formed the basis of a new identity among his followers, so we read much more about faith in the New Testament than in the Old. But simple belief was never enough. Faith in Christ always implied that the faithfulness of Christ was a model for his followers. In the words of New Testament scholar Richard Hays, "It is the enactment of a life-pattern into which we are drawn."[39] Paul tells the Philippians, "Let the same mind be in you that was also in Christ Jesus" (2:5). What he means by faith in Christ is acceptance of an approach to life, not just propositional belief. Moreover, Paul's language of faith is only one of several theological formulations in the New Testament. Others, such as the Gospel of Matthew, have a more positive view of Jewish law. The clearest formulation of Christian priorities in the New Testament is arguably the judgment scene in Matthew 25:31–46. There, when Jesus separates the sheep from the goats, nothing is said about belief or faith. What matters is how people acted: whether they fed the hungry, clothed the naked, and visited the imprisoned. Faith in the sense of belief is no guarantee of how a person will act. Faith is commitment. Its value lies in the kinds of action and lifestyle to which it is committed.

THE NEED FOR A CRITICAL APPROACH

Many Jews and Christians worry that a critical approach to the Bible subordinates it to modern values. That is not the intention here. The Bible deserves a hearing, but to give it a hearing, we must respect the fact that it was written long ago and in another culture. Its values are often at odds with our own. We have much to learn from it, but the dialogue is not a one-way street. The Bible must be appreciated in its complexity, with the recognition that it is also often at odds with itself.

Biblical values are not normative or acceptable for modern society simply because they are found in the Bible. They must be sifted and evaluated critically like values proposed in any other source. In the case of the Bible, that critique is twofold. On the one hand, it is inner-biblical. Values endorsed in various parts of the Bible must be measured against the central values of love of God and neighbor, affirmed in both Testaments but explicitly prioritized in the Gospels. On the other hand, the critique lies in dialogue with modern values, which have increasingly been developed in terms of human rights and must be credited with clear advances in moral sensitivity on such issues as slavery, the use of violence, and the role of women in society. I believe that these two lines of critique, based on inner-biblical priorities and modern sensibilities, are generally compatible with each other, but it is not my intention to produce a synthesis of normative values for the modern world. Values are inherently debatable. The Bible has much to contribute to that debate, but its contribution is not necessarily decisive. On many issues it may leave us with more questions than answers, but it always gives us food for thought.

Our primary task here is to strive for clarity as to the actual evidence for supposed biblical values. We will find that this is much more complicated than many people assume.

CHAPTER ONE

Frames of Reference

MOST of this book is devoted to probes of biblical attitudes toward such topics as right to life, gender, family values, the environment, and justice. Before we turn to specific issues, however, let us consider the broader frameworks within which these topics are discussed in the biblical texts. Three conceptual frameworks are especially important: creation, covenant, and eschatology. Each of these frameworks entails presuppositions about the world and the human condition that are quite different from those that prevail in modern society.

The basic framework for ethics in the Bible is provided by the idea of creation. This is what establishes the nature of humanity, the role of gender, and relations between humanity and nature. It is in the context of creation that we must consider the question of human rights. No appeal is more basic than appeals to the order of creation.

Most biblical laws, however, are presented in the context of a covenant, which is primarily a covenant with Israel. For Christians, this covenant is modified in the New Testament, but the "new covenant" is not entirely different from the old one, and it cannot be understood apart from the tradition from which it arose.

Both creation and covenant are modified in turn by eschatology and the possibility that creation as we know it will come to an end. The expectation of an ending arises in the later books of the Hebrew Bible, first in the Prophets and then more elaborately in the Book of Daniel. Daniel provides the only example in the Hebrew Bible of a new genre, apocalypse, which blossomed in Judaism around the turn of the era, roughly between 200 BCE to 100 CE, but it takes its name from a New Testament book, the Book of Revelation, or Apocalypse of John. Apocalyptic eschatology, or ideas about the end of the world that are characteristic of the apocalyptic literature, shapes the worldview of the New Testament to a great degree and puts both creation and covenant in a new perspective. That perspective differs from the one that prevails in most of the Hebrew Bible / Old Testament and introduces an interesting tension within biblical values on many issues.

CREATION

Appeals to the order of creation are appeals to the way things basically are. It is important to bear in mind, however, that accounts of creation are not simply factual. By definition, they describe events that had no human witnesses. When people write about creation, they can do so only by using their imagination and whatever traditions are available to them. In the ancient world traditions are preserved in the form of stories or myths. In the modern world the word "myth" is often taken to imply falsehood. In the discussion of religion, however, it means a traditional story, usually involving divine beings, that seeks to explain the world in imaginative terms.

The traditional ways of imagining creation in the ancient Near East are known to us especially through two stories from ancient Babylon, the *Enuma Elish* and *Atrahasis*, both of which date to the second millennium BCE.[1] The *Enuma Elish* tells how the god Marduk created the world from the carcass of his mother, Tiamat. Tiamat was angry because the young gods had killed her husband, Apsu, so she threatened to destroy them. Marduk emerges as the hero who does battle with Tiamat to avert destruction. The centerpiece of the Babylonian myth is the battle of Marduk and Tiamat. This is a variant of a combat myth that was widespread in many forms in the ancient world, in which the creator god defeats a monster, often associated with the sea.[2] We find echoes of this combat myth in the Hebrew Bible. In Genesis 1, the watery deep is called *tehom*, a word cognate to "Tiamat." Tiamat has been demythologized, so to speak, but the Babylonian story is still detectable in the background.

More important for the Bible is *Atrahasis*.[3] This story begins before the creation of humanity, when gods instead of men did the work. The labor of agriculture was imposed on a class of gods called the Igigu. The first section of *Atrahasis* deals with the rebellion of these worker gods, which leads to the creation of humanity "to bear the load of the gods." Human beings are created from the flesh and blood of an intelligent god, mixed with clay. The second part of the story deals with the problems caused by the proliferation of humanity. The gods make several attempts to reduce humanity by plague and other means, culminating in a flood, intended to wipe humanity off the face of the earth. A man named Atrahasis (the name means "very wise") is instructed by one of the gods to build a boat that is big enough to ride out the deluge, and so humanity survives. The relevance of this story to the biblical Flood story in Genesis is obvious. In both stories, humanity is constituted of clay plus a divine element and is created to till the earth. In both the survival of humanity is threatened by a flood but is ensured by a boat or an ark.[4]

The differences between these myths and the biblical accounts are considerable, as indeed are the differences between the different Babylonian creation stories, but it is clear that the biblical stories were influenced by the older ones from Mesopotamia and rely on a common ancient Near Eastern idiom. Even the biblical idea of creation by a word, in Genesis 1, which is often thought to be distinctive, is paralleled in ancient Egypt, where the god Ptah used this mode of creation.[5] We call these stories myths because they are not factual accounts but imaginative stories that are unverifiable. To call them myths is not at all to disparage them. Myths often capture profound truths about life, just as modern plays and novels do. But they are fictions, and not to be confused with history or science. This is how people imagined creation in the ancient world.

It is the nature of myth that stories can be told in different ways. The Bible, in fact, begins with two quite different accounts of creation, one in Genesis 1:1–2:4a and the second in Genesis 2:4b–3:24. Readers of the canonical Bible tend to harmonize these stories and see them as complementary, but they represent quite different understandings of creation.[6] We will return to these accounts shortly. But they are not the only models of creation that we find in the Bible.

One persistent model is derived from the combat myth. Consider, for example, Job 26:7–13:

> He stretches out Zaphon [the north] over the void,
>   and hangs the earth upon nothing.
> He binds up the waters in his thick clouds,
>   and the cloud is not torn open by them.
> . . . .
> He has described a circle on the face of the waters,
>   at the boundary between light and darkness.
> The pillars of heaven tremble,
>   and are astounded at his rebuke.
> By his power he stilled the Sea;
>   by his understanding he struck down Rahab.
> By his wind the heavens were made fair;
>   his hand pierced the fleeing serpent.

It is quite commonly supposed that the creator had to drive back the sea to allow the dry land to appear. (See, e.g., Psalm 104.) The passage in Job implies a battle with the sea and its monsters (Rahab and the serpent). Similarly, Isaiah 51:9 asks, "Was it not you who cut Rahab in pieces, who pierced the dragon?" The story of God's battle with the Sea or Rahab is never told in narrative form in the Hebrew Bible, but the poetic allusions make clear that it was well known in ancient Israel.

Despite the statement that God "hangs the earth upon nothing," this creation does not come out of nothing. The idea is rather that God suspends the earth over a void. It is not clear that Rahab or the serpent, or the Sea for that matter, is created. The work of creation is not making things out of nothing but imposing order on chaos. God sets the sea within bounds and establishes a space where life can prosper.

Moreover, in the combat model, the work of creation is ongoing and never finished. Isaiah 27:1 looks forward to the day when God will punish Leviathan, the twisting serpent, and slay the dragon in the sea. In Daniel 7 four great beasts come up out of the sea, endangering creation. The same imagery is used in the New Testament in Revelation 13; and in the end, when the new heaven and earth are revealed, the sea is no more (21:1).[7] What is at issue in the combat myth is the mastery of the creator god, and his victory is meaningful only if his opponent is a worthy rival, one who still poses a threat.[8] Creation, then, is an ongoing drama, rather than something that happened and was done with long ago.

Yet another model of creation is found in the Book of Proverbs. There "the Lord by wisdom founded the earth; by understanding he established the heavens" (3:19). The process is further described in Proverbs 8, where Wisdom is personified as a master worker, assisting God in the work of creating the earth. The implication is that the world is imbued with order and that a person who understands wisdom can discover that order and live in harmony with it.[9] This is the model of creation that is most congenial to modern ideas of intelligent design, but it is just one of several theologies of creation in the biblical record.

The coexistence of these various models of creation in the Hebrew Bible should warn us against taking any of them literally.

Ever since the work of Charles Darwin in the nineteenth century, the biblical accounts of creation have been thought to be in conflict with modern science.[10] Debate has focused especially on Genesis 1. We may distinguish three approaches to the relation between Genesis and science in the current debate.[11]

The first is creationism, which takes Genesis 1 as literal history. This model assumes the priority of Scripture over science and assumes that Genesis 1 should be read as a scientific text. The difficulties of doing this were already appreciated in antiquity by theologians such as Augustine, who noted that night and day are spoken of before the creation of the sun and the moon.[12] Quite apart from any modern scientific theories, the literalist reading of Genesis rests on a genre mistake. It fails to appreciate the mythic, quasi-poetic idiom of the stories. No reader who is familiar with the genre of creation stories can take them literally.[13]

A second approach to the relation between science and Genesis seeks to harmonize the two. The best-known strategy in this regard is the claim that the days of Genesis 1 are not really days but long periods. As it says in 2 Peter 3:8, a thousand years is as a day for the Lord. But while the Hebrew word *yom* can be used for a longer period of time, there is nothing to indicate that it is being so used in Genesis. Rather, we are repeatedly told that a day is "evening and morning" and that the seven days constitute a week ending in the Sabbath.[14] Other, more recent attempts to correlate the biblical account with science may be more seductive. The novelist Marilynne Robinson has declared, "If ancient people had consciously set out to articulate a worldview congenial to science, it is hard to imagine how, in terms available to them, they could have done better."[15] Those who argue in this vein find various, often far-fetched correspondences between Genesis and the ideas of modern science.[16] So, for example, the firmament in Genesis is what we now call the atmosphere; the primordial waste and void, *tohu wabohu*, of Genesis 1:2 is the primordial "soupy" state of the universe; and much is made of the fact that the process begins with the creation of light. The Big Bang becomes the moment of creation.[17]

This line of argument largely amounts to a kind of allegorizing. Allegory was the kind of exegesis practiced in Late Antiquity, by the Church Fathers among others, as a way of reconciling the biblical text (and also Homer) with a very different view of the world, by claiming that it should be taken as symbolic, not literal. The assumption here is that modern science is right, so the Bible must agree with it, even when it conceives things in an utterly different way. This kind of apologetic exposition is a disservice to the Bible. It is better to let ancient myths be ancient myths than to force them into categories of science that are utterly alien to them. Quantum physics does not disprove the claim that the world was created, but it lends no support to it either.[18] It is fair enough to say that Genesis raises questions about the purpose of the universe that go beyond the remit of science, but this is to recognize that the sphere and concerns of science are different from those that inform the biblical text. The third approach to the relationship between science and Genesis, then, is to recognize that they are not comparable and that they have different spheres of interest.

Attempts to correlate the Bible with evolution are guilty of anachronism and of distorting the biblical text just as much as those that reject evolution in the name of biblical inerrancy.

It is true that creation in Genesis 1 is not instantaneous but extends over seven days. The following chapters of Genesis seem to envision a process of trial and error, analogous to what we find in the Babylonian *Atrahasis* myth. In Genesis 6:9 the Lord regrets the creation of humanity, and he proceeds to wipe out most of it with a Flood. The model of creation expressed in the combat myth is even more open-ended. But these models of creation are far removed from the scientific theory of evolution by natural selection. Neither do they lend support to the quasi-scientific theory of intelligent design. The priestly theology in Genesis 1 and the wisdom theology in Proverbs assume that God designed the world in an orderly way, but they do not arrive at this position by disciplined scientific observation. They are religious, theological models for construing the world.

The biblical idea of creation is not just about beginnings but also about the contingency of the world and its dependence on a higher power. It affirms that God is the ordainer and sustainer of the universe.[19] But whether there is such an ordainer and sustainer is not a question that can be answered by science, nor can the question of how the world began be answered in a scientific way by Genesis.

WHAT DO THE CREATION STORIES TELL US?

If the stories of creation in Genesis are not crypto-science, what do we learn from them? We learn some of the fundamental presuppositions of the biblical worldview.

Genesis 1 provides the worldview of the priestly source, which is a rather distinctive theology within the Bible, found especially in the Book of Leviticus.[20] Genesis 1 has a very orderly world, one that is judged to be good. Humanity is created at the apex of creation and is made in the image of God. In ancient Near Eastern temples, the deity was represented by an image or statue. Some scholars think that Yahweh, the God of Israel, was also represented by a statue before the Babylonian Exile in the sixth century BCE, although clear evidence is lacking.[21] Genesis 1, which was probably written around the time of the Babylonian Exile, asserts that God is represented not by a statue, but by humanity. In this exalted view of humanity, humanity must be treated with dignity and respect. We should note, however, that the worldview of Genesis 1 is very schematic. It sketches the major features of creation; it does not attempt to give a nuanced account of variations.[22] Neither does it attempt to explain how anything ever went wrong with this "very good" creation.

The story in Genesis 2–3 is quite different. Here humanity is created to do the agricultural work in the garden, in a way that recalls the *Atrahasis* myth. Although Christian tradition has often assumed that Adam and Eve were born immortal, this is evidently not the case. Both Adam's creation from dust and the formulation of Genesis 3:22 show that human beings were not initially immortal. Death was thought to be an integral part of human life from the very beginning of creation. Adam and Eve had a chance to attain immortality by eating from the tree of life, which was not initially forbidden.[23] The view that the story is about a lost opportunity to gain immortality, rather than the loss of an original immortal state, is in line with other stories from the ancient Near East, such as the famous story of Gilgamesh and also a myth about a figure named Adapa. Moreover, the threatened punishment for eating from the tree appears to be imminent death rather than loss of immortality.[24] In the Genesis case, the snake seems to have gotten it right: disobedience is not followed by instant death. For many interpreters, the discrepancy between the threat and the eventuality loses its significance because the possibility of attaining immortality is foreclosed, but James Barr has argued cogently that the punishment simply was not carried out. "Of course Adam died," he writes, "but he would have died anyway."[25]

Adam and Eve are eventually expelled from the garden lest they eat from the Tree of Life and live forever. They apparently had a chance to become immortal but failed to take it. Instead, they ate from the tree of the knowledge of good and evil, which was forbidden to them. That it was forbidden shows that God intended to set limits to what humans could do, even though he otherwise gave them the run of the garden. In this respect, the God of Genesis resembles the deities of other ancient myths, who do not want their creatures to become too powerful. (Compare the Greek story of Prometheus, who was punished for giving fire to humanity.)

The key to the story in Genesis 2–3 is provided by the curses God pronounces when he discovers that they had eaten the forbidden fruit. The snake is condemned to go on its belly and eat dust (which snakes do not actually do but were apparently thought to do). The woman is told that she will have greater pain in childbirth than was originally intended. (Evidently some pain in childbirth was always part of the plan.) Also, she will be subject to her husband. The man is told that the ground will be cursed because of him, and he will have to labor to get his food until he returns to the earth from which he was taken. These curses describe the human condition as the author understood it. Life was nasty, brutish, and short. The story provided an explanation as to why this was so. Adam and Eve had disobeyed a divine command and reached for more than was given to them.

The story of Adam and Eve is often characterized as the story of "the Fall." "Who," asks James Kugel, "does not automatically think of the fundamental change that took place in the human condition, or what is commonly called the Fall of Man?"[26] Genesis does not speak of a "Fall." It is arguable that the term as used in Christian theology is derived from Plato and Orphic thought,[27] although there are also stories of the "fall" of heavenly beings in the Hebrew tradition, notably Lucifer, the Son of Dawn, in Isaiah 14. Neither do we find Hebrew words for "sin" in Genesis 2–3, in contrast to the Cain and Abel story in Genesis 4, where sin is lurking at the door. Nonetheless, it is undeniable that Adam and Eve disobey a divine command and are cast out of the garden as a result, so the act of eating from the tree of the knowledge of good and evil must be construed negatively. What is not so clear is how their punishment is thought to affect subsequent generations. The curses pronounced in chapter 3 describe what might be called the common human condition. Accordingly, it is reasonable to see that condition as the consequence of the act of disobedience. There is no suggestion, however, that the descendants of Adam are born in a sinful state or that guilt is transmitted to future generations. Not until Genesis 6:5–6 does the Lord see that human wickedness is so great that he regrets that he made humanity and resolves to blot it out by the Flood. The disobedience of Adam and Eve does not bear sole or unique responsibility for this state of affairs. Human history is also complicated by the example of Cain and by the descent of the "sons of God" in Genesis 6:1–4. The disobedience of Adam can be taken as paradigmatic, an illustration of typical human behavior, rather than as a first cause.

The curses, then, show that the story is essentially an explanation for the way life is. They should not be taken as permanent commandments. No one has ever inferred that every man must earn his bread with the sweat of his brow. Neither should we conclude that pain in childbirth is the lot of women and do nothing to mitigate it. Neither, as we shall argue, is the subjection of a wife to her husband to be viewed as a law, but simply as a reflection of how things were in the ancient world.

Perhaps the most controversial aspect of the story, from a modern perspective, is the assumption that human misery is due to disobedience and the refusal to accept limitation. This contention is completely contrary to modern Western sensibilities. It is especially un-American. In the modern world, people are urged to "go for it"; the sky is the limit. The story of Adam and Eve is typical of the ancient world in this respect. People were expected to accept their station in society and not try to rise above it.

We should not be too quick to reject the worldview of Genesis. There are surely situations in life in which it is appropriate, and we can learn from it. But neither should we be too quick to accept it. It is a product of an ancient society, a relic of a different time and place. It cannot be accepted automatically as normative.

What both creation stories in Genesis share is the insistence that we, and the world, are indeed created. As creatures, we are subject to a higher power, the power that created us. This conviction runs contrary to modern secular humanism, but it is a foundational principle of the biblical worldview.

THE MOSAIC COVENANT

Most of the Old Testament laws are presented in a context that is more specific than that of creation: as part of a covenant, or contractual agreement, between God and Israel. The covenant is formalized at a mountain called Sinai in Exodus, Horeb in Deuteronomy. This covenant was designed specifically for Israel, but it is paradigmatic for anyone who wants to consider biblical values.

The Mosaic covenant was modeled on the international treaties of the ancient Near East, specifically vassal treaties, between a more powerful party and a subordinate one.[28] At the heart of the treaties were stipulations, the provisions by which the subordinate party must abide. These stipulations were reinforced by two kinds of material. On the one hand, there was the "historical prologue," the recollection of the events that led to the making of treaty. In the biblical covenant, this is primarily the story of the Exodus. On the other hand, there were curses, usually fearsome, on those who broke the treaty and promises of well-being for those who kept it. In the Hebrew Bible, the curses and blessings figure prominently in the Books of Leviticus and Deuteronomy.

One of the most remarkable points of correspondence between Deuteronomy and the ancient Near Eastern treaties is that the subject people or vassals are told to "love" the over-lord. The *Vassal Treaty of Esarhaddon*, an Assyrian king in the seventh century BCE, specifies: "If you do not love the crown prince designate Ashurbanipal . . . as you do your own lives . . . ," retribution will follow. In Deuteronomy, the Lord (Yahweh) takes the place of the Assyrian king: "Hear O Israel: The Lord is our God, the Lord alone. You shall love the Lord, your God with all your heart and with all your soul, and with all your might." The command to love God is arguably the most important commandment. Love here is not a matter of feeling or emotion, but rather of loyalty and obedience.[29] This remains true in the New Testament, where Jesus tells his disciples in the Gospel of John (14:15): "If you love me, you will keep my commandments."

Biblical laws presuppose a relationship both with God and with a human community. They are not commanded arbitrarily. The covenantal attitude toward law is called covenantal nomism.[30] The covenant provides a context for the command-ments. It is important to keep that context in mind when we encounter criticism of Jewish law in the New Testament.

The covenantal laws are addressed to Israel. Some, espe-cially those in Leviticus, are designed to distinguish Israel as holy, from the other nations: "Speak to all the congregation of the people of Israel and say to them: You shall be holy, for I the Lord your God am holy" (19:2). The special status assigned to Israel can be problematic. In Deuteronomy 7, the Israelites are told to destroy the people of the land utterly, "for you are a people holy to the Lord your God; the Lord your God has chosen you out of all the peoples on earth to be his people, his treasured possession" (7:6). Does being set apart justify inhumane treatment of outsiders by the people of God?[31] We will have occasion to return to this issue in a later chapter.

Do the specifically Israelite laws apply to Christians, who are not part of historic Israel? The claim in 1 Peter 2:9 is that Christians, too, are "a chosen race, a royal priesthood, a holy nation, God's own people." Yet Saint Paul dispensed Gentile converts from the ritual requirements of the Law (such as circumcision and the food laws). Jewish tradition distinguishes between the Noahic laws, which are binding on all humanity, and laws that are peculiar to Israel. Hellenistic Jewish writers, such as Philo of Alexandria, also distinguished between moral laws, binding on everyone, and distinctive ritual laws. They tended to emphasize the moral laws while insisting that Jews should also keep the ritual ones.[32] One might argue that even laws designed specifically for Israel have at least relevance for other people by analogy. Both Jesus and Paul seem to assume the ongoing validity of most of the Old Testament laws as an expression of the moral law. Even in the Old Testament, laws that are proclaimed as part of the covenant often have their grounding in creation, in natural law.[33] The morality or immorality of killing is in no way peculiar to Israel, and neither are matters of gender and family or, indeed, basic issues of justice.

ESCHATOLOGY AND APOCALYPTICISM

Both the doctrine of creation and the Mosaic covenant are this-worldly in their orientation. After the Flood, God makes a covenant with Noah in which he sets his rainbow in the clouds as a sign that the waters will never again become a flood to destroy all flesh (Genesis 9:15). The implication is surely that the earth is safe from destruction. In fact, most people in the ancient world believed, like Qoheleth (Ecclesiastes), that "a generation goes, and a generation comes, but the earth remains forever" (1:4). Even in the time of Christ, the philosopher Philo allowed that God could, if he wished, destroy the world, but asked why he would want to do that, since creation is so perfect.[34]

The expectation that the world will last forever, or at least indefinitely, has important implications for biblical values. If the earth is not passing away, it is important to conserve it for future generations. Also, in ancient Israel human destiny was thought to have its fulfillment on earth. After death, the shade of the person went down to Sheol, where it was not possible even to praise the Lord. The blessings of the covenant promised that the people of Israel would live long in the land, and see their children and their children's children. No judgment was expected after death. If justice was to be realized, it must be realized in this world.

This view of the world underwent a radical change at the end of the Old Testament period. Some passages in the Old Testament books of the Prophets intimate a sense of impending doom, but they do this usually as a metaphor for some catastrophe that is about to occur. Jeremiah looked at the earth and saw waste and void, as there had been before creation (4:23), but the impending catastrophe was the Babylonian invasion of Judah. Isaiah 24 speaks of the windows of heaven being opened and of the earth being utterly broken and torn asunder (24:18–19). In that case, we are not sure of the reference, but again the occasion was probably historical, possibly the destruction of Babylon by the Persians. The idea that this world will come to an end first appears in the apocalyptic literature, in the early second century BCE, in books attributed to the patriarch Enoch.[35]

Apocalyptic literature is represented in the Hebrew Bible only by the Book of Daniel, which was written at the time of the Maccabean revolt, about 164 BCE.[36] Daniel is the only book in the Hebrew Bible that speaks unambiguously about resurrection and about reward and punishment after death (12:1–3). Even Daniel does not speak unambiguously about an end to the present world. This kind of literature became more common in the following centuries and is well represented in the Dead Sea Scrolls. At the end of the first century CE, *4 Ezra*, which is included in the Old Testament Apocrypha as *2 Esdras* 3–14, speaks of a decisive end of this world, marked by seven days of primeval silence and followed by the resurrection and judgment of the dead.[37] It also affirms that God has made not one world, but two (7:50). Salvation is to be found in the hereafter: the second world.

Not all Jews around the turn of the Common Era accepted the apocalyptic worldview. The Sadducees allegedly denied the resurrection of the dead; the Pharisees accepted it. The Essenes, the people who are thought to have preserved the Dead Sea Scrolls, affirmed a judgment of the dead and some form of afterlife but not, apparently, bodily resurrection. They also anticipated a final, decisive war between the forces of light and darkness, and one passage in the Dead Sea Scrolls alludes to a final conflagration.[38]

In the New Testament, however, the apocalyptic worldview is pervasive.[39] Saint Paul declares that "if for this life only we have hoped, . . . we are of all men most to be pitied" (1 Corinthians 15:19). Since this world is passing away, those who use it should act as if they did not (1 Corinthians 7:29–31). The most vivid expression of the apocalyptic worldview is found in the Book of Revelation, but even the Gospels presume a coming judgment, when the Son of Man will come on the clouds of heaven and preside at a final judgment.

The implications of an apocalyptic worldview are vastly different from those of the Mosaic covenant or from the creation theology of the Old Testament. The goal of life is no longer to see your children and your children's children, but eternal life with the angels in heaven. Consequently, some people argue in the name of Christianity that we do not need to be concerned about the environment, since the world is headed for destruction anyway, or that justice in this world is of secondary importance compared to the salvation of souls for the next. Such arguments may be specious, but the eschatological perspective of the New Testament poses questions for biblical values that need to be addressed.

Eschatological scenarios of the end of the world are just as mythical as stories about creation. Indeed, it is a dictum of biblical scholarship that the end-time is like the primeval time.[40] The apocalyptic myths of Daniel and Revelation, replete with monsters rising from the sea, are heavily indebted to the combat myths of the ancient Near East.[41] Attempts to translate these myths into historical predictions are doomed to frustration, as can be seen from a long history of failed millennial predictions.[42] Paul expected that people living in his time would witness the Second Coming of Christ. Two thousand years later, Christians are still waiting. This is not to suggest that the apocalyptic worldview can be dismissed as irrelevant to modernity. Like the old creation myths, it may well have insights into the human condition. But it requires interpretation before we can apply it in the modern world.

Not all issues to be discussed in this volume are equally affected by the prospect that this world is passing away. Questions of right to life and gender, which are among the most controversial issues in the modern debate, are primarily understood in the context of creation. Several other topics, however, such as the environment and social justice, are profoundly affected by the way we understand the future of the world. The values of the New Testament are not always identical with those of the Old. Nonetheless, the Christian testament stands in the Hebraic tradition and cannot be understood in isolation from it. It behooves Christians in the modern world to wrestle with the legacy of both Testaments.

CHAPTER TWO

A Right to Life?

O NE of the ways the Bible is most clearly at odds with modern sensibilities is in the way ethical issues are framed. For most people in the modern world, ethical issues are formulated in terms of rights, usually human rights but increasingly animal rights, too. The paradigmatic expression of human rights in the modern world is the Universal Declaration of Human Rights, adopted by the United Nations in 1948, which begins:

> Whereas recognition of the inherent dignity and of the equal and inalienable rights of all members of the human family is the foundation of freedom, justice and peace in the world

and goes on to declare:

> All human beings are born free and equal in dignity and rights. They are endowed with reason and conscience and should act towards each other in a spirit of brotherhood [article 1]

and:

> everyone has the right to life, liberty and security of person [article 3].

The UN declaration was a direct descendant of the Enlightenment, specifically of the American and French declarations at the end of the eighteenth century. The American Declaration of Independence begins:

> We hold these truths to be self-evident, that all men are created equal, that they are endowed by their Creator with certain unalienable Rights, that among these are Life, Liberty and the pursuit of Happiness.

The French Declaration of the Rights of Man and Citizen (1789) holds that "ignorance, neglect or contempt of the rights of man are the sole causes of public misfortunes" and presents a resolution "to set forth in a solemn declaration the natural inalienable and sacred rights of man." The first of these is that "men are born and remain free and equal in rights." These rights are specified as "liberty, property, security and resistance to oppression." The idea of human rights had percolated through the eighteenth century. The expression "rights of man" gained currency after it appeared in Jean-Jacques Rousseau's *Social Contract* in 1762, although Rousseau made no attempt to define the rights in question.

Others had asserted rights at earlier times in history, but these were generally more restricted in nature and often concerned with property. As Lynn Hunt has insisted: "Human rights require three interlocking qualities: rights must be natural (inherent in human beings); equal (the same for everyone); and universal (applicable everywhere)."[1] Or, as Nicholas

Wolterstorff puts it, "A human right is a right such that the only status one needs in order to possess the right, the only credential required, is that of being a human being."[2] The English Bill of Rights of 1689 refers to rights and liberties deriving from English law but makes no claim of universality. No doubt there were significant antecedents for the idea of human rights, in Stoic philosophy, Roman law, and medieval canon law, but universal human rights, in the sense outlined by Hunt, are a product of the Enlightenment.[3] The attempt to enforce human rights on an international scale, or even to apply them consistently, is, arguably, a much more recent phenomenon, beginning with the UN charter and developing mainly in the past fifty years or so.[4]

Some claim that human rights are already implicit in the Hebrew Bible / Old Testament. Biblical laws impose restrictions on how human beings can be treated, so we might infer that human beings have a right not to be treated in these ways.[5] In effect, rights are the flip side of obligations. The first article of the UN Declaration of Human Rights, which proclaims that all human beings "should act toward one another in a spirit of brotherhood," reflects the biblical injunction to love our neighbor as ourselves. René Cassin, who received the Nobel Peace Prize for his work in drafting the declaration, wrote:

> The concept of human rights comes from the Bible, from the Old Testament, from the Ten Commandments. Whether these principles were centered on the church, the mosque, or the *polis*, they were often phrased in terms of duties, which now presume rights. For instance, Thou shalt not murder is the right to life. Thou shalt not steal is the right to own property, and so on and so forth. We must not forget that Judaism gave the world the concept of human rights.[6]

But while the influence of the Hebrew Bible on the development of the idea of human rights should not be denied, the Bible frames the issues very differently. The current discourse of human rights is anthropocentric; the rights are inherent in human beings as such. The biblical discourse, in contrast, is theocentric. It is primarily concerned with the will of God, not the putative rights of human beings.[7] The Hebrew word *mishpat* (variously translated as "judgment" or "ordinance") sometimes seems to entail "rights." The *mishpat* of the priests is that they receive certain portions of sacrifices, and it is the *mishpat* of the firstborn to inherit (Deuteronomy 21:17). But limited rights of this sort are of a different order from universal human rights, which all people have by virtue of being human.

We must accept the fact that the Bible does not have a discourse of universal human rights. Such a discourse may be good for human society, but it must find its grounding elsewhere.

The ethical discourse of the Bible is not based on the inherent worth of human beings. Genesis 1 declares that humanity is created in the image of God, which implies considerable worth, but this resemblance is seldom invoked in the rest of the Bible. (An exception is found in Genesis 9:6, where creation in the image of God is cited as a reason for the prohibition of bloodshed. We will return to this passage below.) For better or worse, the Bible is not primarily concerned with the rights of human beings but rather with the justice of God.

The contrast between the modern way of thinking about ethical issues and the assumptions operative in the Bible is nowhere more evident than in the question of whether human beings have a right to life.

Few verses of the Bible are so firmly instilled into popular consciousness as the commandment traditionally translated as "Thou shalt not kill."[8] But this commandment is not nearly as sweeping as it has often been taken to be. The Hebrew verb here is *ratsach*, not one of the normal words for "kill" (*qatal, harag, hemith*), and scholars now agree that it should be translated as "murder" rather than "kill" in this context.[9] Murder is killing that is not sanctioned by society. In fact the Bible leaves a wide scope for human judgment in the taking of life.

Any idea we might have that the Bible affirms a right to life is dispelled by a shocking commandment supposedly given to Israel at Mount Sinai:

> The firstborn of your sons you shall give to me. You shall do the same with your oxen and with your sheep: seven days it shall remain with its mother; on the eighth day you shall give it to me. (Exodus 22:29b-30)

There is little doubt as to how oxen and sheep were given to God. Whether sacrifice of the human firstborn was ever standard practice is more difficult to say. Many would argue that no society could systematically sacrifice firstborn children, who carry the hope for the future.[10] Nothing else in the Hebrew Bible suggests that this commandment was generally enforced. Nonetheless, it remained "on the books," perhaps as a devotional ideal[11] but certainly as a reminder of God's prerogative in the matter of life.

The law is both clarified and modified in Exodus 34:19–20:

> All that first opens the womb is mine, all your male livestock, the firstborn of cow and sheep. The firstborn of a donkey you shall redeem with a lamb, or if you will not redeem it you shall break its neck. All the firstborn of your sons you shall redeem.

God is the giver of life. One way of acknowledging this was to return the firstborn, and the first fruits, to God.

Elsewhere in the Bible, we occasionally encounter human sacrifice in early Israel, but it seems to be exceptional. The most famous instance is the sacrifice of Isaac in Genesis 22. God commands Abraham: "Take your son, your only son Isaac, whom you love, and go to the land of Moriah, and offer him there as a burnt offering on one of the mountains that I shall show you." Abraham does not hesitate. In the end, Abraham is not required to kill the boy. But, he is praised for his willingness:

> Because you have done this, and have not withheld your son, your only son, I will indeed bless you, and I will make your offspring as numerous as the stars of heaven and as the sand that is on the seashore. (22:16–17)

It is not apparent from this story that God intended to abolish human sacrifice, and there is certainly no suggestion that Isaac had a right to life. Abraham has no difficulty in accepting the command to sacrifice his son as a valid divine command.[12]

Jephtah's daughter is less fortunate than Isaac. Her father made a vow to the Lord:

> If you will give the Ammonites into my hand, then whoever comes out of the doors of my house to meet me, when I return victorious from the Ammonites, shall be the LORD's, to be offered up by me as a burnt offering. (Judges 11:30–31)

There can be little doubt that human sacrifice was intended. Jephtah would surely not have sacrificed a dog if the animal had come out to meet him. His vow has often been judged rash by modern critics, but the biblical text passes no judgment on it. Indeed, the Epistle to the Hebrews in the New Testament lists him among the heroes of faith (11:32). He is heartbroken when his daughter comes out to meet him, but father and daughter agree that the vow must be honored.[13] There are parallels for the efficacy of human sacrifice in other ancient cultures. The Spartan king Agamemnon allegedly sacrificed his daughter to gain favorable winds to sail to Troy. In 2 Kings 3:26 the king of Moab reportedly sacrificed his firstborn son to turn the tide of battle against Israel and succeeded. Two kings of Judah, Ahaz and Manasseh, are accused of child sacrifice, and the prophet Micah imagines that an Israelite might think that he should offer his firstborn as atonement for sin (6:7).

To be sure, many voices in the Hebrew Bible, including Micah's, were raised in protest against the practice of child sacrifice. Jeremiah claims that the idea had never entered God's mind (19:4–6). Ezekiel says that God gave the Israelites "statutes that were not good, and ordinances by which they could not live. I defiled them through their very gifts, in their offering up all their firstborn, in order that I might horrify them" (20:25–26). However enigmatic the verse, it is surely evidence that some of Ezekiel's contemporaries thought it appropriate to sacrifice firstborn children, whether or not they based that idea on Exodus 22.[14] The practice is not attested after the Babylonian Exile. Nonetheless, the evidence about child sacrifice in early Israel renders problematic any idea that

46

the Bible guarantees a right to life. Life belongs to God, who can demand it at his pleasure.

CAPITAL PUNISHMENT

One of the strongest affirmations of the sanctity of life is found in Genesis 9:5–6, after the Flood, when God tells Noah:

> For your own lifeblood I will surely require a reckoning: from every animal I will require it and from human beings, each one for the blood of another, I will require a reckoning for human life.
>
> > Whoever sheds the blood of a human,
> >   by a human shall that person's blood be shed;
> > for in his own image
> >   God made humankind.

This passage is exceptional in that it refers to creation in the image of God as a reason why one should not shed human blood, but the penalty for bloodshed is more bloodshed. There is a restriction on what human beings may do, but it is not because there is a right to life. The Hebrew Bible prescribes capital punishment with alarming frequency.

In the laws of the Pentateuch/Torah, murder is delineated as an intentional act. If someone strikes another with an iron implement so that he dies, he is a murderer; the murderer should be put to death. Likewise if he strikes with a stone or a wooden implement (Numbers 35:22–28; cf. Deuteronomy 19:11–13). Cities of refuge are provided for cases of accidental killing: for "someone who has killed another person unintentionally when the two had not been at enmity with each other" (Deuteronomy 19:4). But a person who has lain in wait and murdered someone may be taken even from a city of refuge. The judgment as to whether the act was murder lies with the elders of the city. They are authorized to decide whether someone should live or die. The law, divine or not, is applied as human leaders decide.

Many offenses besides murder are subject to capital punishment. These include striking one's parents (Exodus 21:15), cursing one's parents (Exodus 21:17; Leviticus 20:9), and being a rebellious child (Deuteronomy 21:18–21). In case of adultery, both parties are supposed to be executed (Leviticus 20:10). The death penalty is also prescribed for working on the Sabbath (Exodus 31:14, 35:2; Numbers 15:32–36), consulting a medium (Leviticus 20:27), engaging in pagan worship (Exodus 22:20), and committing a host of other offenses. Remarkably, however, death is not prescribed for property offenses.[15]

Jewish apologists in antiquity, such as Philo and Josephus, boasted of the prevalence of the death penalty as if it were a virtue. "Do we find among the Jews," asks Philo, "anything which so savors of mildness and lenity, anything which permits of legal proceedings or extenuations or postponements of penalties and reductions of assessments? Nothing at all, everything is clear and simple . . . the penalty is the same, death."[16] From a modern perspective, the widespread prescription of the death penalty seems decidedly primitive, something a civilized society should outgrow. In part, it may reflect the lack of a developed penitentiary system. Prisons were known but not on a grand scale. Moreover, a law's being found in the Bible does not necessarily mean that it was applied. So, for example, although the law provides for the death penalty in cases of adultery, Proverbs 6:31–35 warns that the adulterer "will get wounds and dishonor, and his disgrace will not be wiped away" and that a jealous husband may refuse to accept compensation or a bribe. There is no mention of the death penalty here, and the passage implies that negotiation about compensation was envisioned. There are notable countertraditions in the Bible, too, where the death penalty is not applied despite the law. Examples include the story of Judah and Tamar in Genesis 38, where the patriarch relents when he realizes that it was he himself who got Tamar pregnant, and the case of the woman taken in adultery in John 8:1–11. Nonetheless, it would be difficult to build a case against the death penalty on the basis of biblical precedent. We could, perhaps, point to the countertraditions or cite the maxim of Ezekiel that God has no pleasure in the death of anyone (Ezekiel 18:32). But nothing in the Hebrew Bible excludes the application of the death penalty, and many passages demand it.

Our discussion thus far has focused on the Hebrew Bible, especially on the laws of the Pentateuch/Torah. When we speak of the death penalty, we are speaking of communal law. The law codes of the Hebrew Bible were communal laws, however they were meant to be applied. In contrast, the New Testament authors were in no position to legislate for a society. The teaching of Jesus mitigates the severity of the law in some respects, but not all. Where the old law said that anyone who murdered was subject to judgment, Jesus says that anyone who is angry with his brother is liable to burn in the fire of hell (Matthew 5:21–22). This is not a punishment that humans can inflict, but it is hardly less severe. Where the law prescribed "an eye for an eye," Jesus said to turn the other cheek instead of taking revenge (5:38–39). But he did not say that turning the other cheek should be the law of the land, nor did it become the law of the church.

Many considerations besides biblical precedent have to be taken into account in a modern consideration of the morality of the death penalty. Society now has more humane and sophisticated ways to deal with criminals. But opposition to the death penalty receives scant support from the Bible. Perhaps the most important lesson to be drawn here is that decisions as to how the law should be applied ultimately rest with society. The objections to textual agency, noted in the introductory chapter, are cogent here. The Bible provides plenty of precedents for the death penalty, but it does not compel anyone to follow those precedents.

ABORTION

The question of a right to life arises most frequently these days in connection with abortion.

Abortion was certainly known in the ancient Near East. The Ebers Papyrus, an Egyptian medical text from the sixteenth century BCE, contains a prescription "to cause a woman to stop pregnancy," involving "unripe fruit of acacia, colocynth, dates, triturate with a six/seventh pint of honey" and placing moist fiber on the vagina.[17] A medical text from Mesopotamia prescribes a concoction involving beer, a lizard, and some unidentifiable herbs to be taken with wine on an empty stomach "to cause a pregnant woman to drop her fetus."[18] Abortion was specifically forbidden in Middle Assyrian law, but remarkably, this is the only ancient Near Eastern prohibition of abortion that has survived:

If a woman has had a miscarriage by her own act, when they have prosecuted her and convicted her they shall impale her on stakes without burying her. If she died in having the miscarriage, they shall impale her on stakes without burying her.[19]

Notably, punishment is prescribed only for the woman.

Yet abortion is never discussed in biblical law. The nearest the Hebrew Bible comes to discussing abortion is in a passage in Jeremiah, where the prophet wishes he had been aborted:

Cursed be the day
  on which I was born!
. . . .
Cursed be the man
  who brought the news to my father, saying,
"A child is born to you, a son,"
  making him very glad.
Let that man be like the cities
  that the LORD overthrew without pity;
let him hear a cry in the morning
  and an alarm at noon,
because he did not kill me in the womb;
  so my mother would have been my grave. (20:14–18)[20]

This passage shows that at least the idea of abortion was known in ancient Judah, but it gives us no information as to whether it was practiced.

One passage in the Hebrew Bible may entail a practice leading to abortion. The trial of a woman suspected of adultery in Numbers 5:11–31 involves making her drink a mixture of water, dust, and ink from the words of a curse that will make her womb swell and her thighs sag if she is guilty. The Hebrew specifies that the offense in question is "a lying of seed," which is to say, genital intercourse such as might result in pregnancy. It seems plausible, then, that the point of the ritual is to cause the woman to abort if she has become pregnant.[21] It is difficult, however, to attach any weight to such an obscure text, since it does not mention abortion explicitly.

The text that served as the basis for later discussion, Exodus 21:22–25, considers the case of injury to a pregnant woman.[22] "When people who are fighting injure a pregnant woman so that there is a miscarriage, and yet no further harm follows, the one responsible shall be fined what the woman's husband demands, paying as much as the judges determine." But an accidental miscarriage is not the same thing as intentional abortion, initiated by the parents.[23]

The relevance of this text to the discussion of abortion was greatly heightened by the Greek translation of the Hebrew Bible, the Septuagint, made in the third century BCE. In the Hebrew of Exodus 21:22, the rare word *ason* is used for "harm." The Greek translation departs radically from the Hebrew:

> If two men fight and strike a pregnant woman and her child comes out not fully formed, he (the striker) will be forced to pay a penalty . . . But if it is fully formed, he shall give life for life. (My translation)

Here, a fully formed fetus is reckoned as a "life," whereas one that is not fully formed is not.[24] Philo of Alexandria, following the Septuagint, expounds the rationale as follows:

> If the offspring is already shaped and all the limbs have their proper qualities and places in the system, he [the striker] must die, for that which answers to this description is a human being, which he has destroyed in the laboratory of nature, who judges that the hour has not yet come for bringing it out into

the light, like a statue lying in a studio, requiring nothing more than to be conveyed outside and released from confinement. (*Special Laws*, 3.109)

He goes on to note:

The view that the child while still adhering to the womb below the belly is part of its future mother is current both among natural philosophers ... and also among physicians of the highest repute.[25]

Apparently, he acknowledges that there could be a legitimate difference of opinion on that point, but not on the question of infanticide.

Attitudes toward abortion in Greece and Rome varied.[26] Plato recommended abortions for women who conceived after the age of forty (*Republic* 5.9). Aristotle (*Politics* 1335b) allowed abortions before "sense and life have begun," which he estimated as coming after forty days for males and ninety for females. The Hippocratic oath forbade abortion except to expel a fetus that was already dead, but there are reports of Greek physicians who prescribed ways to abort in early pregnancy. An inscription from Philadelphia from about 100 BCE includes prohibitions against the taking of drugs to cause abortions. Abortions seem to have become more common in Rome in the early empire, but there were also protests. The poet Ovid said that the woman who aborted a fetus "deserved to die by her own weapons" (*Amores* 2.14.5–6). But if opinion was divided on abortion, the exposure of unwanted infants was widely tolerated and sometimes even encouraged.[27] The Jews were exceptional in the Greco-Roman world in steadfastly condemning the exposure of infants.

Josephus categorically condemns both abortion and infanticide:

> The Law orders all of the offspring to be brought up and forbids women either to abort or to do away with a fetus, but if she is convicted, she is viewed as an infanticide because she destroys a soul and diminishes the race. (*Against Apion* 2.202, trans. Thackeray)

The written law offers no such stipulation, but it does contain a commandment to be fruitful and multiply (Genesis 1:28).

In the Mishnah (compiled in the late second century CE) the fetus was regarded as a person only after birth, or at least after the crown of the head appeared. *Mishnah Niddah* 3:5 declares that a person is born when the greater part of the head has come forth or, in the case of a breech birth, the greater part of the body. Before that, abortion was permitted, at least in some cases:

> If a woman is suffering hard labor, the child must be cut up while in her womb and brought out member by member since the life of the mother takes precedence over that of the child. (*Mishnah Oholot* 7:6)

But if the greater part of the head has emerged, then one cannot give precedence to the one over the other. A person who kills a one-day-old baby is criminally liable and subject to the death penalty, but there is no such sanction for killing a fetus.[28] The medieval exegete Rashi understood the Mishnah to permit abortion because the fetus was not yet a *nefesh*, or person.[29]

This kind of discussion about the beginning of human life or personhood is not in any biblical source. Again, the closest approximation is in Jeremiah 1:5, "Before I formed you in the womb I knew you, and before you were born I consecrated you" (cf. Isaiah 49:1), and in Psalm 139:13–16: "It was you who formed my inward parts, who knit me together in my mother's womb." In the New Testament, Elizabeth tells Mary that "the child in my womb leaped for joy" (Luke 1:44), and Paul says that God set him apart "from my mother's womb." None of these passages, however, amounts to a discussion of the beginning of life or personhood. The fetus is formed in the womb whether it is already a person or not, and everyone knows that babies move in the womb.

ABORTION IN EARLY CHRISTIANITY

There is no explicit discussion of abortion in the New Testament. It is sometimes suggested that sorcerers (*pharmakoi*), who are consigned to the lake of fire in Revelation 21:8 and 22:15, are abortionists, but this is far from clear. The first explicit condemnations of abortion in the Christian tradition are found in *Didache* 2:2 and *The Epistle of Barnabas* 19:5, both dating to the early second century CE.[30] The *Didache* spells out the implications of the commandment to love our neighbor as ourselves by listing a string of prohibitions, beginning with murder and adultery and going on to abortion and infanticide. *The Epistle of Barnabas* also associates the prohibition with the commandment to love our neighbor as ourselves. The fetus apparently qualifies as a "neighbor."[31]

Tertullian (late second or early third century CE) stated the position that would become standard:

> For us murder is once for all forbidden; so even the child in the womb, while yet the mother's blood is being drawn on to form the human being, it is not lawful for us to destroy. To forbid birth is only quicker murder. It makes no difference

whether one take away the life once born or destroy it as it comes to birth. He is a man who is to be a man; the fruit is always present in the seed. (*Apology* 9, 8)[32]

The second-century *Apocalypse of Peter* assigns special torment in hell, in a gorge full of excrement, for women "who have caused their children to be born untimely, and who have corrupted the work of God who created them."[33]

There is, then, a long history of Christian condemnation of abortion, but it is not explicit in the New Testament. Neither is there any acceptance of abortion in either Testament. Perhaps abortion was not widely practiced. Mention is rare even in Mesopotamian and Egyptian texts. Abortion was a dangerous procedure, not to be undertaken lightly. For whatever reason, the biblical authors apparently did not see it as a problem that required explicit comment.

In view of the lack of biblical guidance on the question of abortion, can we draw any inferences from the symbolic world of the Bible or specifically from the New Testament? Children are generally regarded as a blessing and childlessness as an affliction. "Sons are indeed a heritage from the Lord, the fruit of the womb is a reward" (Psalm 127:3). The New Testament theologian Richard Hays argues that "as God's creatures, we are stewards who bear life in trust. To terminate a pregnancy is not only to commit an act of violence but also to assume responsibility for destroying a work of God, 'for whom are all things and for whom we exist' " (1 Corinthians 8:6).[34] Hays writes as a Christian for Christians. His concern is with a properly Christian way of life, not with legislating for society as a whole. In this context, he insists that "it is not appropriate to set up the issue as a conflict of 'rights' . . . In Scripture, there is no 'right to life.' "[35] Neither is there any basis in the New Testament (or in the Old) for the "sacredness of life," which he describes as a sacred cow: immune from discussion. He also argues that the issue is not when life begins or whether the fetus is a person, although these questions are necessarily determinative for those who view abortion as murder. The Bible provides no way of answering those questions. "Whether we accord 'personhood' to the unborn child or not," he writes, "he or she is a manifestation of a new life that has come forth from God. There might be circumstances in which we would deem the termination of such life warranted, but the burden of proof lies heavily upon any decision to undertake such an extreme action."[36] He readily admits, however, that the New Testament does not explicitly or categorically forbid abortion and that there may be occasions when it might be justified.

This way of construing the biblical worldview as hospitable to new life and resistant to abortion, not as a matter of law but as the higher ideal, has much to commend it. Whether it is a necessary way of construing the biblical worldview may be questioned. Must Christians, or Jews, accept everything in life as the will of God? Or is it only in the case of human life that we should not interfere? We have seen that the biblical authors were quite willing to authorize the taking of human life in many cases. Might we not say that to terminate a life, no less than a pregnancy, "is not only to commit an act of violence but also to assume responsibility for destroying a work of God"? Capital punishment and killing in war should not be sanctioned lightly either, but in the end the Bible does not decide the matter for us. The responsibility lies with us, and the Bible is one of many factors that should inform our decision.

To say that the Bible does not affirm either the fetus's right to life or the mother's right to choose does not mean that such putative rights have no place in the modern discussion. Our concern here is not with the morality of abortion but only with what the Bible says about it. In fact, the Bible does not say anything directly about the subject. At the very least this should warn us that abortion is not a central concern in the Bible, and it certainly cannot be a litmus test for biblical values.[37]

The Bible and Gender

THE priestly account of creation in Genesis 1 reaches its climax in Genesis 1:27:

> So God created humankind [Hebrew:
>   adam] in his image;
>   in the image of God he created them
>   [Hebrew: him];
>   male and female he created them.

We are given little by way of context to explain what it means to be in the image of God. The word translated as "image" is commonly used for a statue. Gods were normally represented by statues in their temples in the ancient world. The statue served to represent the presence of the god. It was "the vehicle through which a god resides in the community, maintains a presence, receives worship and prayer, and can actively participate in society."[1] In the ancient Near East the king was often said to be the image of a god, although he necessarily mediated the divine presence in a somewhat different way. This was commonly said of the Egyptian pharaoh, who was the visible form of a deity on earth. Mesopotamian kings were said to be the images of various gods, Enlil, or Shamash, or Marduk.[2] This is not said of the king in the Hebrew Bible. Here, humanity as such takes on this role. The image entails a likeness, a point noted explicitly in Genesis 1:26: "Let us make *adam* in our image, according to our likeness." One aspect of the likeness lies in humanity's dominion over all other creatures: fish, birds, and land animals. This aspect of the creation story will concern us in a later chapter. For the present let us focus on the last part of Genesis 1:27: "male and female he created them."

If humanity is created in the image and likeness of God, and is also male and female, is God, too, male and female? Not in the context of the Hebrew Bible, or of the Priestly document (P). The idea that God might possess any form of sexuality would have been foreign and repugnant to the priestly writers.[3] The statement that *adam* is created male and female, then, must be understood as a qualification of the likeness of God. Adam resembles God insofar as he shares in the work of creation, but he does this by procreating, which requires sexual differentiation.

The midrash *Genesis Rabbah*, a rabbinic commentary from perhaps around 600 CE, entertains the possibility that God created Adam double-faced and then split him to make "two backs."[4] Like the androgyne in Plato's *Symposium*, "the primeval man was round, his back and sides forming a circle; and he had four hands and four feet, one head with two faces, looking in opposite ways."[5] The original *adam* would then be both male and female. The midrash does not accept this possibility, and it has no basis in the biblical tradition.

It is generally accepted that *adam* is the generic Hebrew term for human being, including both males and females.[6] Indeed, Genesis 5:2 declares that God called them *adam*. On this understanding, male and female were created simultaneously, and both are in the image of God.

We cannot fail to notice, however, that the Hebrew uses the singular pronoun when it speaks of the creation of *adam* but the plural when it speaks of male and female. The second account of creation in Genesis 2 clearly claims that the man was created first and the woman was created from one of his ribs. In the New Testament, Paul says that "a man ought not to have his head veiled, since he is the image and reflection of God; but woman is the reflection of man" (1 Corinthians 11:7). Nonetheless, it seems clear that Genesis 1 envisions binary gender and accords both male and female the status of "image of God."

The assertion that women as well as men are created in the image of God is generally, and rightly, hailed in the modern world as remarkably progressive. But Genesis 1 is also held responsible for much of the gender trouble that has beset humanity. The ambiguous use of the word *adam*, sometimes for inclusive humanity but sometimes as the proper name of a male, undoubtedly contributes to androcentrism, the tendency to regard the male as normative and the female as a deviation. In fairness we must note that androcentrism is in no way peculiar to the Bible, and has flourished in cultures where the Bible was unknown, but it is problematic in the biblical context nonetheless. We will return to the problem of androcentrism in the following chapter. But the declaration that humanity is male and female has also lent support to gender polarization, the assumption that human beings must be unambiguously male or female, and to biological essentialism, the assumption that being male or female entails qualities and dispositions far beyond what is required by their different roles in procreation.[7] It is also frequently cited as evidence that the divine plan is for marriage to be between a man and a woman.

It is neither possible nor necessary here to enter into the modern debates about gender and sexuality and the degree to which they are either determined by biology or culturally constructed.[8] We must content ourselves with delimiting what the Bible does and does not say on the subject. As we noted already in Chapter 1, Genesis 1 is a highly schematic account of creation, sketching its main outlines in a simplified way. To distinguish day and night, or even evening and morning, is not to deny that there are dawn and dusk, when light and darkness are not so clearly distinguished. Equally, to say that human beings are male or female does not address the question of whether there are variations in between. Androgynes and transgender people are presumably also created by God. Genesis says nothing whatsoever about distinctively male or female characteristics or the ways men and women should dress, wear their hair, and comport themselves.[9] Differentiation of social roles emerges in historical contexts later in the Bible, but they are not specified in the initial account of creation in Genesis 1. Neither does Genesis 1 specify that marriage must be between a man and a woman, or indeed that there should be an institution of marriage at all.

The second creation story, in Genesis 2–3, has more to say on social roles and on the subject of marriage, but again, what it has to say is by no means exhaustive. A man will cleave to his wife, and the two will become one flesh. But we quickly find that many of the protagonists of the biblical narrative, such as Abraham, Moses, and David, not to mention Solomon, cleaved not just to one woman but to many.[10] We will return to the biblical view of marriage in Chapter 5. For the present it will suffice to note that the biblical account of creation is by no means definitive on the subject.

BEFORE HOMOSEXUALITY

The supposed biblical view that marriage is between a man and a woman is most often invoked in the context of relations between people of the same sex. At the outset, we should remember that the Bible does not have a concept of homosexuality as a disposition or orientation. Homosexuality in this sense is a modern construct, which arose in the late nineteenth century.[11] The term was introduced into the English language in 1892, in a translation of a German work that had appeared twenty years earlier.[12] In the influential formulation of Michel Foucault:

> As defined by the ancient civil or canonical codes, sodomy was a category of forbidden acts; their perpetrator was nothing more than the judicial subject of them. The nineteenth-century homosexual became a personage, a past, a case history, and a childhood, in addition to being a type of life, a life form, and a morphology, with an indiscreet anatomy and possibly a mysterious physiology. Nothing that went into his total composition was unaffected by his sexuality . . . Homosexuality appeared as one of the forms of sexuality when it was transposed from the practice of sodomy onto a kind of interior androgyny, a hermaphrodism of the soul. The sodomite had been a temporary aberration; the homosexual was now a species.[13]

﹒For much of the twentieth century, homosexuality was regarded as a mental disorder,[14] although Freud had firmly declared that "homosexual persons are not sick," for "would that not oblige us to characterize as sick many great thinkers and scholars of all times whose perverse orientation we know for a fact and whom we admire precisely because of their mental health?"[15] Homosexuality was finally removed from the official listing of mental disorders of the American Psychiatric Association in 1973.[16] It is now recognized that some people have a homosexual orientation, but it is not clear that a clean line can be drawn between heterosexuals and homosexuals. There is a spectrum of sexual attraction, and attitudes are heavily influenced by cultural context.[17]

There are at least some precedents for the modern idea of a homosexual orientation and way of life in the classical world. In Plato's *Symposium*, Aristophanes offers a playful explanation of three different sexual orientations. The primeval human being was round, his back and sides forming a circle; he had four hands and four feet and a head with two faces looking opposite ways. These fearsome primeval beings mounted an attack on the gods. To subdue them, Zeus cut them in two and made them walk upright on two legs. This division of the original human being is the origin of desire:

> Each of us when separated, having one side only, like a flat fish, is but the indenture of a man, and he is always looking for his other half. Men who are a section of that double nature which was once called androgynous are lovers of women . . . the women who are a section of the woman do not care for men, but have female attachments . . . But they who are a section of the male follow the male, and while they are young, being slices of the original man, they hang about men and

64

embrace them, and they are themselves the best of boys and
youths, because they have the most manly nature.

Aristophanes defends such people against the charge of
shamelessness and waxes rhapsodic about their love:

> And when one of them meets with his other half, the actual
> half of himself, whether he be a lover of youth or a lover of
> another sort, the pair are lost in amazement of love and friend-
> ship and intimacy, and will not be out of the other's sight, as I
> may say, even for a moment: these are the people who pass
> their whole lives together; yet they could not explain what
> they desire of one another.[18]

Plato's categories do not correspond to the modern distinction between heterosexuals and homosexuals. They distinguish love between men from love between women and treat
pederasty, the love of boys by adult men, as a special category.[19]
Nonetheless, they suggest that sexual orientation is inborn,
determined by a person's makeup. Such theorizing about sexuality was exceptional in antiquity, however, and is not attested
at all in the Bible.

THE EVIDENCE OF THE HEBREW BIBLE

Only a few passages in the Hebrew Bible address the question
of same-sex relations. Some are narratives. A story about Lot
in the city of Sodom in Genesis 19 gave rise to the name "sodomy" for male homosexual intercourse. Lot, nephew of Abraham, sees two strangers in the city gate. (They turn out to be
angels.) He insists that they come into his house and not spend
the night in the public square. The men of Sodom, however,
surround the house and demand that Lot bring out the strangers "so that we may know them." "To know" is often used as a

euphemism for sex, and Lot's reaction makes clear that this is so here: "I beg you, my brothers, do not act so wickedly." To deter them he offers to give them his two virgin daughters, to do to them as they pleased, but says, "Only do nothing to these men, for they have come under the shelter of my roof" (Genesis 19:8). Readers have often assumed that the wicked deed from which Lot wants to deter the men of Sodom is indeed sodomy—intercourse with his male guests. The issue is complicated, however, by a couple of factors. As Lot's response makes clear, he, as host, feels responsible for his guests.[20] That the people of Sodom wanted to rape *male* guests evidently added to the outrage. But what is involved here is rape. Accordingly the story says nothing about the permissibility of consensual sex between males. The idea that it would be worse to rape a man than to rape a woman persists in Philo, in sophisticated circles in Alexandria around the turn of the Common Era: "If you are guilty of pederasty or adultery or rape of a young person, even of a female, for I need not mention the case of a male . . . the penalty is death" (*Hypothetica* 7.1).[21] Interestingly, the most explicit statement about the sin of Sodom in the Hebrew Bible, in Ezekiel 16:49, does not mention sex at all: "This was the guilt of your sister Sodom; she and her daughters had pride, excess of food, and prosperous ease, but did not aid the poor and needy." The Epistle of Jude, verse 7, associates Sodom and Gomorrah with sexual immorality and says that the residents went after "other flesh," and 2 Peter 2:6–10 associates them with licentiousness, without further specification. The "other flesh" in Jude may refer to the flesh of angels. The earliest author to condemn the Sodomites for sex between males was Philo of Alexandria (*Abraham* 135).[22]

Lot's guests were angels, and they could escape by striking the people of Sodom with blindness. Lot's daughters suffer no ill effects. The woman in a related story in Judges 19 is not so fortunate. She is the concubine of a Levite, who is bringing her back from Bethlehem to the hill country of Ephraim. He stops in Gibeah to spend the night, and an old man offers him hospitality. Again, the men of the city, "a perverse lot," demand that the stranger be brought out so that they might "know" him. The host pleads with them not to do such a vile thing and offers them his virgin daughter and the stranger's concubine to ravish or do what they want with them. The Levite thrusts out his concubine. In the morning the concubine is dead on the doorstep. Here again the story is complicated by the demands of hospitality and the fact that what the people of the city wanted was rape. Again, the rape of a man seems to be regarded as worse than the rape of a woman, but the story does not address the permissibility of consensual relations.

Also inconclusive is the evidence for homosexual prostitution in connection with a cult in ancient Israel. Scholars have speculated that sexual acts were performed with a priest or a priestess as a way of ensuring fertility. This whole theory of sacred marriage has fallen into disrepute in recent years, as it rests on dubious evidence. There are however condemnations in the Bible of functionaries called *qadesh* (male) and *q^edeshah* (female). In Deuteronomy 23:17–18 (Hebrews 23:18–19) we read:

> None of the daughters of Israel shall be a temple prostitute [*q^edeshah*]; none of the sons of Israel shall be a temple prostitute [*qadesh*]. You shall not bring the fee of a prostitute or the

wages of a male prostitute into the house of the LORD your
God in payment for any vow, for both of these are abhorrent
to the LORD your God.

The word q*deshah* is also associated with *zonah*, "prostitute"
in Genesis 38:21–22 and Hosea 4:14. The Hosea passage
speaks of sacrificing with q*deshoth*. The texts give no clear
evidence about the role of the q*deshim*.[23] They had quarters in
the Jerusalem temple that were destroyed in Josiah's purge of
the cult (2 Kings 23:7). They appear to have a cultic role that
was unacceptable to the biblical authors, but the evidence is
too unclear to warrant any firm conclusions about their supposed homosexual activity.

The most intriguing story of same-sex love in the Hebrew
Bible is undoubtedly that of David and Jonathan. According
to 1 Samuel 18:1, "the soul of Jonathan was bound to the soul
of David, and Jonathan loved him as his own soul." In 1 Samuel 19:1–2, Jonathan warned David that his father Saul planned
to kill him because "Jonathan took great delight in David." In
1 Samuel 20:16–17, Jonathan made a covenant with the house
of David, saying, "May the Lord seek out the enemies of
David." Jonathan made David swear again by his love for him,
for he loved him as he loved his own life. In 1 Samuel 20:30,
Saul's anger was kindled against Jonathan. He said to him:
"You son of a perverse, rebellious woman! Do I not know that
you have chosen the son of Jesse to your own shame and to
the shame of your mother's nakedness?" Finally, after Saul
and Jonathan are killed in battle with the Philistines, David
mourns Jonathan: "I am distressed for you, my brother Jonathan; greatly beloved were you to me; your love to me was
wonderful, passing the love of women" (2 Samuel 1:26).

The relationship described in these passages has given rise to an enormous amount of literature but little consensus. Interpretation may often be guided by the interpreter's predisposition on the question of homosexuality. At no point does the text say explicitly that David and Jonathan had sex. Accordingly, many commentators see here a case of close friendship or male bonding. Martti Nissinen, for example, writes that "it is also possible to interpret David's and Jonathan's love as an intimate camaraderie of two young soldiers with no sexual involvement."[24] He notes that there is no distinction of active and passive roles, as we might expect in a sexual relationship. Famous parallels for intimate male friendship are found in the stories of Gilgamesh and Enkidu from Mesopotamia, and Achilles and Patroclus in Homer's *Iliad*. Moreover, the rhetoric of love has roots in discourse about treaties and covenants in the ancient Near East. Covenant partners, whether equal or unequal, were said to love each other and referred to each other using language of kinship, such as "brother."[25] "Love" in this context essentially meant "loyalty." David and Jonathan are explicitly said to have made a covenant in 1 Samuel 20. David appeals to Jonathan to "deal kindly with your servant, for you have brought your servant into a sacred covenant with you" (1 Samuel 20:8). Some commentators consequently suggest that the love has a political dimension: it prepares the way for David to take over the kingdom of Saul.[26] Two statements in the text, however, suggest a more emotional or erotic relationship. One is Saul's complaint that Jonathan has chosen David to his shame and the shame of his mother's nakedness. It is possible that the shame here arises from Jonathan's disloyalty to his father and implicitly to the mother who bore him, but it may also have sexual implications. The other is David's statement that the love of Jonathan was better than the love of women.

Nissinen remarks, aptly enough, that "the text thus leaves the possible homoerotic associations to the reader's imagination."[27] Homosexual love, however, like heterosexual love, is about much more than sex. It is about bonding, fidelity, and emotion, all of which seem to be in evidence in the case of David and Jonathan. Some interpreters assume that the biblical heroes could not have consummated their love because "homosexual acts were condemned in Israelite law (Leviticus 20:13). So David's apologists would hardly have described him as homosexual or included a piece that described him that way."[28] But this judgment is problematic on two counts. First, as we shall see, the condemnation of homosexual acts is found only in one distinctive strand of biblical law, and it is not at all certain the author or editor of the books of Samuel would have been constrained by it. Second, even Leviticus does not condemn love between males in the emotional sense, and the specific sex acts that are forbidden are a subject of dispute.

THE PROHIBITION IN LEVITICUS

Sexual acts between males are explicitly condemned in only two verses of the Hebrew Bible. Leviticus 18:22 reads: "You shall not lie with a male the lyings of a woman; it is an abomination." Leviticus 20:13 specifies the penalty: "If a man lies with a male the lyings of a woman, both of them have committed an abomination. They shall be put to death. Their blood is upon them." These verses are in the Holiness Code, a subsection of the Book of Leviticus and of the Priestly Laws, usually dated to the Babylonian Exile, although the evidence for dating is not very clear.

The first question here is what is meant by "the lyings of a woman." The corresponding phrase, "the lying of a male," occurs a number of times in the books of Numbers and Judges (Numbers 31:17, 18, 35; Judges 21:11–12). In Judges, a virgin girl is defined as one "who has not known a man with respect to the lying of a male." In Numbers as well, a virgin is one who has not known the lying of a male. The "lying of a male," then, appears to mean vaginal intercourse. Saul Olyan argues by analogy that the "lyings of a woman" must refer to anal intercourse and that this is the only activity between males that is prohibited in Leviticus.[29] Richard Friedman and Shawna Dolansky, in contrast, note that while "the lying of a male" is always singular, "the lyings of a woman" are plural. They infer that more than one kind of sexual activity is involved.[30] We might also note that the passages that speak of the lying of a man speak of the woman "knowing" or experiencing it. Leviticus speaks rather of a man who lies the lyings of a woman, not of a man who lies the lying of a man with a man. This might suggest that a man who lies the lyings of a woman is one who plays the role of the woman in sex. Both partners, however, are judged worthy of death.

On any interpretation, this law is exceptional in the ancient Near East. The only parallel is provided by a Middle Assyrian law:

> If a man lie with his neighbor, when they have prosecuted him and convicted him, they shall lie with him and turn him into a eunuch.[31]

In this case, however, the issue seems to be the subjugation of the "neighbor," presumably a man of equal status, rather than the homosexual activity, which is repeated in the punishment. In Greece, it was considered shameful for a man of status to be penetrated but not to be the penetrator. Plato, in the *Laws*, regarded as "womanly" men who played the role of the woman (*Laws* 837 C), and Plutarch, writing in the Roman era, allowed no respect or friendship to those who played the passive role (*Moralia* 768 E). Leviticus, however, condemns both parties to death.

Remarkably there is no law on relations between women. It can hardly be that love between women was not known in Israel or Judah. Neither is it the case that the authors were indifferent to what women did. Leviticus 18:23, the verse immediately after the prohibition against lying with a male, forbids relations with an animal but specifies that it is equally forbidden for a woman to give herself to an animal. So the question arises, How did sex between males differ from sex between females?

The obvious answer to this question is that it involved the ejaculation of semen. This suggests that the problem is waste of seed. Yet there is no mention of seed in this passage, and other actions that involve a waste of seed, such as sex with a pregnant woman, are not prohibited. (Neither is masturbation. The problem with Onan in Genesis 38 is that he fails to honor the law of levirate marriage, which required him to raise up a son for his dead brother.) Alternatively, since a mingling of bodily fluids is involved, the issue might concern purity, perhaps because of the mingling of semen and excrement. (Excrement is not regarded as defiling in biblical law, but Ezekiel expresses revulsion when he is asked to cook his food over human dung in 4:12–13.) So none of the explanations on offer is entirely satisfactory, although each of them may have some validity.

It is important in any case to see these laws in the context of the Holiness Code and of Leviticus more generally. The tone for many of the purity laws is set by the list of forbidden foods in Leviticus 11. An animal that has divided hooves and is cleft-footed and chews the cud is permitted. Such an animal is "normal." But those that chew the cud but do not have divided hooves (such as the camel) or have divided hooves but do not chew the cud (such as the pig) are declared unclean. Mary Douglas famously argued that the problem was that the impure animals were regarded as anomalous, or rather that anomalous animals, those that deviated from some norm, were regarded as impure.[32] This kind of reasoning may play a part in the prohibition of sexual relations between males, but it does not explain why the prohibition is not extended to women. Relations between women would seem to be as anomalous as relations between men.

John Boswell claimed that the Hebrew word *toevah*, "abomination," "does not usually signify something intrinsically evil, like rape or theft ... but something which is ritually unclean for Jews, like eating pork or engaging in intercourse during menstruation.[33] But this comparison is misleading.[34] Leviticus recognizes occasions of ritual uncleanness that are not sinful, such as childbirth, seminal emission, heterosexual intercourse, and menstruation. In these cases, purification is accomplished through ritual, sacrifice, and washing.[35] The word *toevah* is not used to refer to them. It is used for a wide range of offenses, many of them moral in nature (murder, lying, robbery).[36]

In the New Testament, Paul dispensed Gentile Christians from following the food laws of Leviticus. Many of the specific laws are generally disregarded in the modern world, except by the ultra-Orthodox. Leviticus 19:19 says, "You shall not let your animals breed with a different kind; you shall not sow your field with two kinds of seed; nor shall you put on a garment made of two different materials." Few people in the modern world regard these commandments as binding. This does not mean that all commandments in Leviticus can be disregarded. Moral laws such as we find in the Ten Commandments are interspersed with the ritual laws of Leviticus 19. But the mixture shows that laws are not automatically binding because they are found in the Bible. Anyone who argues that Leviticus 18:22 is binding but 19:19 is not needs to provide a rationale.

The most striking thing about the Hebrew Bible on the subject of same-sex relations, however, is how little it has to say on the subject. The prophets have nothing to say about it. Neither do the sages who compiled the Wisdom Literature (Job, Proverbs, Qoheleth [Ecclesiastes]) or the scribes who edited Deuteronomy and the Deuteronomistic History. That the subject is addressed explicitly in only two verses, in a distinctive strand of Priestly Law, shows that it is a marginal concern in the Hebrew Bible.

THE NEW TESTAMENT

In the New Testament, too, we find large swathes of material that do not address same-sex relations at all. Jesus never touches on the subject in any of the Gospels.[37] The exceptions are in the writings of Paul. The most important passage is found in Romans 1. The passage begins by declaring that the wrath of God is revealed from heaven against those who suppress the truth. Ever since the creation, the power and nature of God have been visible through the things he has made. Therefore, those who do not acknowledge him are without excuse. Paul draws here on an argument that is also found in the Wisdom of Solomon, a Jewish Hellenistic work from the early first century CE. The Wisdom of Solomon is more sympathetic than Paul to the Gentiles, allowing that they may have tried to find God but gone astray. Paul regards them as culpable. Because they failed to acknowledge God, God punished them. The manner of punishment is startling:

> For this reason God gave them up to degrading passions. Their women exchanged natural intercourse for unnatural, and in the same way also the men, giving up natural intercourse with women, were consumed with passion for one another. Men committed shameless acts with men and received in their own persons the due penalty for their error. (Romans 1:26–27)

Same-sex relations here are said to be a punishment: God gave Gentiles up to their lusts. The punishment consists in deviation from nature, from the order of creation.

NATURAL AND UNNATURAL

Paul enters here into a discourse on nature that had a long history in Greek philosophy, dating back to the Sophists in the fifth century, and no precedent in the Hebrew Bible. While Plato had written positively about homosexual relations in the *Symposium*, in his last work, the *Laws*, he wrote:

> I think that the pleasure is to be deemed natural which arises
> out of the intercourse between men and women, but that the
> intercourse of men with men, or of women with women, is
> contrary to nature, and that the bold attempt was originally
> due to unbridled lust. (1.636)

Later he adduces the animals as proof that such unions were monstrous, although the behavior of animals was a matter of dispute (4.836).[38] In Greco-Roman culture generally, "natural" sexual relations involved a superior active partner and an inferior passive partner (boys, women, slaves). Sexual relations between women, accordingly, were "unnatural."[39] The contrast between "in accordance with nature" and "contrary to nature" figures prominently in Greco-Roman popular philosophy. For example, a character in Plutarch's *Dialogue on Love* disparages union with males as contrary to nature, as contrasted with the love between men and women, characterized as natural.[40]

Hellenistic Jewish literature generally maintained a hard line against same-sex relations, especially relations between males. One of the most explicit passages on the subject is found in Pseudo-Phocylides, a collection of moralizing sayings that probably dates to the first century CE:

> Do not outrage your wife for shameful ways of intercourse.
> Do not transgress the natural limits of sexuality for
>   unlawful sex,
> For even animals are not pleased by intercourse of male
>   with male,
> And let not women imitate the sexual role of men.
> Do not deliver yourself wholly unto unbridled sensuality
>   towards your wife.
> For *eros* is not a god, but a passion destructive of all.
>   (189–94)[41]

Philo of Alexandria uses the expression "contrary to nature" (*para physin*) with reference to relations between a man and a woman in her menstrual period, relations between a man and a boy, and relations between different species of animals (*Special Laws* 3.7–82). His primary concerns seem to be for procreation and clear distinctions between species.[42] Josephus writes:

> The Law recognizes no sexual connections, except the natural union of man and wife, and that only for the procreation of children. But it abhors the intercourse of males with males and punishes any who undertake such a thing with death. (*Against Apion* 2.199, trans. Thackeray)[43]

In Paul's time, the categorization of same-sex relations as *para physin* was commonplace in the world of Hellenistic Judaism.[44] Paul writes in a Hellenistic Jewish cultural context.

While various female acts (or even positions) might be construed as imitating the sexual role of men, and therefore as unnatural, most interpreters agree that Paul is referring to sex between women in Romans 1:26. The word "likewise" in the following verse clearly refers to sex between men. Moreover, this is the type of sexual relations most frequently called contrary to nature in the contemporary Greco-Roman literature.[45] It seems clear, then, that Paul condemns lesbianism as well as male homoerotic relations.

Some interpreters have suggested that Paul was objecting only to heterosexuals who performed homosexual acts.[46] But Paul does not recognize homosexuals as a category at all. For him everyone is heterosexual, and all homosexual acts are expressions of lust. This understanding is deficient by modern lights, but the apostle was a man of his time. Again, others have suggested that Paul's objection was to sex between men and boys, which is normally understood as abuse in the modern world but was widely practiced in Greek and Roman culture.[47] But Paul, like Leviticus, holds both active and passive parties equally responsible and liable for the death penalty. Unlike Philo, Paul was not concerned about procreation, as we shall see in the next chapter. Neither was he concerned about purity laws, such as those involving menstruating women. He may well have been influenced by the prohibition of sex between males in Leviticus, and he was surely influenced by Greco-Roman conceptions of what was natural and unnatural.

But Paul's attempt to argue on the basis of nature is not very satisfactory. As the classical scholar John J. Winkler comments with regard to distinctions of natural and unnatural in Greek culture, "what 'natural' means in many such contexts is precisely 'conventional and proper.' The word 'unnatural' in contexts of human behavior quite regularly means 'seriously unconventional.' "[48] The point can be illustrated easily from 1 Corinthians 11, where Paul strains to make an argument that any woman who prays or prophesies should veil her head. "Judge for yourself," he writes. "Is it proper for a woman to pray to God with her head unveiled? Does not nature itself teach you that if a man wears long hair, it is degrading to him, but if a woman has long hair, it is her glory? For her hair is given to her for a covering" (11:13–15). But nature teaches this only in specific cultural contexts. In the United States, nature stopped teaching that long hair was degrading for a man in the 1960s (except for the Okies from Muskogee of Merle Haggard's song). Paul himself seems to have sensed the weakness of his argument, for he concludes: "But if anyone is disposed to be contentious, we have no such custom, nor do the churches of God." Custom, not nature, is what was at stake, and this was no less true in Romans 1 on the subject of same-sex relations.

THE GREEK TERMS *ARSENOKOITAI* AND *MALAKOI*

Apart from the passage in Romans, the only other passages in the New Testament that condemn same-sex relations are 1 Corinthians 6:9 and 1 Timothy 1:10. As translated in the New Revised Standard Version of the Bible (NRSV), 1 Corinthians 6:9–10 reads:

> Do you not know that wrongdoers will not inherit the kingdom of God? Do not be deceived! Fornicators, idolaters, adulterers, male prostitutes, sodomites, thieves, the greedy, drunkards, revilers, robbers—none of these will inherit the kingdom of God.

The Greek word translated here as "male prostitutes" is *malakoi*, literally "soft people (masculine)." To call them "male prostitutes" is clearly an overinterpretation. The word is widely used and with a wide range of meanings. A male who allowed himself to be penetrated might be characterized as "soft," but the word cannot be restricted to this meaning. In a sexual context, it means "effeminate."[49] It is unlikely, however, that Paul was condemning people for their disposition or just for an effeminate lifestyle. He most probably used the word in its narrower sense of passive sexual partner.

The Greek word translated as "sodomite" in the NRSV, *arsenokoitai*, is more controversial. It recurs in the list of evildoers in 1 Timothy 1:10. The Greek word is a compound of *arsen*,

THE BIBLE AND GENDER

"male," and *koite*, "bed." John Boswell argued that the first term denotes the subject, and so the sense would be "a male lying," that is, a man having intercourse, suggesting a fornicator or a male prostitute.[50] But the word is probably coined on the basis of the Greek translation of Leviticus 20:13: *meta arsenos koiten gynaikos* (with a male, the couch of a woman).[51] The objection is raised that the meaning of a word is not necessarily determined by its etymology. In *Sibylline Oracles* 2.70–77 the verb *arsenokeitein* occurs in connection with other terms that relate to injustice rather than to sexual offenses.[52] But the *Sibylline Oracles* regularly include male homosexual relations in lists of vices. In *Sibylline Oracles* 3.185 the vice is expressed as "male will approach male." In *Sibylline Oracles* 3.595–96 the Jews are praised because they "are mindful of holy wedlock and do not engage in impious intercourse with male children." Again, in *Sibylline Oracles* 3.764 the Sibyl urges people to "avoid adultery and indiscriminate intercourse with males." Since warnings against male homosexual intercourse is a topos in Sibylline literature, there can be little doubt about the meaning of *arsenokoitai* in *Sibylline Oracles* 2 or indeed in Paul. The word suggests an allusion to Leviticus, but Paul's position on the subject is absolutely in conformity with the prevalent position in Hellenistic Judaism.

In the New Testament, as in the Old, we find explicit condemnation of homosexual acts, but only in a few passages, in the Pauline and pseudo-Pauline epistles.[53] Neither Jesus nor the evangelists have anything at all to say on the subject, which should raise questions about the importance of homosexuality as an issue in the biblical world. Moreover, Paul's comments are clearly indebted to the Hellenistic cultural context and to the assumptions of Hellenistic Jews. The Bible provides no direct support for gay rights in a modern context. Anyone who wishes to use the Bible to argue for gay rights would have to argue from the general command to love our neighbor and would then have to face the difficulties of determining what love of the neighbor requires. Conversely, the explicit biblical condemnations of homosexual activity are confined to narrow strands of tradition in both Testaments. Modern discussions of gender and sexuality provide a very different context for this issue than is envisioned in the Bible. Many other considerations besides the few scriptural passages we have discussed would have to be taken into account in a responsible discussion of the ethics of homosexuality.

CHAPTER FOUR

Marriage and Family

I N 2012, Christopher Rollston, a respected Hebrew Bible scholar, then teaching at Emanuel Christian Seminary in Tennessee, published a piece in the *Huffington Post* entitled "The Marginalization of Women: A Biblical Value We Don't Like to Talk About."[1] He had no difficulty citing examples from both Testaments to support his case. A notable example is found in the Ten Commandments. The tenth commandment reads: "You shall not covet your neighbor's house, you shall not covet your neighbor's wife, or his male slave, his female slave, his ox, his donkey, or anything which belongs to your neighbor" (Exodus 20:17; Deuteronomy 5:21). Here the wife is apparently classified as her husband's property, since she is listed with slaves and work animals.[2] Many scholars would say that Rollston was belaboring the obvious. Nonetheless, and even though he was a tenured professor, he was told that he was alienating donors and should find employment elsewhere, which, happily, he did.[3]

The following year, Carol Meyers, a distinguished feminist scholar of the Hebrew Bible, gave the annual presidential address to the Society of Biblical Literature.[4] She addressed the question "Was ancient Israel a patriarchal society?" and answered in the negative: "The term 'patriarchy' is an inadequate and misleading designation of the social reality of ancient Israel."[5] Meyers was not responding to the piece in the *Huffington Post;* her concern was with the implications of the specific term "patriarchy." She is not suggesting that there was gender neutrality in ancient Israel, and she does not dispute that female sexuality is subjected to male control in the Bible, as in many traditional societies. Nonetheless, she paints a very different picture of the portrayal of women both in the Bible and in ancient Israel as we know it from archeology. She insists that "male control of female sexuality does not mean male control of adult women in every aspect of household or community life. In short, male dominance is real; but it was fragmentary, not hegemonic."[6] Wives were not, in fact, placed on the same level as slaves and cattle, regardless of the formulation in the Decalogue.

There is some truth on both sides of this debate. The sweeping condemnation of the marginalization of women is oversimplified and disregards the nuances of the ancient evidence. Nonetheless, it has a clear biblical basis and is no more oversimplified than the way the Bible is generally perceived in popular culture.

FEMINIST BIBLICAL SCHOLARSHIP

Of all the developments that roiled the field of biblical studies in the last third of the twentieth century, none has proved more fundamental than feminist scholarship.[7] Prior to this development, few people saw a problem with the androcentric perspective of the biblical text, typified in the use of the masculine *adam*, "man," as the designation for humanity in general. The pioneers of feminist biblical scholarship, such as Phyllis Trible for the Hebrew Bible and Elisabeth Schüssler Fiorenza for the New Testament, must be credited with removing scales from the eyes of their readers.[8] What they helped them see was not a pretty picture. At the least, the Bible as traditionally interpreted seldom takes account of female perspectives and is often guilty of sexism. For interpreters with religious commitments, whether Jewish or Christian, this new perspective on the Bible was problematic.

Interpreters have adopted various apologetic strategies to deal with this problematic perspective. Phyllis Trible, in an early formulation, claimed that "the intentionality of biblical faith, as distinguished from a general description of biblical religion, is neither to create nor to perpetuate patriarchy but rather to function as salvation for both women and men . . . the hermeneutical challenge is to translate biblical faith without sexism."[9] But the attempt to salvage a pure grain of biblical faith from the husk of cultural context is problematic and presupposes a commitment to vindicate the biblical text, appearances notwithstanding. Carol Meyers moved in a different direction.[10] In her view, the biblical text is admittedly androcentric, but the social reality was more complex. Women had their own spheres of power and influence.

Much of biblical feminist scholarship has been driven by a theological impulse to redeem traditions that seem utterly incompatible with feminist interests.[11] In contrast, the approach of Elisabeth Schüssler Fiorenza has been characterized as a "hermeneutic of suspicion."[12] Schüssler Fiorenza is willing to reject the authority of texts she sees as promoting oppression, but she also engages in the retrieval of tradition. In her most influential book, *In Memory of Her*, subtitled *A Feminist Theological Reconstruction of Christian Origins*, she seeks to reconstruct the early Jesus movement as a resource for feminism.[13] She is not interested in producing an objective history. "My question," she writes, "was not 'did it actually happen?' but do we still have sufficient information and source texts to tell the story of the movement carrying Jesus' name *otherwise*, envisioning it as that of a discipleship of equals?"[14] Moreover, she argues: "If one cannot prove that wo/men were not members of this group and did not participate in shaping the earliest Jesus traditions, one needs to give the benefit of the doubt to the textual traces suggesting that they did."[15]

All of these scholars have contributed greatly to our understanding of the biblical texts, but like most people who have asked questions relating to gender in the Bible, they have been engaged, in their different ways, in a work of advocacy. My objective here is different. It is simply to assess, as dispassionately as possible, what may reasonably be inferred from the biblical text, whether it supports our modern agendas or not. Schüssler Fiorenza calls for an "ethics of accountability," for taking responsibility for "the ethical consequences of the biblical text and its meanings."[16] But an ethically responsible reading must first of all be clear on what meanings are actually supported by the text. It is not ethically responsible to claim that the Bible condemned slavery, when it manifestly did not. Neither is it ethically responsible to claim that the Bible, in either Testament, advocates a discipleship of equals.

If we find a particular biblical position reprehensible, the ethically responsible course is to say so, not to give the benefit of the doubt to whatever positions we find congenial.

The story of Adam and Eve in Genesis 2–3 has had inordinate influence on perceptions of the biblical view of women, both in antiquity and in modern times. Remarkably, we find no reference to it in the Hebrew Bible outside Genesis, but it enters the discussion in the period between the Testaments, notably in the Book of Ben Sira (Ecclesiasticus), which is included in the Catholic Old Testament and the Protestant Apocrypha. The story looms large in the New Testament.

Several points in the story bear on the role of women. One of the oldest arguments for the subordination of women, found already in the New Testament, in 1 Timothy 2:13, is that "Adam was formed first, then Eve." It has been argued that before the creation of Eve, Adam was undifferentiated, neither male nor female.[17] The argument has a certain logic, but it is undercut by the use of the same word, "Adam," for the male *after* the creation of Eve. It is "the man" (*ha-adam*) who acknowledges Eve as "flesh of my flesh and bone of my bone" in Genesis 2:23. That she is taken from Adam's body (rib) also accords priority to Adam, even reversing the order of nature in the birth process.[18] The reversal does not in itself imply the subjection of women in any severe sense, but it establishes a pecking order.

Woman was created in the first place because "it is not good that the man should be alone" (Genesis 2:18). God proposes to create for him "a helpmate corresponding to him." The animals do not qualify. The woman fits the bill, and the two become one flesh. The implications for male-female relations are ambiguous. On the one hand, the story suggests that the woman was created to meet a need on the part of the man. A helper is not necessarily inferior to the one being helped, but *qua* helper, he or she is taking a subordinate or secondary position. The goals of the person being helped remain primary.[19] On the other hand, the emphasis is on companionship and partnership. Again, the story does not suggest repression, but it nonetheless gives precedence to the male.

The only passage in Genesis 2–3 that clearly subordinates the woman to the man is found in Genesis 3:16, when God discovers that Adam and Eve have eaten the forbidden fruit:

> To the woman he said,
>
> > "I will greatly increase your pangs in childbearing;
> > in pain you shall bring forth children,
> > yet your desire shall be for your husband,
> > and he shall rule over you."

This pronouncement has the character of a punishment. The snake is condemned to crawl on its belly and eat dust. The man is to eat his bread by the sweat of his brow. Life will be hard, because humanity grasped for more than it was given. The story places the blame for this on humanity. It is concerned to acquit the creator of responsibility for all the suffering and misery of life.[20]

The ethos of this story is antithetical to that of the modern world, where we are taught to reach for the stars and challenge every limit. The ancient world was not geared toward progress but tended to accept the limits of life as inevitable. (Compare Greek tragedy, where the sin that leads to downfall is *hybris*, the attempt to rise above one's station.) The punishments of Genesis 3 are simply a description of life as the author saw it. No one in the modern world would conclude that men should not find alternatives to physical labor, or indeed that women should not try to mitigate the pain of childbirth. In short, the meaning of the passage is quite clear; what is not so clear is its force. Should it be taken as prescriptive or just as descriptive?

In Genesis, Adam and Eve are both responsible for the act of disobedience. If either bears greater responsibility, it is Adam, insofar as he seems to hold primacy, and in fact the act became known traditionally as the "sin of Adam." Nonetheless, we read in the Book of Ben Sira (early second century BCE): "From a woman sin had its beginning and because of her we all die."[21] Even more egregiously, 1 Timothy 2:14 says: "Adam was not deceived, but the woman was deceived and became a transgressor." Such claims cannot be justified by exegesis of Genesis. Adam may not have been deceived by the snake, but he was deceived by Eve, and he was just as much a transgressor as she was. At this point, the text seems to be subordinated to the cultural prejudices of a later era.

WOMEN IN THE HEBREW BIBLE

There is a wide spectrum of material relating to women in the Hebrew Bible, too wide to review here in any detail.[22] Much seems problematic from a modern viewpoint, although it may have been readily accepted in the ancient world.[23] Women did not inherit, unless there were no sons, but in that case the inheritance passed to the daughters (Numbers 27). A woman's religious vows could be nullified by her father or her husband (30:3–15). Polygamy was accepted down to the common era, although it is rarely attested in the postexilic era (roughly, after 500 BCE). Adultery was understood as having relations with the wife of another man. Both parties were liable to death (Leviticus 20:10; Deuteronomy 22:22), but Proverbs 6:29–35 suggests that the aggrieved husband had some discretion in the matter: the man who commits adultery "will get wounds and dishonor, and his disgrace will not be wiped away. For jealousy arouses a husband's fury, and he shows no restraint when he takes revenge. He will accept no compensation and refuses a bribe no matter how great." According to Deuteronomy, a woman who was found not to be a virgin when she married was to be stoned (22:20–21). If a man falsely accused his bride of not being a virgin, he was to be fined one hundred shekels (which went to the woman's father), but she would remain his wife and he could not divorce her (22:13–19). If a man lay with a woman who was engaged to be married to another man, both were liable to death, but if it happened in the open country where she could not cry for help, only the man was liable. If a man raped a virgin who was not engaged, he was to pay fifty shekels to the young woman's father and marry her. He could not then divorce her (22:28–9). According to Exodus 22:17, the father could refuse to give the young woman to her rapist, but the rapist still had to pay the bride-price.

The laws about marriage have a clear economic aspect.[24] The bride-price, or *mohar*, is a sum of money paid by the groom to the family of the bride.[25] While biblical law never stipulates such a payment for normal marriage, the references in the discussion of rape and seduction show that it was customary. The term occurs only three times in the Hebrew Bible, in the passage in Exodus 22 to which we have just referred, Genesis 34:12 (in the aftermath of the rape of Dinah, when Hamor, the rapist, offers to pay any bride-price her family should demand), and 1 Samuel 18:25 (where Saul demands of David a bride-price of one hundred Philistine foreskins for the hand of his daughter Michal). The amount could vary, depending on social status. Although the payment may give the impression that marriage was a purchase, the reality was more complex, and anthropologists prefer to speak of "bride-wealth."[26] Such payments are known in many traditional societies. In part, they compensated the father for transferring control of the young woman to her husband. Later, they served as a deterrent to divorce, since the payment would be forfeited. In the postexilic period, the main marriage payment was the dowry, the money that the bride brought with her into the marriage, which remained her property. In marriage contracts from the fifth century BCE, from a garrison of Judean mercenaries in the south of Egypt, it appears that the bride-price was added to the dowry. Eventually, the bride-price was given by promissory note, payable only in the event of divorce. Both the bride-price and the dowry provided security for the wife in the case of divorce.[27] Even the law requiring a rapist to marry his victim was designed for the economic protection of the woman, who would probably not find another husband, since she was "damaged goods."

It should be borne in mind that the laws do not necessarily reflect actual practice. Exceptions could certainly be made.

The story of Judah and Tamar in Genesis 38 provides a good example. Tamar, daughter-in-law of Judah, had been widowed. Her brother-in-law, Onan, was supposed to raise up offspring on his brother's behalf, but instead he spilled his seed on the ground and was consequently put to death by the Lord (method unspecified). Judah hesitated to give Tamar to his third son, Shelah, lest he die also. So Tamar took matters into her own hands. She dressed as a prostitute and waited for Judah at a sheep-shearing. When she became pregnant, Judah, in righteous anger, ordered that she be brought out and burned. But she had taken tokens from him, which she produced to show that he was the father. At that point, the execution was called off, and Judah admitted that she was more righteous than he was. In the New Testament, too, Jesus intervenes to save a woman taken in adultery, in John 8. Even when laws are severe, people find a modus vivendi.

DIVORCE

The right of a man to divorce his wife is taken for granted in the Hebrew Bible. The classic passage is found in Deuteronomy 24:

> Suppose a man enters into marriage with a woman, but she does not please him because he finds something objectionable about her, and so he writes her a certificate of divorce, puts it in her hand, and sends her out of his house; she then leaves his house and goes off to become another man's wife. Then suppose the second man dislikes her . . .

The point in this passage is that the first husband may not take her back once she has been married to another man. There is no discussion of the permissibility of divorce. That is assumed.

The grounds cited for divorce in this hypothetical case are notoriously vague. The phrase "something objectionable"[28] means some improper or indecent behavior, but it was open to diverse interpretations. It was invoked in a famous debate between the rabbis Hillel and Shammai in the first century BCE. The Shammaites tried to restrict the grounds for divorce to cases of unchastity, but the school of Hillel ruled that divorce was permitted "even if she ruined a dish for him." Rabbi Akiba went further: "even if he found another fairer than her" (*Mishnah Gittin* 9–10).

The word "hate" (*sane'*), which is used in Deuteronomy 24 in connection with the second husband who divorces the woman, is a technical term for divorce and should be translated as "repudiate" rather than "dislike." To say "I hate my wife/husband" serves as a formula of divorce.

In biblical law, women are not allowed to initiate divorce. That right is taken for granted, however, in the fifth-century BCE papyri from the Judean colony at Elephantine, in Egypt.[29] Josephus mentions two cases where women in the Herodian household initiated divorce,[30] but the practice of a royal house may have been exceptional, and indeed Josephus comments that the divorces were "not in accordance with Jewish law."[31] Josephus also says that his first wife left him when he followed Vespasian to Rome.[32] He was divorced a second time on his own initiative.[33] The evidence of the papyri from the Judean desert, from the early second century CE, is ambiguous and disputed.[34]

Only one prophet in the Hebrew Bible raised his voice against divorce. This was Malachi, an anonymous prophet from the Persian period. (*Malachi* means "my messenger." The name is taken from Malachi 3:1, which says: "See, I am sending my messenger"). The passage addressing divorce, Malachi 2:14–16, is difficult and often mistranslated. It begins with a denunciation of people who have been unfaithful to the wives of their youth. Malachi 2:16 is usually translated: "I hate divorce and covering one's garment with violence." The word "hate," however, is simply a term for divorce. The verse should probably be translated: "For one divorces and sends away and covers his garment with violence."[35] Even so, it is clear that Malachi disapproves of divorce, which no doubt imposed hardship on the women who were sent away.

Malachi's protest against divorce was exceptional in the Hebrew Bible. Some of the Greek translators read the line this way: "But if you hate, send away!" This reading conforms to the general acceptance of divorce but makes little sense in the context.[36] Probably the translator could not believe that a prophet would condemn divorce.

Malachi's objection to divorce may have been based on Genesis 2:24, where man and wife are said to become one flesh. (Malachi 2:15 says elliptically: "Did he not make one, flesh and spirit in it?" [My translation].) If so, this was the first instance in the biblical tradition where Genesis was invoked against the practice of divorce.

Another example of criticism of divorce is found in the Dead Sea Scrolls, in the *Damascus Document* (CD), a sectarian rule book from the first century BCE. The text denounces those who are "caught in fornication by taking two wives in their lifetime, whereas the principle of creation is, male and female he created them" (CD 4.20–5.2). Here, the objection is not to divorce, which was accepted in the *Damascus Document*, but to remarriage. Such an objection was highly unusual in

Jewish tradition, since remarriage was often thought to be the whole reason for divorce, but it reflects the unusually strict interpretation of the Law characteristic of the sectarians of the Dead Sea Scrolls.

Even if the Hebrew Bible is not consistently patriarchal in a technical sense, it is consistently androcentric. Women are sometimes viewed positively. There are a few female leaders, such as Deborah in the Book of Judges, but they are exceptions. Proverbs 31 contains a remarkable paean to the "capable wife." But even there, the woman is praised because of the honor she brings to her husband while he sits in the city gate. Women had their place in Israelite and Judean society, but it was a place tightly circumscribed by the men in their lives.

Ben Sira, whose book is in the Roman Catholic Old Testament and the Protestant Apocrypha, although it is not found in the Hebrew Bible, sums up the obstacles that confronted young women, at least from a father's perspective:

> A daughter is a secret anxiety to her father,
>   and worry over her robs him of sleep;
> when she is young, for fear she may not marry,
>   or if married, for fear she may be disliked;
> while a virgin, for fear she may be seduced
>   and become pregnant in her father's house;
> or having a husband, for fear she may go astray,
>   or, though married, for fear she may be barren.
>   (Ben Sira 42:9–10)

We may assume that Ben Sira was genuinely concerned for his daughters, but he does not seem to have placed much trust in them or, indeed, to have allowed them much agency. He engages in a bitter tirade against the "headstrong daughter," in Ben Sira 26:10–12, that borders on the obscene, although he balances it with praise of the good wife, again from an androcentric perspective: "A silent wife is a gift from the Lord."[37]

To say that the Hebrew Bible is androcentric and greatly concerned with controlling women's sexuality is not to say that it is misogynistic. Only a few passages raise concerns in this regard. The comment of Qoheleth (Ecclesiastes), "I have found more bitter than death the woman who is a trap" (7:26), does not necessarily apply to all women. His further comment— "One man in a thousand I have found, but a woman among these I have not found"—is surely the atypical jaundiced view of a disillusioned individual.

The most troubling passages with regard to misogyny are found in the prophets, who sometimes compare Israel or Jerusalem to an adulterous woman. The prophet Hosea, who lived in the northern kingdom of Israel in the eighth century BCE, compared the covenant between Yahweh and Israel to a marriage in which Israel had been unfaithful, "whoring after other gods." Yahweh would divorce Israel but also threatens that if she does not desist, he will "strip her naked and expose her as on the day she was born" (2:3) and "uncover her shame in the sight of her lovers" (2:10).[38] Ezekiel is more extreme:

> I will judge you as women who commit adultery and shed blood are judged, and bring blood upon you in wrath and jealousy . . . [T]hey shall strip you of your clothes and take your beautiful objects and leave you naked and bare. They shall bring up a mob against you, and they shall stone you and cut

you to pieces with their swords. They shall burn your houses and execute judgments on you in the sight of many women. (16:38–41)

Both of these passages are metaphorical. Neither prophet is inciting violence against actual women. But the force of the metaphor depends on the credibility of the literal meaning. Readers are expected to agree that this is an appropriate way to deal with an adulterous woman, at least in principle. If God treats his unfaithful wife this way, would it not be appropriate for a human husband to do likewise? Accordingly, some feminist scholars refer to such passages as "prophetic pornography."[39]

These metaphorical passages are not representative of the view of women in the Hebrew Bible as a whole, and they were never meant to be prescriptive for the treatment of women. Nonetheless, they provide language that lends itself to supporting abusive views of women. At the least, it is language to be handled with care.

THE NEW TESTAMENT

Family concerns have a central place in the Hebrew Bible. The ideal blessing was to see your children and your children's children. The situation in the New Testament is different. Because of the belief that the end of this world is at hand, most New Testament authors do not think about seeing their grandchildren or even about seeing their children.

Jesus does not often preach about families in the Gospels, and when he mentions them at all, what he has to say can be quite shocking. Consider Luke 14:26:

> Whoever comes to me and does not hate father and mother, wife and children, brothers and sisters, yes, and even life itself, cannot be my disciple.

The word "hate" is used here as it was used in Aramaic marriage contracts, to mean "repudiate." Matthew 10:37 has a milder form of the saying:

> Whoever loves father or mother more than me is not worthy of me; and whoever loves son or daughter more than me is not worthy of me.

The more radical formulation of Luke may be more authentic. We should note, however, that Luke says disciples of Jesus must even "hate" life itself. Elsewhere he tells a disciple to follow him rather than bury his father (Luke 9:59–60; Matthew 8:21–22). Another disciple is told not to turn back to say farewell to those at home. In the Gospel of Mark 3:33-35 (Matthew 12:48), he brushes off his mother and brothers (and sisters in some manuscripts) by asking, "Who are my mother and my brothers?" and then supplying the answer: "Whoever does the will of God is my brother and sister and mother" (cf. Matthew 12:50; Luke 9:21).

Do these sayings show that Jesus was anti-family?[40] Not necessarily. The sayings are addressed to those who would be Jesus' disciples. His movement was new and revolutionary, and like many such movements, it required nothing less than total dedication. Jesus himself was not married. Those of his followers who had families seem to have left them behind. We should expect some tension, although relations with Peter's mother-in-law seem genial (Matthew 8–14; Mark 1:29–32; Luke 4:38–41). Jesus and his disciples visited her house, and Jesus healed her.[41]

But Jesus evidently did not consider marriage to be the higher calling. He allowed that some people might "make themselves eunuchs for the kingdom of God" (Matthew 19:11–12), but he also allowed that "not everyone can accept this teaching, but only those to whom it is given." He affirmed that "in the resurrection of the dead, people neither marry nor are given in marriage, but are as the angels in heaven" (Mark 12:25; Matthew 22:30). Perhaps those who "made themselves eunuchs for the kingdom of God" were already anticipating the resurrected state.[42] Celibacy was unusual in ancient Judaism, but there is a celebrated, if controversial, parallel in the case of the Essenes, the people of the Dead Sea Scrolls, at least some of whom were celibate, and who also thought that they were mingling with the angels.[43] It is also true, as we shall see momentarily, that Paul thought the time left before the Second Coming of Christ was too short to bother with marriage, although it might be necessary for some people. We cannot be entirely sure, however, that this was the thinking of Jesus. As we shall see in a later chapter, Jesus preached a gospel of radical detachment from this world and its material things. Whether this detachment was based on eschatological expectation is uncertain and controversial.

JESUS ON DIVORCE

Although Jesus had chosen not to marry (although he could in principle have married if he had lived longer), he certainly did not reject the institution of marriage for most people. His views on divorce are found in all three Synoptic Gospels—Matthew, Mark, Luke—and also in Paul.[44] Paul writes in 1 Corinthians 7:10–11:

> To the married I give this command—not I but the Lord—that
> the wife should not separate from her husband (but if she does
> separate, let her remain unmarried or else be reconciled to her
> husband), and that the husband should not divorce his wife.

This seems to be an absolute prohibition of divorce, and it cor-
responds to the saying attributed to Jesus in Mark 10:2–12 and
Luke 16:18. Both Mark and Luke say bluntly that any man who
divorces his wife and marries another commits adultery. Mark
spells out the rationale, by citing Genesis, to the effect that
God created male and female and ordained that the two should
become one flesh. "Therefore, what God has joined together,
let no one separate" (Mark 10:9; cf. Matthew 19:3–8). Moses
allowed otherwise only as a concession to human weakness.

Matthew muddies the waters by allowing an exception in
the case of unchastity (5:32; 19:3–9). Paul also allows an exception where a believer was married to an unbeliever. If the unbeliever was willing to persevere in the marriage, they should
not separate, but if the unbeliever wanted to separate, the believer was not bound.[45] The Markan and Lukan Jesus, however, allowed no exception, and one suspects that the more
radical formulation is the more likely to be authentic. Interestingly, many modern churches disregard the teaching of
Jesus on this issue. Perhaps, like Moses, they make a concession to human weakness.

As we have seen, Jesus' stand on divorce was unusual in
the context of Judaism, but not unprecedented. The *Damascus
Document* in the Dead Sea Scrolls also invoked Genesis and
denounced those who married a second wife while the first
one was alive. In that case, remarriage rather than divorce was
the issue.[46] It is the prohibition of remarriage that evokes the

protest of the disciples in Matthew 19: "If such is the case of a man and his wife, it is better not to marry." This statement prompts the comment about eunuchs who make themselves such for the sake of the kingdom.

Jesus' stand on divorce shows that he upheld marriage understood monogamously on the basis of Genesis, although he apparently dispensed his followers from the command to increase and multiply. He was not much of a family man, however, whether because of eschatological expectation or because of his ethic of radical detachment. Leaving family was the price to be paid for membership in the new community of the kingdom. The cost is acknowledged in Mark 10, where Peter says to Jesus, "Look, we have left everything and followed you," and Jesus responds that those who have left "house or brothers or sisters or mother or father or children or fields, for my sake and for the sake of the good news," will receive family a hundredfold in this life (in the new community of disciples) and eternal life in the age to come.

Jesus' disciples included women as well as men. Some feminist scholars have entertained a romantic view of a "discipleship of equals" freed from the constraints of the patriarchal family because the disciples called no one father in this world (Matthew 23:9).[47] This is surely an overstatement. There was never any doubt as to who was the leader in the Jesus movement and who were the followers. The people singled out as twelve apostles are all male.[48] Their being male is not a valid argument against the ordination of women, however; the apostles were not "ordained" in the sense that modern clergy are. But it shows that the community of Jesus' followers was not quite a discipleship of equals. It is true that the female followers of Jesus were freed from the constraints of family life just as much as the men were. It is also true that that freedom came at a cost, for the women as well as the men.

PAUL ON MARRIAGE AND WOMEN

In the case of Paul, the role played by apocalyptic expectation is indisputable. He lays out his views on marriage in 1 Corinthians 7.[49] He begins by declaring that "it is well for a man not to touch a woman," but he realizes that this is an unrealistic ideal. So, to avoid sexual immorality, each man and each woman should have a spouse, and they should not deny one another.[50] But his preference is that each one remain in the state in which he or she was called to join the movement of the followers of Christ. Marrying is not a sin, but "those who marry will experience distress in this life." The unmarried, supposedly, are anxious about the affairs of the Lord, how to please the Lord, while the married man is anxious about the affairs of the world, how to please his wife. Paul explains:

> The appointed time has grown short; from now on, let even those who have wives be as though they had none, and those who mourn as though they were not mourning, and those who rejoice as though they were not rejoicing, and those who buy as though they had no possessions, and those who deal with the world as though they had no dealings with it. For the present form of this world is passing away. (1 Corinthians 7:29–31)

Perhaps the most striking thing about this passage is that it appears to endorse an ideal of celibacy for women as well as for men.[51] Celibacy was controversial in early Christianity because it was disruptive of Roman family values.

It is in light of this imminent expectation, too, that Paul's famous statement in Galatians 3:28 must be understood:

> There is no longer Jew or Greek, there is no longer slave or free, there is no longer male and female; for all of you are one in Christ Jesus.

Two other passages in the Pauline corpus (1 Corinthians 12:13 and Colossians 3:11) repeat the abolition of distinction between Jew and Greek and slave and free but omit the mention of male and female. The formula in Galatians is thought to be pre-Pauline and to have originated as part of a baptismal liturgy.[52] It is a strikingly novel sentiment in the context of the ancient world, for it undermines the distinctions on which the order of society was based.[53]

In the Pauline context, what this declaration means is that whether one is Jew or Greek, slave or free, male or female, makes no difference for one's standing with Christ. It does not mean that social differentiation has disappeared. Paul still thought that women should cover their heads when they prophesied and that men should not. He did not demand the emancipation of slaves. On the contrary, he argued that people should stay in the state in which they were and not cause social upheaval, for the present order was passing away in any case. The declaration is nonetheless highly progressive, for it meant that Greeks, slaves, and women were all welcome in the Christian community. As Schüssler Fiorenza puts it, "Patriarchal marriage—and sexual relationships between male and female— is no longer constitutive of the new community in Christ."[54] The declaration disputes the value most people attached to freedom as against slavery, or to maleness as against femaleness. But it disputes them because the time remaining is short, so they no longer matter. Apocalyptic expectation here is a great leveler, undermining the importance attached to societal distinctions. Nonetheless, it did not abolish patriarchal marriage (or slavery) for the present, and the conventional distinctions reemerged very quickly in the Pauline tradition.

Already in 1 Corinthians 11, Paul reminded the Corinthians that "Christ is the head of every man, and the husband is the head of his wife" (11:2).[55] Accordingly, he held that women should not pray or prophesy with their heads uncovered.[56] But he did not say that women should not prophesy at all. Again, in a dubious exegesis of Genesis, he argued that man was not made from woman, but woman from man. Neither was man created for the sake of woman, but woman for the sake of man (11:8–9), but he qualified all of this by saying that "in the Lord woman is not independent of man or man independent of woman. For just as woman came from man, so man comes through woman, but all things come from God" (11:11–12). In the end, he seems to realize that his attempted exegesis is not very convincing, and he falls back on an authoritarian appeal to the practice of the churches.

Paul seems to have recognized that women had a legitimate role to play in spreading the Gospel. In Romans 16, Paul sends greetings to several women whom he acknowledges as co-workers, including Prisca, the companion of Aquila; Mary, "who worked hard among you"; and Junia, "who was prominent among the apostles."

In 1 Corinthians 14:34–35, however, we have a much more extreme statement:

> Women should be silent in the churches. For they are not permitted to speak, but should be subordinate, as the law also says. If there is anything they desire to know, let them ask their husbands at home. For it is shameful for a woman to speak in church.

It is difficult to reconcile this statement with 1 Corinthians 11, where there was no objection to women speaking in the congregation, whether praying or prophesying, so many scholars, though not all, regard it as later insertion.[57] The purpose of the insertion would have been to bring the Pauline congregations into line with prevalent views of the place of women in society in the Greco-Roman world.

THE HOUSEHOLD CODES

The concern for conformity to Greco-Roman mores finds clear expression in a series of passages that address the proper social demeanor of women, children, and slaves. These passages are commonly called household codes.[58] They are found in Colossians 3:18–4:1; Ephesians 5:21–6:9; 1 Peter 2:13–25; 1 Timothy 2:11–12 (in a passage concerned with deacons); and Titus 2:3–5. The tone of these passages is reflected in 1 Peter 2:13–15:

> For the Lord's sake accept the authority of every human institution, whether of the emperor as supreme, or of governors, as sent by him to punish those who do wrong and to praise those who do right. For it is God's will that by doing right you should silence the ignorance of the foolish.

The concern is for Christians to appear to act appropriately to avoid giving scandal.

The proper order of the household, in the Greek tradition, had been articulated in an authoritative way by Aristotle.[59] A father should rule over his children, a husband over his wife, and a master over his slaves:

> For the male is by nature better fitted to command than the female . . . and the older and fully developed person than the younger and immature. It is true that in most cases of democratic government the ruler and ruled interchange in turn . . . but the male stands in this relationship to the female continuously. The rule of the father over the children, on the other hand, is that of a king. (*Politics* 1.1259b)[60]

Aristotle argued that this household order was in the interest of the state (2.1269b).

This view of the relationship between men and women was standard in the Hellenistic and Roman world and was also accepted in Hellenistic Judaism. Philo held that "a woman should not be a busybody, meddling with matters outside her household concerns, but should seek a life of seclusion."[61] Josephus went further:

> The woman, says the Law, is in all things inferior to the man. Let her accordingly be submissive, not for her humiliation, but that she may be directed, for the authority has been given by God to the man. (*Against Apion* 2.201, trans. Thackeray)[62]

This is not the only occasion on which Josephus claims the authority of the Law for things it never actually says. We saw another example of this in the case of abortion. In the ancient world, as in the modern, people tended to project their beliefs into the Bible, whether it provided a basis for them or not.

The New Testament epistles sometimes temper this hierarchy. Colossians 3:18 tells husbands to love their wives and never treat them harshly and not to provoke their children. Ephesians 5:25 tells husbands to love their wives as Christ loves the church. Sometimes this well-intentioned exhortation reinforces the underlying patriarchal attitude, as when 1 Peter 3:7 tells husbands to honor their wives "as the weaker sex." Do not try this at home in the twenty-first century!

The most extreme example of biblical sexism is found in 1 Timothy 2:11–12: "Let a woman learn in silence with full submission. I permit no woman to teach or to have authority over a man; she is to keep silent." The author repeats the faulty exegesis of Paul, that Adam was formed first and was not the one who was deceived. The passage grants, condescendingly, that a woman can be saved through childbearing.

It has been argued, reasonably, that the so-called Pastoral Epistles (1 and 2 Timothy and Titus), represent a reaction against another strand of early Christianity, represented by *Acts of Paul and Thecla*, which glorified young women such as Thecla who rejected marriage and family life in order to embrace Christianity and thereby caused scandal and disruption in the socially conservative Roman world,[63] and also against the teaching of Marcion, who rejected marriage and procreation and also rejected the God of the Hebrew Scriptures.[64] Nonetheless, it was the reactionary epistles, not the radical Acts, that were included in the biblical canon.

We will revisit the Pastoral Epistles in connection with biblical attitudes to slavery. They are sharply in contrast with modern Western values, but they are arguably equally in conflict with the teachings of Jesus and even those of Paul. These epistles are a long way from the ideal that in Christ there is no male or female. More than most parts of the Bible, they render any concept of biblical authority problematic in the modern world.

CHAPTER FIVE

The Bible and the Environment

THE role of the Bible in shaping attitudes toward the natural world was thrust into the center of debate by a famous article by Lynn White Jr. in 1967.[1]

White held, correctly, that what people do about their environment depends on their beliefs about their nature and their identity, and in the Western world, these were shaped to a great degree by the Bible. Specifically, White traced the human exploitation of nature to the mandate provided by Genesis 1:26–30:

> Let us make humankind in our image, according to our likeness; and let them have dominion over the fish of the sea, and over the birds of the air, and over the cattle, and over all the wild animals of the earth, and over every creeping thing that creeps upon the earth.

The natural world, he inferred, exists "explicitly for man's benefit and rule; no item in the physical creation had any purpose save to serve man's purpose."[2] White was primarily concerned with the way Christian tradition interpreted this text to establish a dualism of humanity and nature. The root of the problem, however, was in the biblical text, which at least admitted of such an interpretation.

Reactions to this thesis cover the full range of opinion. The supposed biblical mandate for exploitation has been welcomed gleefully by some politicians and media pundits, as well as by some conservative theologians.[3] "The ethic of conservation," writes Ann Coulter, paraphrasing the Bible rather freely, "is the explicit abnegation of man's dominion over the earth. The lower species are here for our use. God said so: Go forth, be fruitful, multiply, and rape the planet—it's yours."[4] Champions of conservation are "politically correct, biblically ignorant false prophets," according to Jim Grove.[5] Some (not all) evangelical commentators insist that continued population growth will lead to increased abundance of resources and the transformation of the earth from wilderness to garden.[6]

Most biblical scholars, however, including some evangelicals, have rallied to the defense of the Bible as supporting conservation, not exploitation.[7] Here again we find a spectrum of positions, ranging from enthusiastic affirmation of the Bible[8] to more nuanced critical readings.[9]

GENESIS I

The view that the Bible affirms human dominion over the natural world relies almost exclusively on a single passage, Genesis 1:26–28, cited above. This passage grants humanity dominion over the earth, using the Hebrew verb *radah*, and authorizes it to fill and subdue (*kabash*) it. These verbs admittedly convey a sense of strong, forceful subjugation.[10] But the context must be kept in mind. This is the dawn of creation, when the earth is almost entirely uninhabited by humans and mostly uncultivated. The mandate is to clear wilderness and subdue nature to allow human life to flourish.[11] The biblical authors had no concept of the kind of exploitation of the earth made possible by modern technology.

In a similar vein, Psalm 104 speaks of God setting a boundary that the sea may not cross so that space may be left for life on earth. The relation between humanity and the natural world is adversarial to a degree. In Genesis 9:2 fear and dread of humanity will rest on every animal and bird, fish and crawling thing. This does not mean that there are no limits to what humans can do to animals or to nature.[12] In fact, some limits are clearly implied in Genesis 1. Humanity is given the plants, but not the animals, for food. The arrangement is revised after the Flood in Genesis 9, but even then, there is a restriction: "You shall not eat flesh with its life, that is its blood" (9:4). Also, the week of creation ends with the Sabbath rest, an idea elaborated later in the biblical laws.[13]

Genesis 1 is not the last word on creation. The account in Genesis 2–3 emphasizes that Adam is taken from the earth and will return to it eventually. He is created to till the garden and keep it (2:15).[14] We might infer that he has a fiduciary responsibility for the earth. In modern debates about ecology, this responsibility is often characterized as stewardship.[15] Insofar as Adam is charged with taking care of the garden on God's behalf, this characterization is reasonable, but the image of steward is not developed in the Bible.[16] Nonetheless, the dominion of humanity over the earth, such as it is, clearly comes with responsibility.[17]

The relationship of human beings to the earth is complicated in Genesis 3, where Adam is told that the earth is cursed because of him and will bear thistles and thorns. As we already saw in the discussion of relations between men and women, the curses in Genesis are descriptive, not prescriptive. It is simply the case that people contend with thorns and thistles and have an adversarial relationship with snakes and other animals. The relationship is not the ideal originally envisioned in creation. Rather, it is said to be the result of human sinfulness, which later tradition called fallen human nature. But the relationship is not entirely adversarial. Humanity still depends on the earth for its sustenance, and its fate is intimately bound up with it. Moreover, humanity and the earth are part of a moral continuum. Human behavior affects the earth. We meet this idea repeatedly in the Hebrew Bible. Take, for example, Isaiah 24:5: "The earth lies polluted under its inhabitants." To be sure, the pollution is not due to oil spills or toxic chemicals, as it is in the modern world, but it is due to human behavior nonetheless: "For they have transgressed the laws, violated the statutes, and broken the everlasting covenant." After the Flood, God promises that he will never again curse the earth because of human behavior (Genesis 8:21).[18]

A somewhat different view of creation is implied in Psalm 104 and in the divine speeches at the end of the Book of Job.[19] In both cases, it is clear that the natural world does not exist just to serve the purposes of humanity. In modern parlance, all creatures have intrinsic worth; in biblical parlance, all are objects of God's providential care. God provides grass for the animals as well as food for human beings. The trees are for birds to build their nests, the high mountains are for the wild goats, the rocks for the rabbits (Psalm 104:15–18). Darkness allows the animals of the forest to come creeping out. God puts Job in his place by asking whether he knows when the mountain goats give birth, or can observe the calving of the deer (Job 39:1). Throughout the book, Job assumes that God should be preoccupied with the fate of human beings, even specifically with Job and his family. The speeches from the whirlwind shunt that assumption aside. God has many more, and more important, things on his mind.[20] Some of the hymns in the Psalms (e.g., Psalm 148) call on the elements of nature to praise God;[21] indeed, Job 38:7 says that the morning stars sang together at the foundation of the earth. It may be argued that snow and rain and mountains and hills praise God just by their existence[22] or, inversely, that their existence is reason to praise God. Again, in modern parlance, these passages affirm the intrinsic worth of nature, quite apart from its utility for humanity.

Neither the psalm nor the Book of Job offers a romantic view of creation. The psalm notes that young lions roar for their prey, and God gives them food. This is nice for the lions, not so nice for their prey. Job notes that the eagle and hawk swoop for their prey (39:26–29). In this universe birds and animals eat each other to survive. Humanity is at the top of the food chain but can still be vulnerable to other species on occasion. Eating one another does not mean that there is conscious warfare between species. Rather, creation is an ecosystem where things balance out; the whole is greater than its constituent parts. In a world so constituted, human dominion is rather severely qualified. Passages such as these put in perspective the impression of anthropocentrism that might emerge from Genesis 1 and that is assumed in some parts of the Bible.

THE SABBATICAL LAWS

Perhaps the clearest indication of Israelite attitudes to nature can be seen in the laws governing the use of the land. The basic law is found in the Book of the Covenant, in Exodus 23:10–11:

> For six years you shall sow your land and gather in its yield; but the seventh year you shall let it rest and lie fallow, so that the poor of our people may eat; and what they leave the wild animals may eat. You shall do the same with your vineyard, and with your olive orchard.

This law may be regarded as an extrapolation of the law of the Sabbath, which follows immediately:

> Six days you shall do your work, but on the seventh day you shall rest, so that your ox and your donkey may have relief, and your homeborn slave and the resident alien may be refreshed.

These sabbatical laws have a practical rationale. In an era before chemical fertilizers, crop rotation was essential to preserve the land. Similarly, animals, slaves, and servants last longer and are more productive if they are allowed to rest. The key to the ecological perspective in the Hebrew Bible is the symbiosis of people and land. Ancient Israel was primarily an agricultural society whose survival depended on the land. The goal of the covenant was for the people to live long in the land and see their children and their children's children. The children, too, would depend on the land, and preserving it for them was important.

The Priestly Laws in Leviticus 25 lose sight of the practical rationale for crop rotation. They call for a Sabbath of complete rest for the whole land in the seventh year, during which people and animals alike live off whatever the land yields of itself. Moreover, they provide for a jubilee in the fiftieth year, when the land must lie fallow for two consecutive years. The obvious question, what shall we eat?, is answered blithely by the assurance that the Lord would order a blessing in the sixth year so that the land would provide a crop for three years. It is doubtful that this assurance was ever tested in practice. Leviticus insists that the land is the Lord's (25:23). Not only do people not have a license to exploit the land, they do not even own it. Here again the idea of stewardship seems apt: the people manage the land on God's behalf. However impractical the system of Leviticus may seem, it has a clear message of restraint in the use of the land.

Deuteronomy does not provide its own version of the sabbatical year. Perhaps it assumes the law of the Book of the Covenant. Still, it provides several examples of the need for restraint. If the Israelites besiege a town, they must not destroy its trees (as the Assyrians did in siege warfare): "are trees in the field human beings that they should come under siege from you?" (Deuteronomy 20:19). Only trees that do not bear fruit may be cut down for use in siegeworks. If you see your neighbor's donkey or ox fallen on the road, you must help lift it up (22:4). Anyone who finds a bird's nest must not take the mother with the young "in order that it may go well with you and you may live long" (22:7). Arguably, the treatment prescribed for nature in Deuteronomy is more humane than that described for human enemies, especially the Canaanites! Humane treatment of animals is also required in other parts of the Bible. "The righteous know the needs of their animals," says Proverbs 12:10. As always in Proverbs, the righteous are the wise, who take a long view of things. In all of these verses, the assumption is that humanity depends on natural resources, including animals, and that it is in the interest of humanity to make these resources last for future generations.

In the Hebrew Bible, the assumption is, in the words of Qoheleth (Ecclesiastes), that "a generation goes, and a generation comes, but the earth remains forever" (1:4). The idea that this world will pass away does not enter the tradition until the end of the Old Testament period, although it comes to dominate the New Testament. This changing view of the duration of the world has far-reaching implications for the attitude toward the natural environment.

RESIDUAL WILDERNESS

At no point do the biblical authors outside of Genesis 1 envision that humanity will subdue the whole earth. There is always wilderness and desert on the fringes of inhabited land. Reduction to wilderness is a destructive punishment for a land. Isaiah 34 declares that Edom shall lie waste from generation to generation, but "the hawk and the hedgehog shall possess it; the owl and the raven shall live in it . . . Thorns shall grow over its strongholds, nettles and thistles in its fortresses. In it shall be the haunt of jackals, an abode for ostriches. Wildcats shall meet with hyenas, goat-demons shall call to each other" (34:13–15). The Edomites may face a destroyed land, but creatures, too, need a place to live, and the Lord has portioned it out for them.

The eschatological visions of the Hebrew prophets have little place for wilderness as such. Rather, "the wilderness and the dry land shall be glad, the desert shall rejoice and blossom . . . the haunt of jackals shall become a swamp . . . no lion shall be there, nor shall any ravenous beast come up on it" (Isaiah 35:1, 7, 9). The famous vision of utopia in Isaiah 11 is one where "the wolf shall live with the lamb, the leopard shall lie down with the kid, the calf and the lion and the fatling together," where the lion shall eat straw like the ox, and children will not be harmed by poisonous snakes. Nature is often destructive for humans, and the prophets dream of a harmonious state. That state is not necessarily one of human dominion.

It remains true that the prophets are more concerned with social than with environmental ethics.[23] The Wisdom Literature, rather, especially Proverbs and Job, is concerned with nature and projects a sense of human nature as part of the complex web of life of which God is the creator and sustainer.[24]

The biblical authors were not modern environmentalists: "The question of safeguarding the environment did not enter into their thinking."[25] They were certainly not aware of the threats to nature from abusive human behavior that have come to preoccupy many in the modern world. They did not imagine that human beings would ever have the power to destroy the earth. That could only happen by divine judgment, and humanity could do nothing to prevent it. Nonetheless, to claim that the biblical authors were not concerned with safeguarding the environment is misleading. That, after all, is what the sabbatical laws were all about. The earth was a renewable resource; it had to be treated with care. The key to the appreciation of nature in the Hebrew Bible is the conviction that this world is not passing away and that human beings must live in harmony with it.

THE GOSPELS

The New Testament, in contrast, is written in the conviction that this world *is* passing away.

Jesus does not address the way human beings should treat the environment, at least not directly, so we need to look at the implications of his actions and the view of nature reflected in his sayings and parables.[26] The passage most frequently cited in this regard is in the Sermon on the Mount:

> Look at the birds of the air; they neither sow nor reap nor gather into barns, and yet your heavenly Father feeds them . . . Consider the lilies of the field, how they grow; they neither toil nor spin, yet I tell you, even Solomon in all his glory was not clothed like one of these. But if God so clothes the grass of the field, which is alive today and tomorrow is thrown into the oven, will he not much more clothe you—you of little faith? (Matthew 6:26–30; cf. Luke 12:22–31)

Birds and flowers have importance in the eyes of God or, in modern idiom, have intrinsic worth.[27] The parables are replete with imagery drawn from nature or agriculture—sowers sowing, fields ripe for the harvest, mustard seeds, and so on. It is often claimed, reasonably enough, that Jesus "lived in full harmony with creation."[28] Again, it may reasonably be argued that the disciples of Jesus are called to live lightly on the earth. The Gospels certainly give no support to the idea of a consumer society.[29] Some of the miracles are ambiguous. Stories of the calming of the storm (Mark 4:35–41), the destruction of the Gerasene swine (Mark 5:11–13; Luke 8:32–3), and the withering of the fig tree (Mark 11:12–13, 20–21; Matthew 21:18–20) demonstrate dominion over nature even if these stories are symbolic and do not reflect real actions.[30] Even the sayings about the birds of the air and the lilies of the field are anthropocentric; the ultimate concern is with the fate of human beings. Jesus lived in an agrarian society and made many of the assumptions we have seen in the Hebrew Bible. He drew illustrations from the world around him, which was primarily the world of rural Galilee. But nature as such is not a primary focus of the teaching of Jesus, any more than it was of the Hebrew prophets. Perhaps the main import of the teaching of Jesus for ecology is that it promotes a human lifestyle that is not acquisitive and, in doing so, runs counter to the ethos of modern society that is the root cause of exploitation of the environment. The implications of the Gospels for ecology, then, are indirect but not insignificant.

PAUL AND THE COSMOS

The agrarian context of early first-century Galilee, which pervades the parables of Jesus, disappears in the letters of Paul. Paul's discourse is more abstractly theological. He touches, however, on the fate of creation in one celebrated passage in Romans 8:18–23:

> I consider that the sufferings of this present time are not worth comparing with the glory about to be revealed to us. For the creation waits with eager longing for the revealing of the children of God; for the creation was subjected to futility, not of

> its own will but by the will of the one who subjected it, in hope
> that the creation itself will be set free from its bondage to de-
> cay and will obtain the freedom of the glory of the children of
> God. We know that the whole creation has been groaning in
> labor pains until now; and not only the creation, but we our-
> selves, who have the first fruits of the Spirit, groan inwardly
> while we wait for adoption, the redemption of our bodies.

This passage seems to play on the creation story in Genesis 2–3, where the ground is cursed because of Adam.[31] The "bondage to decay" is a consequence of human sinfulness. The "futility" of life is the leitmotif of the Book of Qoheleth (Ecclesiastes), where the term is usually rendered as "vanity." This is the frustrating condition of existence without a goal, where generations come and go but the earth remains forever (1:4). In Paul's view, however, existence most certainly has a goal: revelation of the children of God. Paul's theology, like much of the New Testament, is informed by Jewish apocalyptic ideas, which hold that this world is transient and that a new glorious world is about to be revealed. The question is whether there is continuity between this world and the glorious world to come: is this world to be replaced, or is it to be transformed and perfected?

Paul does not expound his expectations as fully as we might wish. He says more about the transformation of human beings than he does about the transformation of nature. He affirms the resurrection of the dead in a bodily form that is continuous with what they have in this life, but he qualifies the continuity significantly:

> Flesh and blood cannot inherit the kingdom of God, nor does
> the perishable inherit the imperishable. Listen, I will tell you a
> mystery! We will not all die, but we will all be changed, in a
> moment, in the twinkling of an eye, at the last trumpet . . . For

this perishable body must put on imperishability, and this mortal body must put on immortality. (1 Corinthians 15:50–53).

Resurrected bodies will not be bodies of flesh and blood but some kind of "spiritual bodies," composed of finer stuff.[32] Elsewhere, Paul says that the followers of Jesus who are still alive at the time of the Second Coming will be caught up alive ("raptured") to meet the Lord in the air (1 Thessalonians 4:17).

The passage in Romans 8 suggests that the redemption of creation is analogous to the redemption of the human body. This world will not be simply replaced by the world to come. It will be transformed and will be freed from corruption and death. Paul does not elaborate on the form that this transformed world will take. It is not clear whether it will be the habitat of transformed humanity. Paul is primarily interested in human destiny rather than in the natural world. Nonetheless, he insists, in the passage cited from Romans 8, that all creation has a destiny in store. It has its own value in the eyes of God, or, in modern terms, its own intrinsic worth. The image of labor pains is often associated with the coming of the messianic age in Jewish tradition. So even if Paul's interest in the transformation of creation is limited, he does affirm it.

He does not, however, suggest that humanity should work to bring this transformation about. Rather, it is the work of God and will happen in God's appointed time.[33] The apostle gives only limited support to modern environmental concerns. The passage in Romans is most eloquent in articulating the travail of nature, the sense that nature suffers the consequences of human behavior and deserves to be redeemed.[34] Paul did not see its redemption as a task for humanity. One might argue that if the degradation of nature is regarded as a consequence of human sin, we should try to avoid it,[35] but the implications for human action are oblique.

COLOSSIANS

Even more oblique is a much-cited passage from the Epistle to the Colossians (which is probably not by Paul but is part of the Pauline corpus). Speaking of Christ as Son of God, the epistle states:

> He is the image of the invisible God, the firstborn of all cre-
> ation; for in him all things in heaven and on earth were creat-
> ed, things visible and invisible, whether thrones or dominions
> or rulers or powers—all things have been created through him
> and for him . . . For in him all the fullness of God was pleased
> to dwell, and through him God was pleased to reconcile to
> himself all things, whether on earth or in heaven, by making
> peace through the blood of his cross. (1:15–20)

The portrayal of Christ as a cosmic figure holding all creation together is modeled on the figure of Wisdom in Hellenistic Jewish literature, which in turn was modeled on the
idea of the Logos (word or reason) in Stoic philosophy.[36] The
Stoics believed that the Logos, a divine rational spirit, pervaded the universe and held it together. This kind of belief
is known as panentheism: a divine spirit is immanent in the
world. Hellenistic Jews, such as Philo of Alexandria and the
author of the Wisdom of Solomon, both of whom lived about
the time of Christ, identified this divine spirit with the figure
of Wisdom, known from Proverbs 8, but unlike the Stoics,
they believed that there was also a transcendent God above it.
According to the Wisdom of Solomon 1:8, the spirit of the

Lord fills the world and holds all things together. Even the natural world, then, is animated by a divine spirit.

Early Christians identified Christ with this spirit, most notably in the prologue to the Gospel of John, where he is called the Logos, or Word.

If the natural world is pervaded by a divine spirit, its status is obviously enhanced. Throughout the Bible, creation is the work of God. The passage in Colossians restates this in an emphatic way. But while this statement may be taken to imply an exalted view of creation and the natural world, it remains quite abstract. It is not at all clear how the reconciliation of all things to God is supposed to work. Colossians is concerned with the exalted nature of Christ and only incidentally with the status of the created world. Moreover, if all things are made through Christ, the presence of evil and destructive forces in the world remains unexplained.[37] This is not to deny that the passage in Colossians implies an exalted view of the natural world, but its relevance to modern environmental concerns remains remote.[38]

THE APOCALYPSE AND THE ENVIRONMENT

The most problematic aspect of the New Testament for ecological concerns are the pervasive expectation that this world is passing away and the frequent assertions that it will be destroyed violently by God. "Heaven and earth will pass away," says Jesus in Mark 13:31. Those who ask, "Where is the promise of his coming? For ever since our ancestors died, all things continue as they were from the beginning of creation," find their doubts countered in 2 Peter, affirming that just as the world was once destroyed by flood, "the present heavens and earth have been reserved for fire, being kept until the day of judgment and destruction of the godless" (2 Peter 3:4–7). If the destruction does not happen promptly, remember that with the Lord a thousand years is as a day. The Book of Revelation is full of images of cosmic destruction. On the opening of the sixth seal (6:12–17) "there came a great earthquake; the sun became black as sackcloth, the full moon became like blood, and the stars of the sky fell to earth as the fig tree drops its winter fruit when shaken by a gale. The sky vanished like a scroll rolling itself up, and every mountain and island was removed from its place." In the end, John the visionary "saw a new heaven and a new earth, for the first heaven and the first earth had passed away, and the sea was no more" (20:1). Religious critics of environmentalism like to refer to the fire of 2 Peter as the "real global warming." If this world is doomed to destruction, why be concerned about its preservation in the interim?

Ecologically minded scholars address this problem in various ways. Some dismiss the imagery of cosmic destruction as a metaphor for radical social change.[39] It is true that cosmic imagery is used in this way in the Hebrew Bible—see, for example, Isaiah 13, where the destruction of Babylon is described in terms of the heavens trembling and the heavenly bodies not giving forth light. The apocalyptic literature around the turn of the Common Era, however, conceives of the destruction of this world in more literal terms.[40] So, for example, according to *4 Ezra* (*2 Esdras*) 7:30–31, "the world will be turned back to primeval silence for seven days, as it was at the first beginnings, so that no one shall be left. And after seven days the world, which is not yet awake, shall be roused, and that which is corruptible shall perish." Likewise, Revelation is insistent that the old heaven and earth pass away. There is little doubt that the writers of these texts imagined that the present world would literally come to an end.

The end is always followed by a new beginning. There is presumably some continuity from this world to the next, as there is in the resurrection of the dead. But the transformation is extreme and presupposes the destruction of the old world. Human life and the life of the natural world are intertwined. Humans and nature suffer a like fate. At no point do any of these texts suggest that human beings may exploit or ravage the earth with impunity, but neither do they provide strong motivation for tending it or preserving it. As David Horrell concludes, the biblical texts, especially the New Testament, "leave us with an uncertain and ambivalent legacy when it comes to the possible contribution of their future visions to theological and ethical views of the environment."[41]

But while there is little doubt that the authors of Revelation and 2 Peter believed quite literally that the physical destruction of the world was imminent, we cannot take these texts at face value two thousand years later. As the skeptical contemporaries of 2 Peter observed, things continue, more or less as they were, despite the passing of millennia. In fact, there is no more reason to take biblical accounts of the end of history literally than there is to take the accounts of creation as factual. The extremes of history lie outside the scope of human experiential knowledge. They are accessible only by visionary imagination; the descriptions of apocalypses, especially in the Book of Revelation, are richly imaginative. As such, they are not sources of information about the future but expressions of human hopes and fears in the present, often expressed in language drawn from ancient myths.[42] The descriptions of cosmic destruction in Revelation should be read not as predictions but as fantasies of catastrophe, inspired by the clash between the temporal dominion of the Roman empire and the emerging faith in the lordship of Jesus.[43]

While the natural world plays a prominent part in the imagery of Revelation, the primary concern of the book is for the followers of Jesus. In that sense, it is anthropocentric, and its relevance to environmental concerns is indirect. The most significant part of the book for the discussion of ecology may well be the vision of the new creation in chapters 21–22. Chapter 21 is devoted to the new Jerusalem, built of gold and precious metals. This city will have no need of sun or moon, for the Lamb will be its light. Chapter 22 goes on to speak of the river of the water of life[44] and the tree of life. Nothing accursed will be found there anymore. This is certainly a vision of a harmonious world, one in which the earth is no longer at odds with humanity.[45] It is concerned more with cultic and social concerns than with the restoration of nature as we know it. (The demise of the sea in Revelation 21:1 is due to its symbolic, mythological significance, not to any ecological concern.) Revelation does not suggest that the envisioned world can be brought about by human endeavor. Insofar as it is a hoped-for ideal, however, we might reasonably be expected to strive toward it.

Concern for the preservation of the earth is less prominent in the New Testament than in the Old. The New Testament writers were swept up in the enthusiasm of their new revelation and believed that this world would soon pass away. The eschatological framework of the New Testament, however, must be recognized as a mythic construct, not something that can be accepted as factual from a modern perspective. Statements about the future do not convey factual information but rather express hopes and fears. The idea of new creation is important as an ideal of renewal, but its relevance to modern environmental concerns is only indirect.

At no point, however, does the New Testament suggest that humanity is free to "rape the planet," as Ann Coulter enthusiastically put it. In fact, the New Testament does not even repeat the commandment of Genesis to increase and multiply and fill the earth. Rather, the teaching of Jesus implies that human beings should not be concerned to accumulate wealth in barns but should live a carefree life like the birds and the flowers. The prospect of an imminent ending undermines the rationale for human acquisitiveness and thereby also undermines the motivation for raping the planet.

CHAPTER SIX

Slavery and Liberation

S LAVERY, the condition where human beings are owned, bought, and sold by other people, is arguably the most degrading condition known to humanity. Much of the appeal of the story of Israel in the Bible is that it begins with slavery in Egypt and proceeds to liberation by the power of God. This is, to be sure, the story of a specific people, at a specific time in history, but already in the Hebrew Bible it was seen as paradigmatic, a story that offers hope of "a new Exodus" in other times and places.[1] It has been appropriated repeatedly down through history, by Puritans and Boers, Zionists and black South Africans, and African Americans in the United States. In modern times, it has given rise to a new approach to theology, called Liberation Theology. (Liberation Theology is a movement that originated in South America but enjoyed broad sympathy in Europe and North America in the last quarter of the twentieth century.)[2] Despite occasional protestations that the story applies only to Israel,[3] other people have found that it resonates with their experience.[4] The relevance of the Bible to the modern world depends on analogical use, and any such use presupposes that biblical stories provide paradigms that can be used in analogical situations.

Liberation theologians see the Exodus as paradigmatic for people in economic, political, social, or cultural bondage.[5] Socially conservative critics object that economic and political freedom is not the purpose of the Exodus in the biblical text. Rather, the Israelites are liberated so that they can serve their God, Yahweh. The Lord instructs Moses in Exodus 7:16: "Let my people go so that they may worship me in the wilderness." Or again, in Leviticus 25:55: "For it is to me that the Israelites are slaves/servants: they are my slaves/servants whom I freed from the land of Egypt."[6] But it is specious to deny that the Exodus is also a story of social, economic, and political liberation. The Lord tells Moses at the burning bush:

> I have observed the misery of my people who are in Egypt; I have heard their cry on account of their taskmasters. Indeed, I know their sufferings, and I have come down to deliver them from the Egyptians, and to bring them up out of that land to a good and broad land, a land flowing with milk and honey. (3:7–8)

The land flowing with milk and honey is not just a place of worship. It is also a place where the liberated slaves can enjoy material well-being.[7] It is true that the Exodus is the prelude to a covenant, that freedom comes with new obligations. But the Israelites can enter into that covenant as free people, and the provisions of the covenant are largely concerned with the constitution of a just society.

The Israelites are repeatedly urged to remember their experience in Egypt. The significance of this memory for biblical morality is that it should lead to empathy with the poor and marginal. In the Book of the Covenant (Exodus 20:22 to 23:33) the marginal people are identified as aliens rather than as slaves: "You shall not wrong or oppress a resident alien, for you were aliens in the land of Egypt" (22:21). Again, "You shall not oppress a resident alien; you know the heart of an alien, for you were aliens in the land of Egypt" (23:9; cf. Deuteronomy 10:18). Leviticus goes further: "The alien who resides with you shall be to you as the citizen among you; you shall love the alien as yourself, for you were aliens in the land of Egypt" (19:33–34). The Bible does not address immigration policy as such. Accordingly, it is possible to argue that the aliens in question are people who have entered the country legally.[8] But none of the biblical passages restricts the understanding of "aliens" in this way. Rather, the concern is a humanitarian one. You should know what it is like to be an alien and treat aliens with compassion accordingly.[9] Again, when Numbers 15:16 declares, "You and the alien who resides among you shall have the same law and the same ordinance," it is assumed that aliens must keep the law, but the emphasis of the passage is on the equality of alien and native before the law.

To be sure, there are cases in the Hebrew Bible where Israelite or Judean authorities are not hospitable to aliens. Ezra's insistence that Judeans who had married foreign women must divorce them is a notorious example.[10] It is not the case, however, that the biblical record is equally divided on this issue nor that it is arbitrary to choose one point of view as the Bible's core value.[11] The founding experience of Israel in Egypt demands that sympathy for the alien take precedence over other considerations.

The sojourn in Egypt was not the only occasion when Israel would know the mind of an alien. After the destruction of northern Israel by the Assyrians, and especially after the conquest of Judah by the Babylonians, the majority of the Israelite/Jewish people lived in Diaspora, scattered outside their homeland.

Equally, the experience of Egypt and the Exodus should mean that the Israelites would know the mind of a slave, and the memory of the Exodus is often invoked in this context, too (e.g., Deuteronomy 15:15).

There is another, more fundamental reason why people should empathize with slaves and aliens. Job, in his great pro-testation of innocence, says of his male and female slaves:

> Did not he who made me in the womb make them?
> And did not one fashion us in the womb? (Job 31:15)

The basic reason for appreciating the common humanity of all, regardless of status, is creation, and that reason is rein-forced by the founding experience of Israel in the Exodus.

Yet at no point does the Bible condemn the practice of slavery. We find condemnation of abuses, to be sure, but no calls for the abolition of slavery as a social practice. This does not mean that the story of the Exodus is not relevant to social conditions at all, as some would have it, since the situation of most of the people was greatly ameliorated by the transition from slavery to freedom. But it does mean that the Bible falls far short of realizing the potential implications of both creation and Exodus.

People came to be slaves in the ancient world in basically three ways. They might be born into slavery, they might be captured, whether in war or by kidnapping, or they might become enslaved because they could not pay their debts.[12] The discussions of slavery in the Hebrew Bible are primarily concerned with debt slavery.

The very first of the ordinances regulating society in the Book of the Covenant, after the altar-law at the end of Exodus 20, is a law about slaves. Like much of the Book of the Covenant, this law is modeled on the laws of Hammurabi, the Babylonian king from the eighteenth century BCE, long before the supposed time of Moses.[13] Section 117 of the laws of Hammurabi reads:

> If an obligation is outstanding against a man and he sells or gives into debt service his wife, his son, or his daughter, they shall perform service in the house of their buyer or of the one who holds them in debt service for three years; their release shall be secured in the fourth year.[14]

The law in Exodus begins:

> When you buy a male Hebrew slave, he shall serve six years, but in the seventh year he shall go out a free person, without debt. (21:2)

Several points about this law are noteworthy.

First, despite the ambiguity of the Hebrew, which uses the same word for "slave" and "servant," this passage refers explicitly to the selling of a human being and therefore to slavery.[15] Second, it is accepted without question that it is legitimate to purchase slaves, even Hebrew— that is, Israelite—slaves. Third, the biblical law allows for a longer period of servitude, for a person who was initially free, than does Hammurabi's. Hammurabi may have been exceptional in the ancient Near East. Usually, the release of slaves depended on the good pleasure of the ruler and was likely to happen only on special occasions. Nonetheless, the biblical law is not especially lenient. The preference for a six-year period may be related to the importance attached to the Sabbath and the number seven in Israelite tradition. Finally, the placement of this law at the beginning of the societal ordinances is unusual in the ancient Near East and may indicate that the issue was considered especially important.[16] It should be noted, however, that the restriction of service applied only to Hebrew slaves. Slaves who were not Israelite could presumably be held in perpetuity.

The law in Exodus goes on to qualify this basic law in several ways. Women sold into debt slavery do not go free as male slaves do. Their new master may designate them for himself or for his son. The law offers some protection to the Hebrew slave woman. She may not be sold to a foreign people. If the master loses interest in her, he must let her be redeemed. If he takes another wife in addition to her, he must still support her. Even the fact that she does not qualify for release may be for the protection of the slave woman. In effect, the new master or his son must marry her, and the marriage is not dissolved after six years.

If the enslaved man is given a wife and has children, these remain the property of the master. If the slave wishes to remain with his wife and family, he must decline his freedom, declaring, "I love my master, my wife and my children" (Exodus 21:5). In that case, his ear is pierced with an awl to signify that he is a slave for life.[17] The law is tilted to the advantage of the slave owner by making it difficult for the slave to go free. A similar tilt in favor of slave owners is evident in Exodus 21:20–21. If an owner strikes a slave so that he dies, the owner is supposed to be punished. But if the slave survives for a day or two there is no punishment, "for the slave is the owner's property."

In all of this, we see at most some slight adjustments to Near Eastern custom, toward providing protection for the slave, but no challenge to the institution of slavery itself.

The slave laws of Exodus are revised in Deuteronomy 15. Again, there are very modest adjustments. Now the same law applies to male and female. (There is no longer any mention of marriage between master and female slave.) Deuteronomy also allows the slave to stay in servitude "because he loves you and your household." Presumably, the slave's children would remain the master's property in any case if they were born in servitude. Deuteronomy exhorts the slave owners to provide liberally for manumitted slaves and invokes the memory of the Exodus: "Remember that you were a slave in the land of Egypt" (15:15). But there is no suggestion that it is wrong in principle to own slaves, even Hebrew ones, and there is no requirement to free foreign slaves. Deuteronomy does provide, however, that "slaves who have escaped to you from their owners shall not be given back to them. They shall reside with you in your midst . . . you shall not oppress them" (23:15–16). The slaves in question appear to be ones who escaped from neighboring peoples, rather than slaves who were already living in Israel.

The Priestly legislation in Leviticus 25:39–40 edges closer to prohibiting the enslavement of fellow Israelites:

> If any who are dependent on you become so impoverished that they sell themselves to you, you shall not make them serve as slaves. They shall remain with you as hired or bound laborers. They shall serve with you until the year of the jubilee.

The difference between being a slave and being a bound laborer was one of degree. The bound laborer did not have the freedom to leave. Moreover, the length of service could be much longer than in the other codes: the year of the jubilee occurred every fifty years (25:11). This legislation is part of the Holiness Code, and we do not know that it was ever followed in practice.

Leviticus further specifies that a slave's children should go free with him (25:41). This would be a significant change in traditional law if it had ever been implemented, as it would deprive the slave owners of a significant source of free labor. There is no restriction, however, on taking slaves from among foreign peoples or from among resident aliens, even when they were born in the land: "You may keep them as a possession for your children after you, for them to inherit as property. These you may treat as slaves, but for your fellow Israelites, no one shall rule over the other with harshness" (25:45–46).

It is sometimes suggested that slavery in the biblical context was quite different from slavery in other contexts, such as classical Rome or the American South. It is true that there were differences. Except for kings and temples, most people did not have very many slaves.[18] This may be a reason why there were no slave revolts. Most people became slaves through debt and were used in agriculture or domestic service. Slaves could be treated as part of the family. They could be acknowledged as fathers, unlike the situation later in Rome. Yet it is clear from the biblical laws that slaves could be subject to abuse. In fact, the passage just cited from Leviticus 25:45–46 implies that to treat someone as a slave meant to treat him or her harshly. Female slaves were at their master's disposal. Sexual use of slaves may not have been as rampant in the ancient Near East as it was in Rome, but it was assumed, nonetheless. Most crucially, slaves did not have freedom to pursue their own lives and interests. Harshness of treatment may have varied, but slavery inherently denied the dignity and agency of the enslaved.

Only rarely are voices raised against slavery in the Hebrew Bible. The prophet Amos railed against those who would "sell the poor for silver and the righteous for a pair of sandals" (2:6; 8:6), but his condemnation does not amount to a rejection of slavery as such. The most eloquent testimony to the reality of debt slavery is found in Nehemiah 5, where people come to Nehemiah to complain:

> Now our flesh is the same as that of our kindred; our children are the same as their children; and yet we are forcing our sons and daughters to be slaves, and some of our daughters have been ravished; we are powerless, and our fields and vineyards now belong to others. (5:5)

It is clear that Nehemiah is only concerned with Judean slaves. He also bought back Judeans who had been sold to surrounding people. But at least he recognized the wrongness of slavery in the context of his own people.

The concern about aliens, too, left something to be desired. Aliens were integrated into the Israelite and Judean communities in various ways,[19] but they were still viewed as second class, and there was no objection to having them as slaves.

SLAVES IN SECOND TEMPLE JUDAISM

We have only fragmentary evidence of the practice of slavery in Second Temple Judaism.[20] The Samaria Papyri from the fourth century BCE consist largely of slave contracts. The names of the slaves are Yahwistic, and this suggests that they were Judeans or Samaritans, but they are sold "in perpetuity" with no provision for their manumission.

Ben Sira, writing in the early second century BCE, occasionally gives advice relating to slaves:

> Fodder and a stick and burdens for a donkey;
>   bread and discipline and work for a slave.
> Set your slave to work, and you will find rest;
>   leave his hands idle, and he will seek liberty.
> . . . .
> and if he does not obey, make his fetters heavy.
>   (33:25–30)

One should not be ashamed of drawing blood from the back of a wicked slave (42:5). If one has but one slave, however, one should treat him like a brother, lest he run away! (33:32).

According to Philo and Josephus, the Essenes had no slaves (Philo, *That Every Good Man Is Free*, 79; Josephus, *Jewish Antiquities* 18.21). Josephus adds that they consider slavery an injustice. If this is so, then they were exceptional in ancient Judaism and indeed in the ancient world. The *Damascus Document*, found in the Dead Sea Scrolls and believed to be related to the Essene sect, contains regulations forbidding the sale of slaves to Gentiles (CD 12.10–11) and the forcing of slaves to work on the

Sabbath (CD 11.12).[21] These regulations, however, are not necessarily specific to the Essenes. There is no mention of slaves in the Community Rule. But even if the reports in Philo and Josephus are idealized and not historically accurate, they still show that it was not inconceivable that a Jewish community should reject slavery, however unusual such rejection may have been.

JESUS AND SLAVERY

Jesus often refers to slaves in his parables without ever questioning the morality of the institution.[22] The faithful and wise slave can expect a reward, but the wicked slave, who begins to beat his fellow slaves and indulge in drunken behavior, will be cut off and left to weep and gnash his teeth (Matthew 24:45–51). No master invites a slave who has been laboring in the fields to eat before he himself does; rather, he demands that the slave serve him at table (Luke 17:7–10). Even those who do what they are ordered to do are worthless (17:10). It has been suggested that the mercy of the king in the parable of the unmerciful servant (Matthew 18:23–35) and the expectation that debtors be merciful in turn "must have struck Jesus' hearers as profound critiques of an exceedingly oppressive practice that produced slaves."[23] Perhaps, but as often in the Gospels, the appeal is for humane implementation rather than for abolition of an oppressive system.

THE PAULINE CORPUS

The status of slaves is discussed more explicitly in the Epistles.

The ringing baptismal formula cited by Paul—"There is no longer Jew or Greek, there is no longer slave or free, there is no longer male and female; for all of you are one in Christ Jesus" (Galatians 3:28)—has been called the Magna Carta of Humanity.[24] There is nothing like it in all of antiquity. Slaves could rub shoulders with owners in the Christian community. As we have seen in our discussion of male and female, however, social distinctions were not, by implication, abolished in everyday life. Even in Galatians, Paul continues his argument using slavery as an allegory, contrasting Hagar (Genesis 16, 21), who represents Mount Sinai and earthly Jerusalem and bears children in slavery, with the free woman Sarah, who represents the Jerusalem above. Paul assures his readers that they are children of the free woman, not of the slave.[25] The distinction between slave and free is too deeply embedded in his consciousness to be erased by the baptismal formula.

Paul's views on slavery are spelled out most explicitly in 1 Corinthians 7:21–24:

> Were you a slave when called? Do not be concerned about it . . . For whoever was called in the Lord as a slave is a freed person belonging to the Lord, just as whoever was free when called is a slave of Christ . . . In whatever condition you were called . . . there remain with God.

He explains the reason for this: the appointed time has grown short. Those who deal with the world should act as if they have no dealings with it, for the present form of the world is passing away (7:29–31).

One of the verses in this passage, elided in this excerpt, is especially controversial. 1 Corinthians 7:21 reads, literally: "Even if you can become free, rather use [*mallon chresai*]." The text is elliptic and does not make explicit what the slave should use or what he should avail himself of. The NRSV translation specifies "make use of your present condition"—implying that slaves should decline the opportunity for freedom. It is questionable, however, whether declining was a legal option for slaves who were offered manumission.[26] The opposite implication is more plausible: if you can become free, use (avail yourself of) freedom.[27] In verse 23, Paul tells the Corinthians not to become slaves of human masters—in effect, not to sell themselves into slavery—because "you were bought with a price" (that is, redeemed by Christ). It seems unlikely, then, that Paul would have told slaves to decline the opportunity of manumission, even if it were possible to do so. The situation of the freedman may not have been so greatly different from that of the slave, since he remained bound to his master in many ways,[28] but freedom was nonetheless to be preferred, as a matter of human, and specifically Christian, dignity.

But Paul did not mean that a slave should pursue freedom actively. In his eyes, the slave was already free "in Christ." Whether he was free in socioeconomic terms was of little consequence.[29]

Was it of little consequence to slaves themselves? Not all slaves were necessarily treated badly. Their status varied with the status of their masters.[30] It could be better to be a rich man's slave than an indigent free person. People sometimes sold themselves into slavery in the hope of being assured of the necessities of life. Some could save money and purchase their freedom. Some acquired skilled trades or became tutors or household managers. Many were awarded Roman citizenship when they were manumitted. But usually slavery was harsh. It has even been defined as the "permanent, violent domination of natally alienated and generally dishonored persons."[31] Slaves could be freed when they reached the age of thirty, but many died young and were worn out by that age. They had no legal rights. Slaves could not be acknowledged as fathers; their children belonged to their masters. They were sexually at the disposal of their masters.[32] They could be beaten or even killed with impunity. In the words of one authority on Roman slavery, "The lot of bad slaves was to be beaten and that of good slaves to internalize the constant threat of a beating."[33] And of another:

> The bare record of fact shows that Roman slaves, like those in the Americas, were bought and sold like animals, were punished indiscriminately and violated sexually; they were compelled to labour as their masters dictated, they were allowed no legal existence, and they were goaded into compliance through cajolery and intimidation.[34]

If some people found slavery preferable to extreme poverty, they must have been in a desperate situation.

Especially important in conveying Paul's view of slavery is the brief letter to Philemon. In it Paul makes an appeal on behalf of a person named Onesimus. The key passage (verses 8–16) reads as follows:

> For this reason, though I am bold enough in Christ to command you to do your duty, yet I would rather appeal to you on the basis of love . . . I am appealing to you for my child, Onesimus, whose father I have become during my imprisonment. Formerly he was useless to you, but now he is indeed useful both to you and to me. I am sending him, that is, my own heart, back to you. I wanted to keep him with me, so that he might be of service to me in your place during my imprisonment for the gospel; but I preferred to do nothing without your consent, in order that your good deed might be voluntary and not something forced. Perhaps this is the reason he

was separated from you for a while, so that you might have him back forever, no longer as a slave but more than a slave, a beloved brother—especially to me but how much more to you, both in the flesh and in the Lord.

Paul goes on to ask Philemon to welcome Onesimus "as you would welcome me" and to charge anything Onesimus might owe him to Paul's own account.

At least since the time of John Chrysostom (ca. 349–407) commentators have inferred that Onesimus was a runaway slave and that Paul was sending him back to his owner. This view is still defended and remains an interpretive option,[35] but in recent years opinion has shifted in favor of the view that he was not technically a fugitive but was at odds with his master in some way and had asked Paul to intercede for him.[36] Another suggestion, that Onesimus had been sent to Paul as a messenger or gift-bearer,[37] is unsatisfactory, both because he is said to have been formerly useless and because it is necessary for Paul to intercede for him on his return. It has even been suggested that he was not a slave at all but was actually Philemon's brother "in the flesh."[38] This suggestion is ruled out by verse 16 ("no longer as a slave").[39] There is a parallel in a letter of Pliny where a friend of the owner intercedes for clemency for a freedman who had displeased his master.[40] Unlike Paul, Pliny sharply reproved the freedman, but Paul's situation is different, given the conversion of Onesimus to Christ.[41]

It seems clear that Onesimus was a slave and that Paul recognized Philemon's rights over him. It is less clear what Paul wanted Philemon to do. He says that Philemon can have him back "no longer as a slave but more than a slave, a beloved brother." Is this a subtle way of asking Philemon to set

Onesimus free?[42] He says, "I wanted to keep him with me . . . but I preferred to do nothing without your consent, in order that your good deed might be voluntary." Is this a subtle way of asking Philemon to let Onesimus return to Paul, to assist him?[43] The subtlety of the letter leaves the reader, at least the modern reader, uncertain. Paul stops short of making explicit requests, either for the manumission of Onesimus or for Onesimus's transfer to Paul's service. On any interpretation, he is asking Philemon to view Onesimus as a brother but stops short of saying that he has an obligation to do so. He concludes by saying he is confident that Philemon will do even more than he asks.

Martin Luther commented that "this letter gives us a masterful and tender example of Christian love. For we see here how St. Paul takes the part of poor Onesimus and, as best he can, pleads his cause with his master."[44] Modern readers are more likely to note the deference to the slave owner. Paul does not denounce slavery in prophetic tones and does not seem to have regarded it as an intolerable evil. His intercession for Onesimus rests on the fact that both he and Philemon were followers of Christ. Nonetheless, his strategy may have been effective in this context. He evinces more sympathy for the situation of this particular slave than we will find in the later epistles that were composed in his name.

THE HOUSEHOLD CODES

As in the case of women, freedom for slaves takes a back seat to social conformity in the household codes in the later epistles. We read in Colossians:

> Slaves, obey your earthly masters in everything, not only while being watched and in order to please them, but wholeheartedly, fearing the Lord. Whatever your task, put yourselves into it, as done for the Lord and not for your masters, since you know that from the Lord you will receive the inheritance as your reward; you serve the Lord Christ. (3:22–24)

In effect, service to slave owners is service to Christ and will be rewarded or punished by Christ. Masters, too, are urged to treat their slaves justly and fairly, "for you know that you also have a Master in heaven" (4:1). Similarly, Ephesians 6:5–7 calls on slaves to "obey your earthly masters with fear and trembling, in singleness of heart, as you obey Christ," and masters are warned to stop threatening their slaves, "for you know that both of you have the same Master in heaven" (6:8). All, it would seem, are slaves before God.

1 Timothy is more explicit as to the rationale behind this demand for obedience by slaves:

> Let all who are under the yoke of slavery regard their masters as worthy of all honor, so that the name of God and the teaching may not be blasphemed. Those who have believing masters must not be disrespectful to them on the ground that they are members of the church; rather they must serve them all the more, since those who benefit by their service are believers and beloved. (6:1–2)

Presumably, the author was concerned that Christians not get a reputation for encouraging insubordination among slaves (or women) and thereby bring the church into disrepute. Rather, as in the Epistle to Titus 2:9–10, faithful slaves are an ornament to the Christian way of life. The logic of this position is that the social mores in question are not matters of importance; the liberation of slaves is not a requirement of the Christian message, and indeed, no such demand is made even of owners who are "believers," even though, supposedly, in Christ there is neither slave nor free.

The New Testament does not demand that Christians manumit slaves, then. It even sometimes commends slavery as a condition that Christians should embrace. So 1 Peter 2:18–21:

> Slaves, accept the authority of your masters with all deference, not only those who are kind and gentle but also those who are harsh. For it is a credit to you if, being aware of God, you endure pain while suffering unjustly. If you endure when you are beaten for doing wrong, what credit is that? But if you endure when you do right and suffer for it, you have God's approval. For to this you have been called, because Christ also suffered for you, leaving you an example, so that you should follow in his steps.

SLAVERY AS A CHRISTIAN IDEAL

It is not only in the later epistles that we find slavery or a slave-like attitude commended. Jesus himself is reported to have said:

> You know that among the Gentiles those whom they recognize as their rulers lord it over them, and their great ones are tyrants over them. But it is not so among you; but whoever wishes to become great among you must be your servant, and whoever wishes to be first among you must be slave of all. (Mark 10:42–45)

Paul tells the Philippians:

> Let the same mind be in you that was in Christ Jesus,
>
> > who, though he was in the form of God,
> > did not regard equality with God
> > as something to be exploited,
> > but emptied himself,
> > taking the form of a slave. (2:5–7)

Paul claims that although he is free, he has made himself a slave to all (1 Corinthians 9:19) and often introduces himself as the slave of Christ (Romans 1:1; Galatians 1:10; Philippians 1:10).[45] Paul's use of slavery as a metaphor is complex. Sometimes slavery refers to servitude to the Law, from which Christians have been delivered (Romans 8:12–17, 21–23). But often it means that he and his fellow Christians are slaves to Christ. To be a slave of Christ was not unambiguously humbling. For a leader like Paul, the title "slave of Christ" "established his authority as Christ's agent and spokesperson."[46] Indeed, in the biblical and Near Eastern tradition, high-ranking officials were often called ʿebed, "slave or servant," of the king. Nonetheless, for most people the metaphor attached a high value to humility, to emptying oneself, as Christ is said to have done in Philippians 2. This is the aspect of Christianity that later drew the disdain of Nietzsche for a "slave religion."

Whatever we make of the spiritual value of humility, which no doubt is admirable, the idealization of slavelike humility did not contribute to agitation for the liberation of slaves. It is often argued that "taking a stand in favor of abolishing slavery in Greek and Roman antiquity would not have occurred to anyone. Slavery was part and parcel of the whole political-economic religious structure. The only way even of imagining a society without slavery would have been to imagine a different society."[47] And yet we are told that the Essenes, who lived in Judea in the time of Jesus, had no slaves, because they regarded slavery as unjust. Whether that report is historically accurate or not, it shows that it was possible to conceive of a society without slaves in the time of Jesus, but that vision was not shared by the New Testament writers.

THE BIBLE AND DEBATE ABOUT ABOLITION

Both sides in the debate on abolition in nineteenth-century America drew on the Bible. The anti-abolitionists could point out, quite validly, that slavery is never proscribed in either Testament. One pro-slavery minister wrote that Jesus must have presumed mightily on the intensity of intellect of his followers if he expected them to infer from the command to love your neighbor that slavery should be abolished. God himself, he wrote, had failed to draw that inference in the Hebrew Bible.[48] That argument was undercut to a degree by the observation of Moses Stuart, the leading American biblical scholar of his day, that those who defended slavery because it is accepted in the Bible should also "insist on the liberty of polygamy and concubinage."[49] Frederick Douglass made an even more telling comment. Insisting that he did not believe that the Bible sanctioned slavery, he added that if someone were to persuade him that it did, he would consign it to the flames.

> For of what value to men would a religion be which not only permitted, but enjoined upon men, the enslavement of each other, which would leave them to the sway of physical force and permit the strong to enslave the weak?[50]

Implicit in that argument is that we must look not to specific laws in the Bible, but to the general principles that inform it, even if they are not well embodied in this particular case.

Slavery is no longer a matter of public debate. No one would now argue that because it is accepted in the Bible it should be accepted in modern society. But for that very reason it provides an illuminating test case in biblical values. In this case, at least, it is indisputable that positions endorsed in the Bible are morally unacceptable. We may still look to more general principles in the Bible for moral guidance. Freedom remains a biblical value, proclaimed ringingly in the story of the Exodus and in the baptismal formula in Galatians 3:28. But we must also acknowledge that the implementation of these principles in the Bible often falls short, even by the Bible's own standards.

CHAPTER SEVEN

Violence and Zeal

"You have heard that it was said, 'An eye for an eye and a tooth for a tooth.' But I say to you, 'Do not resist an evildoer. But if anyone strikes you on the right cheek, turn the other also' " (Matthew 5:38–39).

The legitimation of violence is one of many aspects of biblical tradition with which Jesus takes issue in the Sermon on the Mount. Such legitimation is pervasive in the biblical record. Yahweh, we are told, is a man of war (Exodus 15:3). He can be pictured as a blood-stained warrior, who treads the nations as one treads grapes in a winepress and spatters his garments with blood (Isaiah 63:3). It does not always follow that his followers are authorized to act as Yahweh does, but he sets a powerful example. And while the Hebrew Bible is often concerned to set limits to violence, it universally recognizes that "there is a time to kill" (Qoheleth [Ecclesiastes] 3:3). The advice of Jesus to turn the other cheek stands in flat contradiction to the prevailing wisdom in the

Old Testament on this issue. Oddly, most Christians, through the centuries, have not been bothered by this contradiction; indeed, the New Testament is predicated on the expectation of a very violent divine intervention at the end of history. The growing recognition of the role religious ideology plays in modern terrorist activity, however, especially in the wake of the attacks on the United States on September 11, 2001, calls for a reassessment of the biblical heritage in this regard.[1]

Violence has many dimensions. Most obviously, the word refers to any overt physical destructive act, ranging from striking an individual to an act of war. Increasingly, however, we have also come to recognize as violent anything that "violates the personhood of another in ways that are psychologically destructive rather than physically harmful."[2] Violence, however, is not an end in itself, unless the perpetrator is a psychopath. Rather, it is instrumental, a means to an end.[3] We must always consider the ends for which it is used. But we must also consider the implications of choosing this particular means to attain those ends.

I take it as axiomatic that violence is undesirable, for it has the potential to destroy life, not only by actual killing but also by the multiple forms of physical and psychological damage it inflicts. That which destroys, inhibits, or impairs life is bad. To say that violence is undesirable, however, is not to say that it is always the worse course of action or that it is never justified. Here again my guideline is what most damages or enhances life.

THE CONQUEST

Perhaps the most obvious, and in many ways the most troubling, paradigm of violence in the Hebrew Bible is the story of the conquest of Canaan. Deuteronomy prescribes the total slaughter of the previous inhabitants of the land: "When the Lord your God gives them over to you and you defeat them, then you must utterly destroy them. Make no covenant with them and show them no mercy" (7:2). The Book of Joshua claims that Joshua carried out a campaign of wholesale slaughter. For this, he is not faulted. On the contrary, the Israelites are blamed for falling short of total slaughter and failing to drive out all the Canaanites (Joshua 13:13; Judges 1).

The current scholarly consensus is that the account of the conquest is largely a work of fantasy and that there was no large-scale massacre of the Canaanites.[4] The story is now viewed as an ideological composition from the age of King Josiah, in the late seventh century BCE, aimed at justifying his expansionistic policies, or perhaps from even later, lending justification to the resettlement of the land after the Exile (which, as far as we know, did not involve violence).[5] Fact or fantasy, these texts present a model for the ways Israel should relate to its neighbors. Ownership of the land is conferred by divine grant, not by ancestral occupancy or negotiation, and violence against rival claimants of the land is not only legitimate but mandatory. The fact that the conquest is not historical does not lessen the moral problem.[6] The problem is not that it happened but that it was believed to have been commanded and condoned on divine authority. The paradigmatic potential of the story, as a model for future disputes about territory, is all too obvious.

Immanuel Kant wrote, with reference to the sacrifice of Isaac, that "there are certain cases in which man can be convinced that it cannot be God whose voice he thinks he hears; when the voice commands him to do what is opposed to the moral law, though the phenomenon seem to him ever so majestic and surpassing the whole of nature, he must count it a deception."[7] In the case of the Canaanites, we have a clear conflict between a supposed divine command and what Kant would have called the moral law. Of course, we do not have to look to Kant for guidance on this matter. To say that the Israelites, as described in the Book of Joshua, failed to love their Canaanite neighbors as themselves, or even to respect them as human beings in the image of God, would be an understatement. Using biblical standards to critique the ethics of the conquest narrative would not be difficult. What is remarkable is how seldom it has been so critiqued until very recent times.

Through the centuries, the biblical story of the conquest has served as a paradigm of colonial violence.[8] If God has given a particular land to a people, then they are justified in taking possession of it by any means. The obvious contemporary example is the Israeli occupation of the West Bank, justified, at least in some circles, by the traditional claim to the land on biblical authority. Not all Jews make that claim; Christian Zionists make it more emphatically than anyone. But the use of the conquest paradigm is by no means unique to modern Israelis. Biblical rhetoric, and the sense of being a chosen people, was prominent in the sermons of New England divines who referred to native Americans as "this Amalek annoying Israel in the wilderness" or who thanked God for "extirpating the enemies of Israel in Canaan."[9] The Boers in South Africa also saw themselves as a latter-day Israel surrounded by heathens. The biblical story provides an all-too-handy paradigm for imagining the native population as an unholy other, excluded from the world of moral concern.[10]

Biblical theologians have usually assumed the validity of the biblical viewpoint. Often the conquest is said to be justified by the decadence of the Canaanites, a judgment for which there is little objective evidence.[11] In Genesis 15:16, God promises the land to Abraham, but not immediately, "for the iniquity of the Amorites is not yet complete." This single verse is cited to show that the eventual expulsion of the Canaanites was justified by their sinfulness.[12] Even scholars who are less explicitly theological have found ways to justify the ways of Yahweh and his chosen people. William Foxwell Albright, one of the great historical scholars of the twentieth century, remarked resignedly that "from the impartial standpoint of a philosopher of history, it often seems necessary that a people of markedly inferior type should vanish before a people of superior potentialities."[13] It was left to the Palestinian intellectual Edward Said to adopt a "Canaanite perspective" on the story—to look at the conquest from the perspective of the victims.[14] From that perspective, it is no longer the culmination of Exodus and liberation but an unmitigated disaster, analogous to that which befell the Palestinians in the twentieth century. Only since the controversial monograph of the English scholar Keith Whitelam, *The Invention of Ancient Israel: The Silencing of Palestinian History*, published in 1996, has the moral problem of the conquest become an issue in mainline biblical scholarship.[15]

We live in a postcolonial age, and the problems inherent in colonial violence are now more widely appreciated. The violent conquest of one people by another is now widely recognized as a crime against humanity. But not in all cases. Millions of Americans—Jews and especially right-wing Christians—still think that the ownership of the land of Israel/Palestine was settled by divine decree three thousand years ago. The invocation of divine authority trumps moral concern about the violence. As John Calvin wrote in his commentary on Joshua, "When it is added that God so commanded, there is no more ground for obloquy against him than there is against those who pronounce sentence on criminals."[16]

The attempt to resolve the moral problem by appeal to divine command is facile at best. The consensus of critical scholarship is that the violent conquest never happened. Joshua, in effect, is fictional. But if the story of the conquest is fictional, then the story of a divine command telling Joshua to conquer the land is part of that fiction. If there was no massacre of the Canaanites, as apologists for the biblical text eagerly agree, then there was no divine command mandating the conquest of the land.[17]

In fact, the supposed divine command dovetails too neatly with the interests of one party in the conflict to be accepted without suspicion. The story of the conquest does not necessarily tell us the wishes of God for the land west of the Jordan; it conveys only the aspirations of some Israelites or Judeans.

Jewish tradition has usually dealt with the problem of violence in the conquest tradition by pointing out that the commands in Deuteronomy and Joshua concern specific peoples (Canaanites, Amalekites, etc.) who no longer exist.[18] Extending the commandments by analogy to modern peoples like the Palestinians is not permitted. But if a text is regarded as sacred or canonical, it is difficult to exclude analogical applications. The text would lose its relevance for our time. If the kind of violence that is extolled in these texts now seems unacceptable, the question arises, should these texts still be regarded as authoritative and, if so, in what sense?

Violence in itself is not a biblical value, even in the story of the conquest. It is related, however, to a value that is sometimes proclaimed in the Bible and is often associated with religious fanaticism: zeal.

The paradigmatic zealot in the Hebrew Bible is the priest Phinehas in Numbers 25.[19] When Israel was staying at Shittim, in the course of the Exodus, the people began to have sexual relations with the women of Moab. One man, Zimri, brought a Midianite woman to his tent. When Phinehas, son of Eleazar, son of Aaron, saw it, he took his spear, followed them into the tent, and pierced the man and woman together. By modern standards this is an extreme act of intolerance. Yet Phinehas is rewarded with a covenant of eternal priesthood. For the biblical author, the distinct identity of Israel was at stake. (Intermarriage has remained a sensitive issue in Judaism down to the present day.) The word for "zeal" is the same word that is used to say that Yahweh is a jealous God. It bespeaks an absolute devotion, one that brooks no reflection or compromise. (Phinehas makes no attempt to persuade Zimri of the error of his ways.) In later times, some of the Judeans who resisted Roman occupation by violent means were called Zealots in reference to their religious motivation.

It is sometimes argued that the exemplary dimension of Phinehas's action was not its violence but his zeal for the Lord.[20] But zeal is inherently violent, for it is intolerant. Yahweh is a jealous God who tolerates the worship of no other gods. (Zeal and jealousy are expressed by the same root word in Hebrew.) The jealousy of Yahweh gives rise to what has been called intolerant monolatry in the Hebrew Bible.[21] It is now widely agreed that early Israel was to some degree polytheistic[22] but that some prophets, as reflected in the Elijah stories in 1 Kings and in Hosea, advocated the cult of Yahweh alone, a position that won out after the reform of King Josiah in 621 BCE. Polytheistic societies are, by definition, tolerant of more than one deity, but they certainly were not nonviolent. Monolatry, or the demand for the exclusive worship of a single deity, was not the root cause of violence, as has sometimes been suggested, but insofar as it encouraged intolerance of other gods, it contributed to it on occasion.[23]

Phinehas does not stand alone in upholding zeal as an ideal. Consider the sentiment in Psalm 139:21–22:

> Do I not hate those who hate you, O Lord?
>   And do I not loathe those who rise up against you?
> I hate them with perfect hatred;
>   I count them my enemies.

The psalmist does not, as far as we can tell, act violently against the wicked, but he asks God to do so: "O that you would kill the wicked, O God" (verse 19). Again, in Psalm 69:9, "it is zeal for your house that has consumed me," and that zeal leads to an antagonistic relationship with those who follow a different way.

A VIRTUE OF HATE

In the early years of the twenty-first century, Meir Soloveichik, scion of a prominent Jewish Orthodox family and now a prominent rabbi in New York, spent some time at Yale

Divinity School studying philosophy of religion. In 2004, he published a short article in the journal *First Things*, entitled "The Virtue of Hate."[24] He recounted a story told by Simon Wiesenthal, the Nazi hunter, about an encounter with a dying Nazi who confessed to him the atrocities he had committed against Jews and asked for his forgiveness. Wiesenthal refused, but he was tortured by the experience and submitted the story as the subject of a symposium, eliciting responses from people of various religious commitments. All the Jewish respondents thought Wiesenthal was right in refusing to forgive the Nazi. All the Christian respondents thought he was wrong. Soloveichik concludes that Judaism and Christianity differ fundamentally in their attitudes toward forgiveness and their responses to evil. In his view:

> Judaism . . . does demand love for our fellow human beings, but only to an extent. "Hate" is not always synonymous with the terribly sinful. While Moses commanded us "not to hate our brother in our hearts," a man's immoral actions can serve to sever the bonds of brotherhood between himself and humanity.[25]

One is obligated to hate the hopelessly wicked.

Soloveichik is not insensitive to the dangers of hatred— that in hating one may become like that which is hated or that hating may be misdirected toward people who are not responsible for the evil imputed to them.[26] But he denies that hate is always wrong, and in this he has the support of Qoheleth (Ecclesiastes): there is a time for love and a time for hate, a time for war and a time for peace (3:8). His point is that those who do evil must be held accountable for their deeds.

"To my knowledge," writes Soloveichik, "not a single Jewish source asserts that God deeply desires to save all humanity, nor that He loves every member of the human race."[27] He overlooks the Wisdom of Solomon, a Jewish Hellenistic work from around the turn of the Common Era. (Perhaps he does not accept it as Jewish, since it is written in Greek and is part of the Catholic scriptures.) In Wisdom 11:23–24 we read:

> But you are merciful to all, for you can do all things,
> and you overlook people's sins, so that they may repent.
> For you love all things that exist,
> and detest none of the things that you have made,
> for you would not have made anything if you had hated it.

Admittedly, Wisdom goes on to say, with reference to the Canaanites, that "those who lived long ago in your holy land you hated for their detestable practices" (12:3–4) and adds that "they were an accursed race from the beginning" (12:11). Even God, it would seem, made an exception for the Canaanites. Other texts might be cited in support of a more compassionate view of God. The Assyrians had done Israel unspeakable harm. Yet God asks Jonah,

> And should I not be concerned about Nineveh, that great city,
> in which there are more than a hundred and twenty thousand
> persons who do not know their right hand from their left, and
> also many animals? (Jonah 4:11).

But as a generalization, Soloveichik's characterization of the Jewish scriptures is fair enough. The God who is

> merciful and gracious, slow to anger, and abounding in stead-
> fast love and faithfulness, keeping steadfast love for the
> thousandth generation, forgiving iniquity and transgression
> and sin,

is still

> by no means clearing the guilty but visiting the iniquity of the parents upon the children and the children's children, to the third and fourth generation (Exod 34:6–7).

We should not conclude that all Jews subscribe to hate as a virtue. And despite the words of Jesus, forgiveness of enemies is at best an ideal for Christians, to which only a minority aspire. The New Testament by no means dispenses with punishment of the wicked; rather, it defers punishment to eschatological judgment.

THE ZEAL OF THE MACCABEES

The story of the conquest is set in the early history of Israel, even if it took shape much later. The subsequent history of Israel was not one of conquest, violent or otherwise. On the contrary, the Israelites and Judahites were repeatedly trampled by the great powers of Mesopotamia. The military resistance of Israel and Judah crumpled. Faced with the Assyrians and the Babylonians, there was not much a small people could do.

The great exception was provided by the Maccabees, when they were faced with religious persecution under Antiochus Epiphanes.[28] The officers of the king demanded that Jews offer sacrifice to pagan gods, and one man came forward to comply. Mattathias, we are told, "burned with zeal and his heart was stirred. He gave vent to righteous anger; he ran and killed him on the altar. Thus he burned with zeal for the Law, just as Phinehas did against Zimri the son of Salu" (1 Maccabees 2:25–26).

The Maccabean revolt set a powerful precedent in Jewish history because it showed that Judeans could succeed in winning independence by physical force. Not all Jews approved. To succeed the Maccabees had to agree to violate the Sabbath. If they had not, they would have been sitting ducks for the Seleucid army. Some religious purists preferred to die rather than break the law (1 Maccabees 2:29–38). Two hundred years later, Jewish revolutionaries looked to the example of the Maccabees in their struggle against Rome. In this case, they were not successful, and it was easier to blame them for their religious shortcomings than had been the case with the Maccabees. In the late first and early second century CE, the Jews rebelled three times against Rome, and each revolt ended in disaster. In light of this experience, Jewish tradition turned away from violent resistance until the rise of a new militarism in modern Israel in the wake of the Holocaust. The initial Maccabean resistance to persecution can be justified as self-defense. The aggressive actions of their descendants in making war on their Gentile neighbors are harder to defend. In ancient Judaism, however, the Maccabean revolt is something of an aberration, and it is viewed ambiguously in later tradition. Violence can be glorious when it is successful, but it can also lead to disaster and compounded suffering.

APOCALYPTIC VIOLENCE

If the people of Judah usually lacked the power to take vengeance on their enemies, they could at least fantasize. And they did. The late prophetic and subsequent apocalyptic writings are full of gory fantasies of vengeance.[29] Ezekiel conjures up a fantastic enemy called Gog. (The name is probably inspired by that of Gyges of Lydia, who had no historical dealings with the

Judeans.)³⁰ Gog, we are told, will not be defeated by any human hand. Rather, "I will strike your bow from your left hand and will make your arrows drop out of your right hand. You shall fall upon the mountains of Israel, you and all your troops and the peoples that are with you. I will give you to birds of prey and to the wild animals to be devoured" (39:3–4). The prophet Joel has the Lord summon all the nations to the valley of Jehoshaphat to be destroyed: "Put in the sickle for the harvest is ripe. Go in, tread, for the wine press is full. The vats overflow, for their wickedness is great" (Joel 3:13). In Isaiah 63, the Lord is bespattered with blood, like one who has been treading a winepress.

Similar fantasies of vengeance figure prominently in the Book of Revelation in the New Testament, which has been called "that most consistently and relentlessly violent text in all the canonical literature of all the world's greatest religions."³¹ Here Rome takes on the role of Babylon, the destroyer of Jerusalem. John the visionary eagerly anticipates its fall: "Fallen, fallen is Babylon the great! It has become a dwelling place of demons, a haunt of every foul spirit, a haunt of every foul bird, a haunt of every foul and hateful beast" (18:2). He calls on heaven, and on "saints, apostles and prophets," to rejoice over the violence of its fall. Even more violent is the destruction wrought by the Word of God, a rider who appears from heaven, astride a white horse and with a sharp sword emanating from his mouth. Taking a cue from Ezekiel, John summons the birds of heaven to the "great supper of God"— "to eat the flesh of kings, the flesh of captains, the flesh of the mighty, the flesh of horses and their riders—the flesh of all, both free and slave, both small and great" (19:17–18). The beast (representing Rome) and the false prophet are thrown alive into the lake of fire that burns with sulfur. The vengefulness and gore of this scene are worthy of a Mel Gibson movie. It is ironic that the rider on the white horse, the one who initiates such an orgy of violence, is presumably none other than Jesus of Nazareth, who advocated turning the other cheek. It is also ironic that the conquering Jesus mimics the kind of violence that was so objectionable in the Roman empire.[32]

While Revelation is exceptional in the violence of its imagery, its expectations for the future are not greatly different from what we find in the Gospels.[33] The Synoptic Gospels all have Jesus, shortly before his arrest, issue a prophecy of the coming of the Son of Man from heaven as the eschatological judge. Whether these prophecies reflect the beliefs of the historical Jesus is a matter of endless debate in New Testament scholarship, but this is how his message was framed in the early Christian tradition.

APOCALYPSE AND TERROR

A widespread belief, or at least suspicion, in contemporary society is that apocalyptic beliefs and terrorist violence are directly linked.[34] The charge has substance, but the issue of apocalyptic violence is a good deal more complicated than the paradigm of straightforward aggression offered by the conquest story.

First, apocalyptic literature is primarily the product of people who are, or at least conceive themselves to be, powerless and persecuted. There are exceptions, as when apocalyptic rhetoric is manipulated to serve the interests of empires and rulers. The Book of Revelation was written in the aftermath of the destruction of Jerusalem by Rome, when there was at least sporadic persecution of Christians. Rome may have seen itself as spreading enlightenment and peace in the world, but the people it conquered knew better. In the famous words attributed to the Briton Calgacus by the Roman historian Tacitus, the Romans were "plunderers of the world," who exhausted the land and rifled the ocean. "To ravage, to slaughter, to usurp under false titles, they call empire; and when they make a desert, they call it peace."[35]

The question is whether the outrages committed by Rome justify the fury of the Apocalypse. The British novelist D. H. Lawrence, citizen of another Roman-style empire, dismissed the portrait of Babylon in the Apocalypse as mere envy:

> How they envy Babylon her splendour, envy, envy! How they love destroying it all. The harlot sits magnificent with her golden cup of wine of sensual pleasure in her hand. How the apocalyptists would have loved to drink out of her cup! And since they couldn't, how they loved smashing it.[36]

Many people suspect a similar mixture of envy and resentment on the part of the Muslim terrorists who brought down the twin towers of the World Trade Center. But Lawrence, a scion of the British empire, had little sympathy for underlings. Revelation, in contrast, was clearly written from the perspective of a subject people.[37] For such people, apocalyptic fantasies have a therapeutic effect.[38] In many cases, visions that affirm a radical reversal of the present order give hope to people who otherwise would have no hope at all. If the visions are violent, they are at least honest in representing feelings that are almost inevitable for people who have suffered at the hands of a conquering power. Anger and fantasies of violence may be life-giving for the powerless; even actual violence may be justified if it serves to relieve oppression.

The classic apocalyptic texts in the biblical tradition, however, are not calls to violent action. The Book of Daniel dismisses the Maccabees as "little help" if they are acknowledged at all (11:34). The heroes of the book are not the resistance fighters but the wise teachers, who explain to the people that the course of events is not decided by human action but by heavenly powers and that faithful humans who lose their lives will rise to a glorious hereafter. John of Patmos exhorts his readers, "If you are to be taken captive, into captivity you go; if you kill with the sword, with the sword you must be killed."[39] His message is one of endurance and faith. Similarly, the members of the sect known to us from the Dead Sea Scrolls, who lived in anticipation of a great war between the Sons of Light and the Sons of Darkness, pledged to "pay to no man the reward of evil" and "not [to] grapple with the men of perdition until the Day of Revenge" (1QS [Community Rule] 10:19). In all these cases, and in the case of nearly all ancient Jewish and Christian apocalypses, the message is quietistic rather than violent.

The quietistic ethic is framed and supported by predictions of great eschatological violence, to be unleashed from heaven. There is an intrinsic connection between present forbearance and eschatological vengeance in this literature. In the Epistle to the Romans, Paul tells his readers: "Never avenge yourselves, but leave room for the wrath of God ... No, 'if your enemies are hungry, feed them; if they are thirsty, give them something to drink'; for by doing this you will heap burning coals on their heads" (12:19–21). As Krister Stendhal shows in a famous article, this attitude has more to do with the perfection of hatred than with disinterested love: "With the Day of Vengeance at hand, the proper and reasonable attitude is to forego one's own vengeance and to leave vengeance to God. Why walk around with a little shotgun if the atomic blast is imminent?"[40] From this perspective, the violence of apocalyptic eschatology serves as a kind of release valve whereby the oppressed can vent their frustration and anger without actually translating their feelings into violent action.[41]

The demand for justice and the tendency toward quietism go some way toward rebutting the charge that fantasies of eschatological violence are conducive to terrorism. But the issues are more complicated still. Brutal oppression has always been a fact of life for a significant proportion of the world's population, but fantasies of vengeance are not always justified or excusable. What constitutes "intolerable oppression" can vary greatly from one situation to another. From the letters of Pliny we know something about Roman policy toward Christianity in Asia Minor when the Apocalypse of John was written. It was not benevolent, but it stopped well short of systematic persecution.[42] John found it intolerable because it exalted Rome and its emperor above the God of Jews and Christians. Analogously, American influence in the Arab world may not always be benevolent, but whether it qualifies the United States to be reckoned the Great Satan and warrants calls for jihad is open to dispute. Apocalyptic fantasies can serve to create a sense of crisis where crisis is not generally perceived. This is not to deny that extreme oppression exists, or even is relatively commonplace, but only to point out that the apocalyptic view of the world is not necessarily an objective one, and that it is not necessarily justified by oppression in all cases.

Moreover, while many apocalypses discourage violent action in the present and set little store by human agency, they may nonetheless sow the seeds of violence. Violent language has its own potency.[43] It is a matter of debate whether messianic hopes were a factor in the Jewish revolt against Rome in the late first century BCE. Josephus assigns a measure of responsibility to a series of figures whom we might describe as apocalyptic prophets. After describing the activities of the Sicarii, or Dagger-men, he goes on:

> Besides these there arose another body of villains, with purer hands but more impious intentions, who no less than the assassins ruined the peace of the city. Deceivers and impostors, under the pretense of divine inspiration fostering revolutionary changes, they persuaded the multitude to act like madmen, and led them out into the desert under the belief that God would give them tokens of deliverance. Against them, Felix, regarding them as but the preliminary insurrection, sent a body of cavalry and heavy-armed infantry, and put a large number to the sword. (*Jewish War* 2.259–60, trans. Thackeray)[44]

There was a succession of such sign prophets in the first century CE. Josephus admits that the movements they led were not violent but were inspired by the hope of miraculous divine intervention. But he blames them nonetheless for disturbing the peace of the city and creating an atmosphere congenial to rebellion. He also claims that the rebels were inspired by an "ambiguous oracle, which was found in the sacred texts" (6.312–15) more than by anything else. We do not know which oracle that was. Possibilities include Daniel 7 (the "one like a son of man") and Balaam's prophecy of the scepter and the star in Numbers 24:17. Josephus gives an unsympathetic account of the revolt, but he must be credited with insight into the workings of prophecy, ambiguous or otherwise. If people are told to expect a heavenly deliverer on a white horse who will annihilate their enemies, it may be difficult for them to restrain themselves from giving him a helping hand. There are many examples in both Jewish and Christian history of people who took it upon themselves to "force the end" in defiance of religious authorities and the weight of tradition. In the not-too-distant past, there was a plot to blow up the Temple Mount in Jerusalem in hopes of accelerating Armageddon.[45]

The use of apocalyptic rhetoric in modern times has often been marked by calculated ambiguity. Ambiguity allows extremists to encourage fantasies of violence without directly advocating violent action.[46] This is as true of Christian fundamentalists, such as Ian Paisley, whose anti-Catholic rhetoric, drawn heavily from the Book of Revelation, stoked sectarian violence in Northern Ireland for a generation, as for the Islamic clerics who issue latter-day calls for jihad. It would not be fair to conclude that every apocalyptic-minded preacher is guilty of inciting violence, but the genre has potential in that regard, even when the preacher is not consciously trying to exploit it.

One of the reasons why apocalyptic rhetoric is conducive to violence is that it tends toward dualism. When the world is divided between Good and Evil, Sons of Light and Sons of Darkness, then there is little room for compromise, and without compromise there is little alternative to violence.[47] This kind of dualism can exist outside of an apocalyptic context, but it is especially characteristic of apocalyptic and eschatological language, in ancient Persia as well as in the Bible, and in Islam as well as in Judaism and Christianity. Associated with this dualism is the certainty associated with apocalyptic revelation, which carries with it the conviction that the believer is absolutely right and the enemy absolutely wrong.

Many scholars who are rightly concerned about the prevalence of violence in the Old Testament find an antidote in the New Testament, construing it as a consistent witness against violence.[48] But while the New Testament provides powerful advocacy for peace and nonviolence, it frames its message with the expectation of violent judgment and can easily encourage violent attitudes.[49]

JESUS RECONSIDERED

What then should we do with the saying about turning the other cheek?

Despite occasional attempts to argue that Jesus was a revolutionary, "with zeal as his weapon," who endorsed violence,[50] or that he led armed followers to Jerusalem in anticipation of an apocalyptic battle,[51] the evidence that his career and message were predominantly nonviolent is overwhelming.[52] Most telling in that regard is the fact that he made no attempt to defend himself when he was arrested, whether this was a matter of principle, or reliance on divine deliverance, or an acknowledgement that resistance would be futile.[53] The only violent action attributed to him is the driving of the money changers from the temple with improvised whips (Matthew 21:12–13; Mark 11:15–19; Luke 19:45–6; John 2:13–17). The motivation for this action is much disputed.[54] At the least, it bespeaks respect for the sanctity of the temple. It also shows that Jesus' aversion to violence was not absolute when the honor of God, rather than self-defense, was at stake. But this action stands out because it is exceptional. It does not warrant the conclusion that Jesus was a violent revolutionary.

Many scholars have been troubled by the implication that Jesus was prepared to tolerate injustice in the present rather than take decisive action to defeat it. Accordingly, they have offered ingenious explanations of Jesus' sayings as tactical advice. So it has been suggested that Jesus was proposing a "third way" between violence and pacificism.[55] Turning the other cheek was a way to shame the aggressor. Nonviolence was indeed used as an effective technique by Mahatma Gandhi, but it worked for Gandhi because of mass mobilization and news coverage, neither of which is envisioned in the Gospels. Again, it is suggested that the saying "Love your enemies" was intended to address conflicts within Judean communities, not with the imperial oppressor. Jesus, we are told, was addressing the malaise of village communities that were disintegrating under Herodian and Roman exploitation.[56] The saying in Matthew 5:41, "If anyone forces you to go one mile, go also the second mile," clearly refers to the Roman custom of forcing occupied people to carry a soldier's gear, so it has to be regarded as a Matthean addition.[57] But in fact the whole idea of Jesus revitalizing village communities is a modern romantic construct with no basis in the texts.

In the context of the New Testament as a whole, the saying about turning the other cheek can be understood easily enough by analogy to Paul's advice about feeding the hungry enemy. In effect, divine intervention is at hand. Vengeance should be left to God. One need not share Paul's desire to pour burning coals on the head of the enemy. Paul had been zealous for the Law in his early career and did not lose his zeal when he became a follower of Jesus. The attitude of Jesus may be better reflected in the parable of the wheat and the tares (Matthew 13:24–30), whether he actually spoke that parable or not.[58] Weeds and wheat should be allowed to grow together until the harvest. Trying to pull up the weeds before then would do more harm than good. Again, whoever wants to save his life will lose it (Matthew 16:25; Luke 9:24). This saying, with its corollary that anyone who loses his life for Jesus' sake will save it, may well have been fashioned by the disciples after the death of Jesus, when they were more likely to encounter persecution. But Jesus, as reflected in the Sermon on the Mount, taught that his followers should not be concerned for their self-preservation in this world but should trust in the creator, like the lilies of the field and the sparrows of the air. That kind of trust does not necessarily presuppose a coming judgment, but it would certainly be facilitated by a belief in an afterlife.

If Jesus' sayings about turning the other cheek and loving one's enemy are predicated on the expectation of an apocalyptic judgment, they may not be as radically different from Jewish apocalyptic ideas as is usually thought. To be sure, they are still different. Many sources in the ancient world counsel against retaliation: "Do not say, 'Just as he did to me, so I shall do to him; I shall repay the man according to his deed' " (Proverbs 20:22). No ancient Jewish text, however, demands that people love their enemies or refuse to defend themselves.[59] Indeed, the command to love one's enemies is not found in the

New Testament outside the Gospels. Typically, the expectation of a final judgment encourages the perfection of hatred and extreme polarization. It may be that the originality of Jesus lay in the way he used apocalyptic expectation to encourage freedom from worry about this life. It is not apparent, however, that even Jesus dispensed with the need for some ultimate retribution. The expectation of ultimate retribution continues to play an important role in the Gospels and the rest of the New Testament.

Modern theologians and biblical scholars point quite rightly to the multiplicity of viewpoints within the biblical text. Even in the Old Testament, we find inclusion and integration as well as rejection and violence. The violence toward the Canaanites can be balanced against the concern for slaves and aliens in Deuteronomy, or one can hold up as exemplary the model of the suffering servant or the teaching of Jesus. It is not unusual for Christian theologians to say that "the biblical witness to the innocent victim and the God of victims demystifies and demythologizes" the sacral order in which violence is grounded.[60] Such an approach is well intentioned, and salutary up to a point. But while violence is not the only model of behavior on offer in the Bible, it is by no means peripheral. Jesus may have preached nonviolence (money changers in the temple excepted), but the canonical text of the New Testament claims that he will come back and be much less indulgent the second time around. In short, the Bible testifies not only to innocent victims and to the God of victims but also to the hungry God who models violent behavior and the zeal of his human agents.

If we are going to use the Bible as a guide to behavior in the modern world, then we must use it judiciously. If the devil can cite scripture for his own purpose, he would certainly have no trouble finding texts that seem to support violence. Neither is it difficult to find texts in support of tolerance or even pacifism. To derive guidance from the Bible on this subject, as on any other, it is necessary to see individual passages in perspective and to establish priorities, whether we do this on inner-biblical grounds or derive our criteria from elsewhere.

CHAPTER EIGHT

Social Justice in the Hebrew Bible

> Anum and Enlil named me, to promote the welfare of the
>   people,
> me Hammurabi, the devout, god-fearing prince,
> to cause justice to prevail in the land,
> to destroy the wicked and the evil
> that the strong might not oppress the weak.[1]

So proclaimed Hammurabi, king of Babylon, in the eighteenth century BCE, roughly five hundred years before Moses. Hammurabi was not necessarily a champion of social justice, but his proclamation was de rigueur for any self-respecting king in the ancient Near East. Kings were divinely appointed to uphold what was right:

> The great gods called me, so that I became the beneficent
>   shepherd
> Whose scepter is righteous
> . . . .
> In order that the strong might not oppress the weak,
> That justice might be dealt to the orphan and the widow.[2]

These proclamations show, on the one hand, that there was a common perception of justice throughout the ancient Near East, along with a consensus that kings and rulers had a responsibility to provide it.[3] On the other hand, they show what justice entailed: the strong should not oppress the weak. It was the obligation of rulers to protect the most vulnerable members of society, typically the widow and the orphan.

How far ancient rulers concerned themselves with the plight of the orphan and the widow is another matter. There is evidence of sporadic release of slaves and remission of debt in Mesopotamia throughout the period before the common era, much of it from the middle of the second millennium.[4] Records of these acts of liberation are often found in royal inscriptions, which may exaggerate the benevolence of the king. So we read of a prince of Lagash[5] about 2430 BCE: "He established liberation for Lagash. To the mother he restored her children, and to the children he restored their mother. He instituted liberation for the interest on barley."[6] Another king, about a century later, "freed the sons of Lagash, who were imprisoned because of debts, taxes, theft and murder" and made a covenant "not to hand the widow and orphan over to the powerful."[7] We also find provision, as late as Hellenistic Egypt, that people be allowed to return to their own estate or property.[8] The abuse that these measures sought to remedy was debt slavery, the custom by which men surrendered their children, wives, or themselves into slavery in payment of their debts. In the ancient Near East, remedial measures were most likely to be taken when a new king came to power. Like tax cuts in modern politics, they were a way of winning the good will of the populace and thereby strengthening the ruler's hold on power.[9]

In the Hebrew Bible, too, the rhetoric of justice is part of the royal ideology:[10]

> Give the king your justice, O God,
>   and your righteousness to the king's son.
> May he judge your people with righteousness,
>   and your poor with justice.
> . . . .
> May he defend the cause of the poor of the people,
>   give deliverance to the needy,
>   and crush the oppressor. (Psalm 72:1–4)

The king

> delivers the needy when they call,
> The poor and those who have no helper.
> He has pity on the weak and the needy,
>   and saves the lives of the needy. (72:12–13)

The ideal king

> shall not judge by what his eyes see,
>   or decide by what his ears hear,
> but with righteousness he shall judge the poor,
>   and decide with equity for the meek of the earth.
> (Isaiah 11:3–4)

The demand for justice was not a social contract between ruler and ruled. It was required by the divine cosmic order, which the king was expected to uphold.[11] It is said of God that "righteousness and justice are the foundation of your throne" (Psalm 89:14), and the king was his agent on earth. Nonetheless, it is amply clear, especially from the prophetic books, that Israel and Judah were rife with injustice.

The classic biblical preaching against injustice is found in the Prophets, especially in those of the eighth century BCE, Isaiah, Amos, and Micah, but also in Jeremiah at the beginning of the sixth century.[12] Some of their critiques still seem all too relevant today.

Amos inveighs against dishonest business practices, then as now often coupled with the trappings of religious observance:

> Hear this, you that trample on the needy,
>   and bring to ruin the poor of the land,
> saying, "When will the new moon be over
>   so that we may sell grain;
> and the sabbath,
>   so that we may offer wheat for sale?
> We will make the ephah small and the shekel great,
>   and practice deceit with false balances,
> buying the poor for silver
>   and the needy for a pair of sandals,
>   and selling the sweepings of the wheat." (8:4–6)

As in all ancient Near Eastern discourse on the subject of justice, the issue here is the exploitation of the poor, who are viewed as expendable in the pursuit of profit. It is sometimes claimed that the objective here is distributive justice, to redistribute social goods and social power.[13] But this is true only to a limited degree. At no point do the prophets advocate equal distribution of wealth or challenge an order where some people have more than others. It is assumed that "there will never cease to be people in need on the earth" (Deuteronomy 15:11). The problem for the prophets is that the poor are deprived of the necessities of life and degraded to a subhuman condition.

The rich "trample the head of the poor into the dust of the earth and push the afflicted out of the way" (Amos 2:7). There is always a question as to what the threshold is, what should be deemed sufficient for the poor. But the examples cited by Amos and the other prophets seem clear enough. If people have to sell themselves into slavery to cover their debts or get food to eat, that is surely unacceptable. Moreover, it is a problem when the gap between rich and poor becomes disproportionate. Amos rails against

> those who are at ease in Zion,
> and . . . those who feel secure on Mount Samaria,
> . . . .
>
> . . . those who lie on beds of ivory,
>   and lounge on their couches,
> and eat lambs from the flock,
>   and calves from the stall;
> who sing idle songs to the sound of the harp,
>   and like David improvise on instruments of music;
> who drink wine from bowls,
>   and anoint themselves with the finest oils,
>   but are not grieved over the ruin of Joseph! (6:1–6)

The point here is not necessarily that beds of ivory and bowls of wine are bad in themselves,[14] but that they make a painful contrast with the "ruin of Joseph" and the poverty of Israelite peasants. Similarly, Amos's younger contemporary Isaiah rails against those who "join house to house, who add field to field, until there is room for no one but you, and you are left to live alone in the midst of the land" (5:8). They could add field to field because the poor had to forfeit their ancestral plots to pay their debts. Again, the gap between rich and poor is part of the problem. The prophets see society organically, and that the balance of society is out of joint is what brings it to ruin.

THE BASIS OF JUSTICE

The Hebrew word *mishpat*, which is often translated as "justice," is derived from the verb *shaphat*, "to judge," and can also mean "judgment" or "commandment." Accordingly, it is sometimes suggested that *mishpat* refers to the enforcement of a judicial system and that the word implies a judicial performance. The moral philosopher Oliver O'Donovan contrasts this juridical view of justice with another widespread view, derived from Aristotle: "justice as receiving one's own and being in social equilibrium."[15] O'Donovan claims that "when Amos calls for *mishpat* to 'roll on like a river,' he means precisely that the stream of juridical activity should not be allowed to dry up."[16] A brief perusal of the oracles of Amos and Isaiah, however, shows that this view is mistaken. Some of the conduct condemned by the Prophets involves breaking laws (e.g., the dishonest trading in Amos), but some does not. Even if the rich of Judah were acting quite legally in joining house to house and adding field to field, their actions were unconscionable given the poverty of their compatriots. While this view may not quite amount to an Aristotelian view of justice, social equilibrium is definitely a consideration. It rests not so much on positive covenantal law as on an intuition into the order of nature or of creation.[17] This is also true of some of the best-known stories illustrating the problem of injustice in the Hebrew Bible. Take, for example, 2 Samuel 11, where the prophet Nathan confronts King David for having Uriah the Hittite killed and taking his wife Bathsheba. Nathan tells the king a story about a rich man who took a poor man's little ewe lamb to make a meal for his guest, although that was all the poor man had. David is outraged, not because a law had been violated but because the action was patently unjust. The prophet is able to entrap the king by telling him, "You are the man." Equally, in the story of Naboth's vineyard, in 1 Kings 21, Elijah's condemnation of King Ahab is not a technical judgment on a legal case but outrage at an action that was obviously unjust because of the abuse of royal power.

The Prophets are engaged not in articulating a theory of justice but only in protesting egregious abuses. If a theory is implicit in their protests, it is first of all that everyone should have enough to live a satisfying life, each with his own vine and fig tree, and free from fear (Micah 4:4). Also, the discrepancies in wealth should not be too great. Great discrepancies invariably arise from exploitative practices, which in turn give rise to resentment and tensions that disrupt the peace of society.

THE CENTRALITY OF JUSTICE

For the Hebrew Bible, no value is more central or fundamental than the demand for social justice. Demands for cultic worship pale in significance, to the point that sometimes the prophets seem to reject the ritual cult.[18]

"With what shall I come before the LORD," asks the prophet Micah, "and bow myself before God on high?" (6:6). He considers burnt offerings or rams or calves and even raises the possibility of human sacrifice:

Shall I give my firstborn for my transgression,
    the fruit of my body for the sin of my soul? (6:7)

But he brushes these options aside:

He has told you, O mortal, what is good;
    and what does the LORD require of you
but to do justice, and to love kindness
    and to walk humbly with your God? (6:8)

Similarly, Amos declares:

I hate, I despise your festivals,
    and I take no delight in your solemn assemblies.
Even though you offer me your burnt offerings and grain
    offerings,
    I will not accept them;
and the offerings of well-being of your fatted animals
    I will not look upon.
Take away from me the noise of your songs;
    I will not listen to the melody of your harps.
But let justice roll down like waters,
    and righteousness like an ever-flowing stream. (5:21–24)

We should probably not conclude that the prophets rejected the sacrificial cult entirely. Such a rejection would be hard to conceive of in the eighth century BCE. But they certainly questioned its value and significance. Amos reminded his listeners that the Israelites could not have offered large numbers of sheep and cattle in their time in the wilderness and that God had been with them nonetheless (5:25). Moreover, generous offerings to the cult made people feel that they were pleasing God and blinded them to the social problems. In that sense, the cult was more a hindrance than a help. For the prophets, and indeed also in the laws of Moses, nothing was more important than social justice.

As we have seen, the concern for the most vulnerable members of society, specifically the widow and the orphan, was part of the common idea of justice in the ancient Near East. Nonetheless, in a perusal of the literature of the ancient Near East on the question of justice, the Hebrew Bible stands out in several respects.

First is simply the degree of emphasis on the importance of justice in the biblical writings. Although Hammurabi and his fellow kings professed their commitment to protecting the widow and the orphan, their laws are primarily concerned with the land-owning gentry. More significantly, no people of the ancient world other than Israel produced a corpus of literature critical of the practice of monarchy. On purely humanistic grounds, the Hebrew Bible holds a distinctive place within ancient literature because of the passion it displays on this subject.

Second, while monarchy in Israel and Judah was very much like monarchy in other countries, Israel remembered a time when there was no king in Israel, and the biblical writings were actually compiled after the demise of the monarchy. This does not necessarily mean that all human beings were "created equal."[19] The idea that earliest Israel, the tribes that occupied the central highlands of Canaan toward the end of the second millennium BCE, constituted an egalitarian society is a modern romantic myth.[20] Tribal societies were not egalitarian, even if they were not as stratified as their monarchical counterparts. But there surely were tendencies in the direction of egalitarianism both in early Israel and in post-monarchic Judah. The law of the king in Deuteronomy 17 is the prime example. Here the role of a king is acknowledged, but he is subordinated to the Law, so Deuteronomy has reasonably been said to provide the first instance of constitutional monarchy.[21] In postexilic Judah, the High Priest took the place of the king to a great degree, but the principle of equality before the Law was widely accepted.

Third, the Hebrew Bible typically modifies the common ancient Near Eastern concern for the widow and the orphan, by adding another marginal figure, the alien. We find this already in Exodus 22:21: "You shall not wrong an alien, or abuse a widow or an orphan." Leviticus 19:34 even says: "You shall love the alien as yourself." The concern for aliens is distinctive to Israel in the ancient Near East.[22] Biblical law distinguishes between the resident alien (*ger*) and the foreigner (*nokri*). Resident aliens had a well-defined place in Israelite law.[23] They could join in the celebrations of the harvest festivals (Deuteronomy: 16, 11, 14), though not the Passover unless they chose to undergo circumcision and join the Israelite community. (In the Second Temple period and later Judaism, the word *ger* came to connote "convert.") They were expected to refrain from work on Sabbaths and Holy Days. In the laws of Deuteronomy and Leviticus, the alien is often mentioned with the poor. Special care should be taken to pay the alien for his labor, "for he is poor and urgently depends on it" (Deuteronomy 24:14–15). The gleanings at the edges of the field should be left for the poor and the alien (Leviticus 19:9–10; Leviticus 23:22).

The concern for the alien is repeatedly grounded in Israel's own experience. Abraham was a resident alien in the land of Canaan, dependent on the kindness of the local population

(Genesis 23:4). His descendants were aliens in a land not theirs (15:13). Most frequently, the Israelites are reminded that "you were aliens in the land of Egypt" (Exodus 22:20). Accordingly, they should "know the heart of the alien" (23:9), for they have experienced what it is to be an alien. In that sense, concern for the alien is an instance of the Golden Rule, to do unto others as you would have them do unto you. But there is also an intuition that care for the alien and other vulnerable members of society is a fundamental human obligation. God is the guarantor and protector of such people. God, we are told, "watches over the alien; He encourages the orphan and widow" (Psalm 146:9). Even more forcefully, Deuteronomy proclaims that God "executes justice for the orphan and the widow, and loves the aliens, providing them food and clothing. You shall also love the alien, for you were aliens in the land of Egypt" (Deuteronomy 10:18).

It may seem a short step from passages like these to affirming that aliens, and widows and orphans, have rights under biblical law. If people have an obligation to treat the poor and the alien in a certain way, does that not imply that they have a right to be treated that way?[24] Perhaps, but the Bible does not put it that way. Society has an obligation to provide for such people as part of its obligation to God. Whether aliens would have a legal claim under Israelite law is not clear. They could only appeal to the compassion of a judge and the force of Israelite tradition. But the obligation on the society is none the less for that.

Affirmations that God loves the poor and the alien and watches over them have given rise to the claim of Liberation Theology that God has a "preferential option" for the poor.[25] If this claim is understood to mean that God is especially concerned for the poor, it has some basis in the biblical tradition. How a society treats its poor determines how it stands in the sight of God. But the biblical writers certainly did not think that the judicial system should give preferential treatment to the poor.[26] On that point, the laws are explicit: "You shall not render an unjust judgment; you shall not be partial to the poor or defer to the great. With justice you shall judge your neighbor" (Leviticus 19:15). Similarly, Exodus 23:2 says: "When you bear witness in a lawsuit, you shall not side with the majority so as to pervert justice; neither shall you be partial to the poor in a lawsuit." In Deuteronomy 1:16–17, the judges are charged thus:

> Give the members of your community a fair hearing, and judge rightly between one person and another, whether citizen or resident alien. You must not be partial in judging: hear out the small and the great alike; you shall not be intimidated by anyone, for the judgment is God's.

This vision is not of a distributive justice but rather of a right order where both rich and poor have their obligations. It remains true that the rich are much more likely to encroach on the poor than vice versa, and it is the poor, not the rich, who need assurances of divine protection.

AN END TO THE PRESENT ORDER?

The prophets were not Marxist revolutionaries.[27] At no point do they urge the poor to rise up against their wealthy oppressors. But they do call for an end to the present order. Amos says the eyes of the Lord are on the sinful kingdom of Israel and that he will wipe it from the face of the earth (9:8). Isaiah says the nobility of Jerusalem must go down into the open maw of the netherworld, Sheol (5:14). When the prophets call for human action to remedy the situation, it involves "returning" to the true way. In Jeremiah 7:5–7 the prophet assures his listeners:

> For if you truly amend your ways and your doings, if you truly act justly one with another, if you do not oppress the alien, the orphan, and the widow, or shed innocent blood in this place, and if you do not go after other gods to your own hurt, then I will dwell with you in this place.

The Book of Jeremiah is heavily edited, and this conditional pronouncement is likely to come from an editor rather than a prophet. The prophets more typically announce doom and destruction, implying that the unjust society cannot and must not endure, but they look to divine intervention rather than human revolution to bring it to an end. Society as a whole stands condemned. The situation is not one that can be ameliorated by individual acts of kindness.

Beyond the prophecies of destruction, we get occasional glimpses of the kind of society for which the prophets hoped. One such passage is found in Isaiah 65:17–25, where the prophet envisions a new heaven, a new earth, and a new Jerusalem.

> No more shall there be in it
>   an infant that lives but a few days,
>   or an old person who does not live out a lifetime;
> for one who dies at a hundred years will be considered a
>   youth,
>   and one who falls short of a hundred will be considered
>   accursed.
> They shall build houses and inhabit them;
>   they shall plant vineyards and eat their fruit.
> . . . .

They shall not labor in vain,
   or bear children for calamity;
for they shall be offspring blessed by the LORD.

The ideal is a world of modest self-sufficiency where each family has its own vine and fig tree.

This state of affairs can be brought about only by divine intervention. The prophets are not revolutionaries. But by enunciating this eschatological vision, the prophets hold up a goal that can guide society.

FROM JUSTICE TO CHARITY

In the late Second Temple period, the view of poverty and injustice changed. We still find denunciations of the rich and powerful, especially in apocalyptic literature, but we also find a new emphasis on almsgiving as an expression of righteousness.[28] In fact, the Hebrew word *tsedaqah*—which with *mishpat* was part of the word-pair "justice and righteousness," the basic vocabulary of justice in the Hebrew Bible—came to mean simply "almsgiving." We find this shift already in the second century BCE in the Book of Daniel, chapter 4, where Daniel tells Nebuchadnezzar to "atone for your sins by almsgiving and for your iniquity by mercy to the poor."[29] Ben Sira, a little before Daniel in the early second century BCE, tells his readers to "help the poor for the commandment's sake, and in their need do not send them away empty-handed" (29:9).[30] Moreover, he advises his readers to

Lay up your treasure according to the commandments of the
   Most High,
and it will profit you more than gold.

Store up almsgiving in your treasury,
    and it will rescue you from every disaster. (29:11–12)

Similarly, Tobit, who may be roughly contemporary with Ben Sira, expressed his righteousness by giving food to the hungry, offering clothes to the naked, and burying the dead (1:17). He also charges his son to

> give alms from your possessions, and do not let your eye be-grudge the gift when you make it. Do not turn your face away from anyone who is poor, and the face of God will not be turned away from you. If you have many possessions, make your gift from them in proportion; if few, do not be afraid to give according to the little you have. So you will be laying up a good treasure for yourself against the day of necessity. For almsgiving delivers from death and keeps you from going into the Darkness. Indeed, almsgiving, for all who practice it, is an excellent offering in the presence of the Most High. (4:7–11)

Neither Ben Sira nor Tobit was laying up treasure for the hereafter. Both supposed that one could acquire credit with the Lord for this life. Tobit, ironically, was blind when he gave this advice to his son, but he had not lost hope that his good deeds would be rewarded. The prospect of laying up treasure in heaven became much more alluring when belief in reward and punishment after death began to take hold in Judaism in the second century BCE.

For our present purposes, the shift in emphasis from the social orientation of the prophets to the concern for individual merits in Ben Sira and Tobit is significant. To be sure, the shift was not absolute. There were still apocalyptic writers who railed against the excesses of the rich and the powerful.[31] It is also true that biblical law always had a place for charity—compare the

Deuteronomic injunction to leave gleanings for the poor and the alien. But the increased emphasis on individual almsgiving, coupled with the belief in reward and punishment in the here-after, complicate the situation considerably when we turn to the New Testament.

AN ETHIC OF PROSPERITY?

Social justice has to do with material prosperity in this world. In the Hebrew Bible, material prosperity is promised in the blessings of the covenant:

> If you will only obey the LORD your God, by diligently observing all his commandments . . . all these blessings shall come upon you . . .
> Blessed shall be the fruit of your womb, the fruit of your ground, and the fruit of your livestock, both the increase of your cattle and the issue of your flock.
> Blessed shall be your basket and your kneading bowl. . . .
> . . . The LORD will make you abound in prosperity, in the fruit of your womb, in the fruit of your livestock, and in the fruit of your ground in the land that the LORD swore to your ancestors to give you. The LORD will open for you his rich store-house, the heavens, to give the rain of your land in its season and to bless all your undertakings. You will lend to many na-tions, but you will not borrow. The LORD will make you the head, and not the tail; you shall be only at the top, and not at the bottom—if you obey the commandments of the LORD your God. (Deuteronomy 28:1–5, 11–13)

Such prosperity is the ideal for the people of God. There is no virtue in poverty.

In some circles of American Christianity in the twentieth and twenty-first centuries, prosperity has been elevated as a goal of religion.[32] The Book of Chronicles mentions an obscure figure named Jabez who is said to have been honored more than his brothers. This Jabez, we are told, "called on the God of Israel, saying, 'Oh that you would bless me and enlarge my border, and that your hand might be with me, and that you would keep me from hurt and harm!' And God granted what he asked" (1 Chronicles 4:10). This verse has been singled out as a formula for Christian self-help. A book entitled *The Prayer of Jabez: Breaking Through to the Blessed Life*, published in 2000, became an international best-seller, sold nine million copies, and received the Evangelical Christian Publishers Association Gold Medallion Book of the Year award in 2001.[33] It promised that those who used the prayer of Jabez would soon notice significant changes in their lives.

The biblical credentials of Jabez notwithstanding, the "prosperity gospel" is a caricature of biblical teaching on wealth, poverty, and justice. The blessings of the covenant were promised to the people as a whole and were contingent on keeping the commandments, which were largely concerned with social justice. The idea that suffering and poverty are punishment for sin and that the righteous prosper is critiqued decisively in the Book of Job. Job is portrayed as a paradigmatically righteous person who loses everything. Fundamentally, both the Law and the Prophets are focused on concern for other people, especially the less fortunate in society. The God of Israel is not an ATM machine for personal advancement. The desire for prosperity is too easily corrupted by greed. The prophets especially were acutely attuned to the usual progression: that those who "join house to house, who add field to field" often do so by exploiting the less fortunate.

The prosperity promised in the covenantal blessings is more modest. It is a state of sufficiency where everyone has enough to live on. This concern is fundamental to the Hebrew Bible and remains an important part of the biblical tradition. The New Testament allows even less scope for the prosperity gospel and changes the focus by urging people to lay up their treasure in heaven.

CHAPTER NINE

Social Justice in the Shadow of the Apocalypse

SURPRISINGLY, despite the centrality of justice in the Hebrew Bible, some people question its importance in the context of Christianity. The objections are of various kinds.

The provocative moral theologian Stanley Hauerwas has claimed that "justice is a bad idea for Christians."[1] He does not deny that Christians should feed the hungry and care for the sick, but he objects to thinking of such activities in terms of the liberal, secular ideal of justice; it is, rather, a matter of following the Gospel of Jesus.[2] For anyone who does not share Hauerwas's aversion to secular liberalism, however, his objection seems like a quibble. The important question is what the foundational Christian texts say about the treatment of our fellow human beings, not whether their prescriptions are peculiarly Christian.[3]

Another objection pretends to a higher ideal. Love rather than justice is supposed to be the ideal for Christians. The Swedish theologian and bishop Anders Nygren declared that "fellowship with God is not governed by law but by love. God's attitude to men is not characterized by *justitia distributiva* but by *agape*, not by retributive righteousness but by freely giving and forgiving love."[4] This kind of love was the ideal for Christians. It stood in contrast with *eros*, the kind of love that seeks to enhance the well-being of the agent. *Agape*, says Saint Paul, "seeks not that which belongs to it" (1 Corinthians 13:5). However admirable such an ideal of unconditional love may be, however, it cannot be set in antithesis to justice. Justice, in the biblical tradition, is primarily about the welfare of the weaker members of society. One cannot claim to love those people, in any sense of the word, without being concerned that justice be done to them. In short, while the Christian ideal may call for more than justice, it cannot be construed as calling for less. The ideal of loving one's neighbor, or one's enemies, requires justice as a baseline, the minimal acceptable behavior.[5]

THE APOCALYPTIC PERSPECTIVE

A far more prevalent challenge to the importance of social justice from a Christian perspective comes from a popular way of construing Christian hope for the Second Coming of Christ, for an eschatological judgment.

The New Testament is pervaded by an eschatological, apocalyptic perspective that seems to diminish the importance of life in this world. The issue is expressed most succinctly by Paul in 1 Corinthians in a passage quoted earlier:

> I mean, brothers and sisters, the appointed time has grown
> short; from now on, let even those who have wives be as though

they had none, and those who mourn as though they were not mourning, and those who rejoice as though they were not rejoicing, and those who buy as though they had no possessions, and those who deal with the world as though they had no dealings with it. For the present form of this world is passing away. (7:29–31)

Slaves should not seek their freedom, since the time until the end is short. Why spend time reforming this world when it is passing away? Paul evidently expected the Second Coming of Christ in his own lifetime. He assured the Thessalonians:

We who are alive, who are left until the coming of the Lord, will by no means precede those who have died. For the Lord himself, with a cry of command, with the archangel's call and with the sound of God's trumpet, will descend from heaven, and the dead in Christ will rise first. Then we who are alive, who are left, will be caught up in the clouds together with them to meet the Lord in the air. (1 Thessalonians 4:14–17)

This catching up of the righteous to meet the Lord in the air is known as the Rapture, an idea popularized by the best-selling series of novels *Left Behind*, by Tim LaHaye and Jerry B. Jenkins.[6] The Book of Revelation provides a much fuller scenario, in which the coming of Christ as a warrior from heaven (chapter 19) is followed by a reign of one thousand years; Satan is confined in a pit (chapter 20). At the end of the thousand years, when Satan is released, he will muster the nations, Gog and Magog, for battle, and attack the righteous in Jerusalem, only to be destroyed by fire from heaven and cast into a lake of fire. Then follows a general resurrection and the creation of a new heaven, a new earth, and a new Jerusalem (chapter 21).

In American Protestant tradition, two traditions can be distinguished by the way they map human history onto the Book of Revelation.[7] Postmillennialists believe that the Second Coming of Christ comes after the millennium, a time of peace and prosperity during which his followers spread the Gospel on earth. For American Protestants, including such notable figures as Jonathan Edwards (1703–58), this belief was long dominant. Postmillennial eschatology generally implies an optimistic view of history. Those who held this view traditionally worked to bring about the millennium on earth and were supportive of social causes such as the abolition of slavery.[8]

Premillennialism, in contrast, holds that the Second Coming must take place before the millennium, which can only come after a period of trials and tribulations and the utter destruction of the earth. This understanding of the end-time, a more pessimistic view of history than that of the postmillennialists, was popularized in North America by the Dispensationalist movement, associated with John Nelson Darby, an Anglo-Irish minister who became the leader of the Plymouth Brethren. According to Darby's system, pieced together from the Books of Daniel and Revelation, the last phase of history will begin with the Rapture, as described in 1 Thessalonians. Next comes the Tribulation, the reign of the Antichrist. The latter part of the Tribulation will be almost unbearable, but it will culminate in the battle of Armageddon and the triumph of Christ over Satan.[9] Only then will the millennium follow.

This view of eschatology offers much less room for human initiative and much less reason to improve conditions on earth. Premillennialist theologians have traditionally had little time for social engineering. Cyrus Scofield, author of the best-selling *Scofield Reference Bible*, declared that "the true mission of the church is not the reformation of society. What Christ did not do, the Apostles did not do. Not one of them was a reformer."[10] An eminent evangelical theologian, John Walvoord, assured his readers that "it is not God's purpose in the present age to have social justice or to have all the ills and problems of life removed now."[11] The Christian task was to save souls from the coming wrath of God. "God didn't send me to clean the fishbowl," wrote Hal Lindsey, author of the best-selling book, *The Late Great Planet Earth*. "He sent me to fish."[12]

THE BOOK OF REVELATION

Despite the theological tradition that social reform is useless in view of the impending apocalypse, the Book of Revelation is the book of the New Testament that comes closest to sharing the outrage of the prophets about social abuses.[13] To be sure, Revelation does not advance any social programs, but it is unsparing in its criticism of Rome. Though often oblique, the criticism clearly targets Rome's economic dominance.[14] The beast from the earth "causes all, both small and great, both rich and poor, both free and slave, to be marked on the right hand or the forehead, so that no one can buy or sell who does not have the mark of the beast or the number of its name" (13:16–17). The mark of the beast was the image of the emperor on Roman coins.[15] Revelation 17 paints an indelible portrait of Rome as the whore of Babylon, "clothed in purple and scarlet, and adorned with gold and jewels and pearls, holding in her hand a golden cup full of abominations" (17:4). The following chapter notes that "the kings of the earth have committed fornication with her, and the merchants of the earth have grown rich from the power of her luxury" (18:3). Revelation does not suggest that this situation can be changed by human power; it calls for divine judgment. It is clear, however, that one of the reasons for divine judgment is economic injustice, dramatized by the conspicuous consumption and luxury of Rome. Economic injustice is clearly seen as grounds for divine judgment, and Revelation registers a protest against it. Eschatology, the expectation of an imminent end to the present order, does not, then, lead automatically to social indifference. On the contrary, the expectation of divine judgment lends power to the denunciations of Revelation, just as it lent power to the protests of the Hebrew prophets. A similar prophetic tone can be found in the Epistle of James, which calls on rich people to weep and wail for the miseries that are coming upon them, because they have lived in luxury and defrauded their workers (5:1–6).[16]

CHRIST AGAINST EMPIRE?

In recent years, many scholars have argued that most of the New Testament can be construed as preaching resistance against the Roman empire.[17] Arguably, the exaltation of a figure who had been crucified by the Romans and the symbolic use of the cross were implicitly critical of the empire.[18] Paul is anti-imperial insofar as he advocates service of Christ rather than service of the emperor. But Paul does not make the alternative explicit. He never suggests that service of Christ is incompatible with service of the emperor. The time remaining is short. There is no need for political revolution. On the contrary, he tells the

Romans that everyone should be subject to the governing authorities, "for there is no authority except from God, and those authorities that exist have been instituted by God."[19] While the authenticity of this passage is sometimes questioned,[20] it coheres with the general advice of the apostle not to upset the social order, since the time remaining is short and the form of this world is passing away. His view is not just a matter of political realism.[21] It is a consequence of apocalyptic conviction.

When Paul uses the Greek word *dikaiosyne*, which can mean either "justice" or "righteousness," he usually means righteousness, the condition of being right with God, applied to individuals. Paul was not indifferent to social issues. He took up a collection for the poor of Jerusalem and cooperated in famine relief in Acts 11:27–28. He objects to discrimination and social distinctions within the Christian community, especially in the Lord's supper.[22] But he was no social reformer, any more than he was an anti-imperial rebel. Social concerns were not at the top of Paul's agenda in the short time that he thought remained.

JESUS

For Christians, the basic values are those propounded by Jesus. There is a long-standing debate as to how far the teaching of Jesus was shaped by eschatological expectations, or, to put the matter another way, as to what he meant by the kingdom of God. I do not propose to rehearse that debate here. On the one hand, attempts to cast Jesus as a social reformer, and to deny that he shared the apocalyptic expectations of his time, lack credibility.[23] It is scarcely conceivable that his followers could have cast him in the role of the Son of Man who would come on the clouds of heaven if he himself had expressed no expectation of imminent divine action. On the other hand, if Jesus was an apocalyptic prophet, as Albert Schweitzer and his latter-day followers have maintained,[24] then we must admit that he was a somewhat unusual one, who expressed his message in parables and sayings rather than in apocalyptic visions. Modern debates about the nature of Jesus' message arise from the ambiguity inherent in his sayings and parables. What concerns us here is the significance of his message, as presented in the Synoptic Gospels, for the question of social justice.

Part of the problem of grasping the message of the historical Jesus is that he is presented differently in the individual Gospels. Leaving aside the Gospel of John, which is written in a style very different from that of the Synoptics and has a distinctive theology, there are still notable differences among the first three Gospels. Matthew declares that Jesus did not come to abolish the Law and the Prophets and that not one jot or tittle of the Law will pass away (5:17–18). In the Gospels, Luke is the one that gives most prominence to social concerns.[25]

Luke sets the tone for his Gospel in the first chapter, with the *Magnificat*, the hymn of thanks and praise put on the lips of Mary. After expressing thanks to God for what he has done for Mary herself, the hymn continues:

> He has shown strength with his arm;
>> he has scattered the proud in the thoughts of their
>>> hearts.
> He has brought down the powerful from their thrones,
>> and lifted up the lowly;
> he has filled the hungry with good things,
>> and sent the rich away empty. (1:51–53)

The hymn strikes themes that are familiar from the Hebrew Bible. In 1 Samuel, Hannah, the mother of Samuel, celebrated her pregnancy:

> The LORD makes poor and makes rich;
>   he brings low, he also exalts.
> He raises up the poor from the dust;
>   he lifts the needy from the ash heap,
> to make them sit with princes
>   and inherit a seat of honor. (2:7–8)

The hymns in both Testaments express the desires of the poor and lowly, typically in terms of simple reversal: cast down the mighty and raise up the lowly. We find very similar aspirations in some of the Jewish apocalyptic literature close to New Testament times, especially in the books of Enoch. The *Similitudes of Enoch*, which probably dates from around the time of Jesus, promises that a heavenly figure called "that Son of Man" will raise the kings and the mighty from their couches and thrones, "loosen the reins of the strong," and overturn kings from their thrones and kingdoms (*1 Enoch* 46:4–5). The inequality between the mighty and the lowly, and the resentment that it breeds, is obviously a big part of the problem.

The use of the perfect tense in the Magnificat is evidently proleptic. The rich and the mighty were not actually overthrown in Judea in the time of Jesus, and neither were the hungry filled. We know that when Judea had a famine in the time of Herod the Great (25–24 BCE), the king had ornaments of gold and silver from his palace converted into coinage to buy grain from Egypt.[26] During another famine, in the reign of the emperor Claudius (41–54 CE), Queen Helena of Adiabene, who had converted to Judaism, bought supplies from Egypt and distributed them in Judea.[27] The latter famine is noted in the Book of Acts (11:27–8). The disciples in Antioch took up a collection for the believers in Judea. Throughout much of the first century, banditry was a problem in Judea and Galilee, and this, too, was a sign of desperate need.[28] The Magnificat is an expression of hope rather than of fact, but it acknowledges the problem of social inequity.

Luke has Jesus pick up similar themes at the beginning of his public career. We are told that he came to his hometown of Nazareth on the Sabbath and stood up to read in the synagogue. He chose a passage from the prophet Isaiah:

> The Spirit of the Lord is upon me,
>   because he has anointed me
>   to bring good news to the poor.
> He has sent me to proclaim release to the captives
>   and recovery of sight to the blind,
>   to let the oppressed go free,
> to proclaim the year of the Lord's favor. (Luke 4:18–19;
>   Isaiah 61:1–2)

The "year of the Lord's favor" was the jubilee year, the time of remission of debt, when all people, in theory, were supposed to return to their ancestral property (Leviticus 25:8–17). By New Testament times, the jubilee year had come to represent more generally the time of salvation.[29] Jesus, on Luke's account, was promising to bring this prophecy to fulfillment.[30] Later, when John the Baptist sends messengers from prison to ask whether Jesus is "the one that is to come," the messiah who would bring about the deliverance of Israel, Jesus tells them:

> Go and tell John what you have seen and heard: the blind receive their sight, the lame walk, the lepers are cleansed, the

deaf hear, the dead are raised, the poor have good news
brought to them. (Luke 7:22; Matthew 11:4–5)

Bringing good news to the poor is a big part of what Jesus was
about.

Admittedly, no other Gospel states this mission as insis-
tently as Luke. Here, the difference between Matthew and
Luke can be seen in the Beatitudes, in the Sermon on the
Mount in Matthew and the corresponding Sermon on the Plain
in Luke. The Lukan version is simple: "Blessed are you who are
poor, for yours is the kingdom of God" (6:20). The Matthean
version reads: "Blessed are the poor in spirit, for theirs is the
kingdom of heaven" (5:3). Again, Luke reads: "Blessed are you
who are hungry now, for you will be filled" (6:21). Matthew
qualifies: "Blessed are those who hunger and thirst for righteousness, for they will be filled" (5:6). Matthew places the stress
on spiritual dispositions rather than on economic conditions.
The expression "poor in spirit" recalls Isaiah 66:2: "This is the
one to whom I will look, to the humble and contrite in spirit,
who trembles at my word." To be sure, the "poor in spirit" are
also likely to be poor in material goods and to belong to the
lowly of society, but the emphasis is different.

In both versions of the Beatitudes, the poor (in spirit) are
assured that theirs is the kingdom of God/heaven. This again
admits of different interpretations. It may mean that the lowly will be exalted when God's kingdom comes to pass on earth.
Alternatively, it may mean that they will go to heaven when
they die, and this is how it has usually been taken in the Christian tradition. But it may also mean that they are pleasing to
God in the present—in effect, that they have already entered

the kingdom that Jesus is proclaiming. On the latter interpretation, Jesus is not promising them a reversal of fortunes but rather, in effect, assuring them of their value in the eyes of God despite their poverty.

A few other statements in the Beatitudes, however, suggest more material rewards. Satisfaction of hunger, as formulated in Luke, is unequivocal. Regardless of when or how the hunger will be satisfied, the Lukan beatitude recognizes that hunger in the present is a problem that needs to be addressed. Matthew's formulation moves the focus away from physical hunger. It makes a difference here whether the word *dikaiosyne* is translated as "righteousness" or as "justice." If as justice, then it implies a critique of an unjust society and a concern for material well-being in this world.[31]

Matthew's third beatitude declares the meek blessed, for they shall inherit the earth. The meek, in this context, are probably the lowly, who are victims rather than perpetrators of power and violence. The promise that the meek will inherit the earth seems to imply an eschatological reversal of fortunes. It suggests discontent with the present order, which is dominated by the rich and powerful. Luke makes this reversal more explicit by adding woes:

> But woe to you who are rich,
> for you have received your consolation.
> Woe to you who are full now,
> for you will be hungry. (6:24–26)

Other passages, too, suggest that the poor will have a special place in the kingdom of God. The parable of the great banquet in Luke 14:15–24 / Matthew 22:1–14 tells how a man invited guests to a banquet, but they declined, for various reasons. He told his servant: "Go out at once into the streets and lanes of the town and bring in the poor, the crippled, the blind, and the lame." The implication is that those who are outcasts in the present will find a place in the kingdom of God, while the privileged will miss out through indifference. The point is made more forcefully in the story of the rich man and Lazarus the beggar (Luke 16:19–31). In the afterlife, their fortunes are reversed. When the rich man appeals to Abraham, he is told: "Remember that during your lifetime you received your good things, and Lazarus in like manner evil things, but now he is comforted here and you are in agony." We are not told that the rich man was especially wicked, except that he does not seem to have done much to help Lazarus, who was sitting at his gate. The point is simply that the gap between rich and poor, which is implicitly unjust, will be reversed in the kingdom.

There are at least occasional hints that this reversal will happen in this life, not only in the age to come. In Mark 10:29–30, Jesus tells his disciples:

> Truly I tell you, there is no one who has left house or brothers or sisters or mother or father or children or fields, for my sake and for the sake of the good news, who will not receive a hundredfold now in this age—houses, brothers and sisters, mothers and children, and fields, with persecutions—and in the age to come eternal life.

The reference to persecutions seems to be a gloss to temper the optimism. At the least, this passage shows that some followers of Jesus were thinking in terms of reversing the present economic order.

Some other purported indications of concern with economic welfare are not so clear. The Lord's Prayer (Matthew

6:9–13; Luke 11:2–4) asks unambiguously for "bread," the basic necessity of life.[32] It also asks God to forgive us our debts as we also have forgiven our debtors. The Gospel of Luke, however, asks for forgiveness of sins, rather than debts. In fact, debt was a standard metaphor for sin in late Second Temple Judaism, so it is not clear whether Jesus was teaching people to pray for debt relief.[33]

Again, there can be little doubt that taxes were burdensome in the early Roman empire, all the more so since Jews also paid tax to the temple.[34] Jesus apparently paid the taxes without protest. According to Matthew 17:24–27, he commented, with respect to the temple tax, that "children of the king" should not have to pay tax. Nonetheless, he told Peter to pay it to avoid scandal. The fact that Peter is to pay it by taking a coin from the mouth of a fish does not inspire great confidence in the historicity of the story. The acceptance of the tax is also reflected in Matthew 22:21: "Render to Caesar the things that are Caesar's." These stories are in practical agreement with the position later articulated at greater length by Paul in Romans 13:1, where he tells everyone to be subject to the authorities. If there is resistance to empire here, it is subtle indeed. The primary concern appears to be avoiding conflict with the Roman authorities.[35] It may be, however, that the story was told by early Christians to distinguish their Teacher, and themselves, from the Zealots, who actually withheld tribute and started the revolt against Rome in 66 CE.[36]

Jesus eventually came into conflict with the Roman authorities anyway. According to the Gospels, he created two disruptions in Jerusalem that might have led the authorities to intervene. One was the driving out of the money changers from the temple (Mark 11:15–17 and parallels). This action, however, was not so much a protest against economic exploitation as against the violation of the sanctity of the temple.[37] The other was his entry into Jerusalem riding on a donkey, greeted by crowds shouting, "Hosanna to the Son of David" (11:1–10 and parallels). Whatever Jesus might have intended to signify by this action, the Romans would surely have seen it as an act of rebellion, an attempt to restore a native Judean monarchy. That action, however, raises the question of messianic expectation, which goes beyond the range of our discussion.[38] Messianism surely entailed the hope for a just society and a rejection of foreign imperial rule, but these concerns were interwoven with a complex web of religious and political traditions.

WHAT GOOD NEWS?

What, then, is the good news that is preached to the poor? Is it that "God loves the poor and hates the rich?"[39] Surely not. Jesus is said to have loved the rich young man who could not bring himself to sell all he had and give to the poor.[40] Even though it is easier for a camel to pass through the eye of a needle than for someone who is rich to enter the kingdom of heaven, it is not impossible with God. But wealth is thought to be more of a hindrance than a help in attaining the kingdom.

Jesus did not preach any form of a prosperity gospel, even one with deferred eschatological payout. The promise of "a hundredfold now in this age" is an outlier in this respect. What we find consistently in the Gospels is an ethic of detachment, which depreciates the value of worldly goods. Luke 12:16–21 tells the story of the rich man who built new barns so that he had ample goods stored up for many years, but that very night God took his life. The rich man was no different from anyone who worries over a retirement account. He was only exercising the basic human instinct for self-preservation. The evangelist draws the lesson: "Be on guard against all kinds of greed, for one's life does not consist in the abundance of possessions" (Luke 12:15). The point is elaborated a few verses later:

> Do not worry about your life, what you will eat, or about your body, what you will wear. For life is more than food, and the body more than clothing. Consider the ravens: they neither sow nor reap, they have neither storehouse nor barn, and yet God feeds them. Of how much more value are you than the birds! And can any of you by worrying add a single hour to your span of life? . . . Consider the lilies, how they grow: they neither toil nor spin; yet I tell you, even Solomon in all his glory was not clothed like one of these. But if God so clothes the grass of the field, which is alive today and tomorrow is thrown into the oven, how much more will he clothe you— you of little faith! (12:22–28; cf. Matthew 6:25–34)

Faith here is not a matter of belief. It is a matter of trust in the providence of the creator. This is perhaps the hardest demand made anywhere in the Bible, for it asks us to let go of our instinct to worry about our own welfare.

The ethic of radical detachment is embodied in Jesus' instructions to his disciples.[41] In Mark, "he ordered them to take nothing for their journey except a staff; no bread, no bag, no money in their belts, but to wear sandals and not to put on two tunics."[42] In Matthew and Luke, they are even denied sandals.[43] They are told to take no payment,[44] but to accept lodging and food, for the laborer is worthy of payment. The viability of this radical itinerant lifestyle depends, of course, on a symbiotic relationship with people of goodwill who have possessions and are able to offer hospitality. The lifestyle could also be subject to abuse. The *Didache*, written early in the second century CE, sets a limit on how long a prophet could stay: "Let him not stay more than one day, or if need be a second as well; but if he stays three days, he is a false prophet" (*Didache* 11:5). Also, if a prophet asked for money, he was a false prophet (*Didache* 11:6).[45] Nonetheless, the lifestyle of the itinerant preachers represents an ideal of detachment from worldly goods.

After the death of Jesus, his followers in Jerusalem experimented with communal living.[46]

> All who believed were together and had all things in common; they would sell their possessions and goods and distribute the proceeds to all, as any had need. (Acts 2:44–45)

We are told that there was not a needy person among them, for those who owned land or houses sold them and gave the proceeds to the apostles, who distributed them according to the needs of the community. The practice of selling property and donating the proceeds appears to have been voluntary, although Ananias and Sapphira were struck dead for withholding part of what they had received. The problem here may have been the deception rather than the partial donation. The practice of donating goods was not absolute, in any case. Peter still had a house when he escaped from prison (12:12), and the custom of breaking bread in homes (2:46) requires that some members of the community retain houses in which to host the gatherings.

The practice of sharing possessions in Acts was predicated on the expectation that the Second Coming was imminent.

It could not be sustained over a lengthy period of time. The proceeds from the sale of property were used up. Already in Acts 11, the Jerusalem community fell into need in a time of famine, and the apostles had to take up a collection in Antioch. Since the people in Antioch contributed according to their individual means, they clearly had private property. The renunciation of worldly goods, then, had to be modified in practice in light of necessity.

Whether the preaching of Jesus was likewise predicated on the expectation of imminent divine intervention is more difficult to say. The Sermon on the Mount recommends that people lay up treasure in heaven rather than on earth (Matthew 6:19–21),[47] and we have seen the promise to the disciples of rewards in this life, but on the whole Jesus seems to emphasize trust in the creator rather than expectation of future judgment. So, for example, one should love one's enemies, for God makes his sun rise on the evil and on the good and sends rain on the righteous and the unrighteous (5:45). In that case, love of one's enemies is not predicated on the hope that they will be punished in the future. But the parable of the wheat and the weeds (13:24–30), in contrast, recommends that wheat and weeds be allowed to grow together until the harvest, when the weeds will be separated out and burnt. In the Gospels, the expectation of a final judgment always casts a shadow.

RENUNCIATION AND JUSTICE

Jesus' preaching on renunciation does not address the problem of injustice directly in the manner of the Hebrew prophets, but it arguably addresses it in a more profound manner.

The root of injustice is greed. If people were not intent on accumulating wealth and in rising above their fellows, there would be no injustice to begin with. To be sure, this way of looking at society is idealistic. Human nature being what it is, the likelihood of overcoming injustice by renouncing greed is virtually nonexistent. Indeed, as Matthew 26:11 acknowledges, "you always have the poor with you." In the Hebrew Bible, it was possible to try to shape society by reforming laws, which, at least in theory and occasionally in practice, had some coercive power. The New Testament, in contrast, is not legislating for society and can only exhort or denounce. In this respect, the position of Jesus is comparable to that of the Prophets rather than that of the Pentateuch/Torah.

The New Testament holds out the prospect that the injustices of the present will be erased in the future. In the meantime, however, something must be done to ease the plight of the poor. Here the New Testament, beginning with Jesus, follows the lead of Second Temple Judaism in advocating almsgiving.[48] When the rich young man asked Jesus for advice, Jesus told him that he lacked one thing: "Go sell what you own, and give your money to the poor, and you will have treasure in heaven." Likewise, he tells his followers in Luke 12:32–34:

> Do not be afraid, little flock, for it is your Father's good pleasure to give you the kingdom. Sell your possessions, and give alms. Make purses for yourselves that do not wear out, an unfailing treasure in heaven, where no thief comes near and no moth destroys. For where your treasure is, there your heart will be also.

If the treasure is in heaven, that is presumably where the kingdom will be, too. There are several instances of almsgiving in the Book of Acts (9:36; 10:2, 4).

Almsgiving is also at issue in the judgment scene in the Gospel of Matthew (25:31–46). Here Jesus separates the sheep from the goats. The criteria for admission into the kingdom are laid out. Those who are admitted are told:

> For I was hungry and you gave me food, I was thirsty and you gave me something to drink, I was a stranger and you welcomed me, I was naked and you gave me clothing, I was sick and you took care of me, I was in prison and you visited me.

When did they do these things? they ask, and are told: "Just as you did it to one of the least of these my brothers [as in the Greek; NRSV paraphrase: one of the least of those who are members of my family], you did it to me." Those who failed to perform such acts of charity are consigned to eternal punishment.

There has been debate as to whether "the least of these my brothers" means the poor wherever they are found or just those in the community of the Jesus movement.[49] But whatever the evangelist may have intended, it is impossible to restrict the application of the passage to the followers of Jesus. One does not have to be a Christian to feed the hungry—or to be hungry. The merit of the act does not depend on whether the hungry person is Christian.

The judgment scene in Matthew 25 arguably gives the bottom line on biblical values, at least for Matthew. The criteria for judgment are based entirely on our treatment of our fellow human beings, especially the weakest among them. The judge in this scene does not ask people whether they believe in Christ or whether they go to the temple. On this point, the evangelist is fully in agreement with Amos and the eighth-century prophets who spoke for all in need.

Whether the practice of almsgiving is an adequate response to the problem of poverty is very questionable. It is arguable that this problem can be addressed only by reforming the structure of society. The Prophets and Revelation recognize this in their way, although they look for divine intervention rather than human action to bring about the change. But the advocacy of almsgiving in the Gospels and elsewhere in the New Testament is by no means negligible. It reminds us that the plight of the poor is a high priority in the biblical tradition. The Bible never states that almsgiving must be left to individuals. Governments also have a responsibility to see that needs are met. In earlier times, the responsibility primarily fell to the king. The emphasis on individual almsgiving arises to fill a need left by the lack of benevolent institutional leadership.

IF A MAN WORK NOT . . .

Given the biblical attitude toward kings' and governments' responsibility to help the poor, it is somewhat ironic that socially conservative Christians in recent decades have been preponderantly opposed to social programs. For many, the biblical view of social welfare is summarized in a passage in 2 Thessalonians, typically cherry-picked out of context:

> Now we command you, beloved, in the name of our Lord Jesus Christ, to keep away from believers who are living in idleness and not according to the tradition that they received from us. For you yourselves know how you ought to imitate us; we were not idle when we were with you, and we did not eat anyone's bread without paying for it; but with toil and labor we worked night and day, so that we might not burden any

> of you . . . For even when we were with you, we gave you this command: Anyone unwilling to work should not eat. For we hear that some of you are living in idleness, mere busybodies, not doing any work. Now such persons we command and exhort in the Lord Jesus Christ to do their work quietly and to earn their own living. (3:6–12)

Socially conservative commentators have pounced on this passage as the definitive expression of "the biblical view." "America has rewarded laziness and we have called it welfare," says John Hagee, a Fundamentalist megachurch leader from Texas. "The Bible says, 'the man who does not work, should not eat.' I know the liberals hate that verse but read it and weep! It is God's position."[50]

2 Thessalonians appears to have been written in part as a corrective to 1 Thessalonians. In the first letter, in a passage cited at the beginning of this chapter, Paul expressed his belief that the Rapture, when believers were caught up to meet the Lord in the air, would happen in his lifetime. In 2 Thessalonians, which many scholars believe was not written by Paul,[51] there is an attempt to cool the eschatological expectation:

> As to the coming of our Lord Jesus Christ and our being gathered together to him, we beg you, brothers and sisters, not to be quickly shaken in mind or alarmed, either by spirit or by word or by letter, as though from us, to the effect that the day of the Lord is already here. Let no one deceive you in any way. (2:1–3)

It may be that the idle people of whom chapter 3 complains were carried away with the expectation of the Second Coming and had abandoned their worldly work. Or perhaps the epistle refers to the itinerant "false prophets" of whom we read in the *Didache*, who overstayed their welcome and were freeloading off the community. What is clear in any case is that 2 Thessalonians is trying to correct an abuse. It is not formulating "the biblical position" on the treatment of the poor.

In fact, the New Testament has a dominant position on the treatment of the poor. Feeding the hungry and taking care of those in need is a high priority for Christians. To be sure, there are abuses, which need to be addressed, but no person of goodwill can allow the occasional abuses to detract from the fundamental importance of providing for the poor as a biblical value.

The Authority of the Bible

A T the beginning of this book we considered whether it is even possible to speak of biblical values. The question has several ramifications.

Strictly speaking, the Bible does not mean anything until it is interpreted. Appeal to textual agency ("but the Bible says") is far too simple an evasion of the reader's responsibility. The more important question, however, is whether it is possible to interpret the Bible with a degree of objectivity so that people who approach it with different prejudices and faith commitments can reach consensus. I hold that a degree of objectivity is possible. Interpretations are always contestable, but in fact there is very little dispute about the meaning of the biblical passages we have discussed. No one doubts that Deuteronomy 7 mandates the slaughter of the Canaanites or that Matthew 25 prioritizes feeding the hungry. Even where the exact meaning of the text is disputed (what is meant by "the lyings of a woman" in Leviticus? what constitutes unnatural intercourse for women in Romans 1?), the range of disagreement is circumscribed and arises from the laconic nature of the text rather than from the philosophical difficulty of interpretation.

A more substantial problem is posed by the diversity of positions within the Bible. The Sermon on the Mount highlights several issues on which Jesus takes positions at variance with the Law of Moses, notably the injunction to turn the other cheek rather than to retaliate and the command to love one's enemies. Yet the same sermon says that not one jot or tittle of the Law will go unfulfilled. Neither is there a simple progression on these issues between the Testaments. The New Testament closes with a fantasy of vengeance in the Book of Revelation that seems to be alien in spirit to the Sermon on the Mount. If we are to appeal to biblical values, it is necessary to have some hierarchy, some criteria, by which the values can be assessed. Isolated verses, taken out of context, are not necessarily representative of "the biblical view." In Chapter 9 we considered the claim of John Hagee that 2 Thessalonians 3:10 ("anyone unwilling to work should not eat") is "God's position" on the subject of welfare. Yet Matthew 25 condemns those who do not feed the hungry to eternal punishment. President Trump's first attorney general, Jeff Sessions, cited "the Apostle Paul and his clear and wise command in Romans 13 to obey the laws of government" as justification for the policy of separating the children of illegal immigrants from their parents. But as Stephen Colbert aptly commented: "If he just read a little bit further into Romans 13 he would have found: 'Love thy neighbor as thyself. Love does no harm to a neighbor. Therefore, love is the fulfillment of the law' " (13:10).[1] Which of these verses should take precedence?

For Christians, at least, this question is answered explicitly by Jesus. The greatest commandments are those that demand love of God and love of one's neighbor.[2] Paul, in the passage that Sessions and then Colbert cited, makes this clear: "The commandments . . . are summed up in this word, 'love your neighbor as yourself.' "[3] But the Hebrew Bible, too, has clear priorities. Concern for the poor and hungry is not contingent on their work ethic, and concern for the alien is not contingent on their legal status. Widows, orphans, and aliens are repeatedly singled out as those who need special care. Individual verses must be weighed in context. Not every statement in the Bible can be taken uncritically as "God's position."

The most acute problem confronting anyone who speaks of biblical values, however, is undoubtedly the Bible's apparent endorsement of positions that now seem reprehensible. The defenders of slavery in the nineteenth century who argued that the Bible never condemns it were unquestionably right. The story of the conquest and utter destruction of Canaan, even though it may be fantasy rather than history, lends ready support to the use of violence as a means of settling disputes. The strictures of 1 Timothy that a woman should learn in silence and that she must not teach or have authority over a man are no longer socially acceptable. It is all too easy for the atheistic scientist Richard Dawkins to argue that the Bible promotes "a system of morals which any civilized modern person, whether religious or not, would find—I can put it no more gently—obnoxious."[4] Dawkins, like many critics of the Bible, may be one-sided in his critique, but his arguments are not without foundation.

Disagreement is not simply a matter of judging the Bible by modern standards. As Nicholas Wolterstorff has written, à propos of the slaughter of the Canaanites:

> The problem is not that we have absorbed modern enlight-ened views about ethical and theological matters and are, as such, morally offended by the picture of genocidal slaughter in Israel's conquest of the land as reported in the book of Joshua, and religiously offended by the picture in Deuteronomy of God as enjoining such slaughter. Our problem is rather that we have been formed in our understanding of God by the bib-lical acclamations of God as just and loving and shaped in our ethical thinking by God's command to do justice and love mercy. But the picture of God that we get in Deuteronomy and Joshua seems in flagrant conflict with those acclamations and with that command.[5]

Equally, the acceptance of slavery and the strictures against women fall short of the ideal of loving one's neighbor and of the utopian ideal where there is neither slave nor free, male nor female.

The Bible is often called the Good Book. In fact, it is more of a proverbial curate's egg: good in spots. The good parts are considerable. No other document from the ancient world ex-hibits the passion for justice or the concern for the vulnerable members of society that we find in the Old Testament books of the prophets.[6] Despite the dominion granted to humanity over the earth in Genesis, the sabbatical laws of the Hebrew Bible show great concern for the sustainability of the land. The idea that we should love our enemies (Matthew 5:44) is an excep-tional ideal by any standard, ancient or modern, as is the ideal of turning the other cheek. Even Dawkins grants that Jesus must be considered one of the great ethical innovators of history.[7] But Dawkins is right that Jesus did not blindly follow the scriptures he had inherited and that the New Testament has its own share of moral problems. If the preaching of the prophets or the Sermon on the Mount still inspires us, this is not because they are found in the Bible but because they appeal to principles that are compelling on broad humanistic grounds.

The humanistic principle of ethics fundamental to all others is some formulation of the Golden Rule, that we should do unto others as we would have them do unto us, or the negative formulation of the Talmud, "What is hateful to you, do not do to your fellow."[8] This principle is affirmed in many cultures, East and West.[9] It is also the principle underlying the concern for the alien in the Book of Exodus: "You shall not oppress a resident alien; you know the heart of an alien, for you were aliens in the land of Egypt" (23:9). It is explicitly formulated by Jesus in the Sermon on the Mount (Matthew 7:12; Luke 6:31). The Bible provides considerable support for this principle, but not everything in the Bible is in accordance with it.

BIBLICAL AUTHORITY?

What, then, should we make of biblical authority?

Not everything in the Bible can be accepted as a divine command even when it is presented as such. Wolterstorff has noted that the supposed divine command to extirpate the Canaanites in Deuteronomy 7 is found in a narrative now widely thought to be fictional. Archeological evidence, or lack thereof, shows that there was no violent conquest of Canaan by the

Israelites. So, Wolterstorff infers, "if there never was a foreign people invading the land of Canaan and taking it by conquest, then there was also no such thing as God mandating a foreign people to do it."[10] The implications of this observation are more far-reaching than Wolterstorff acknowledges. The story of the revelation on Mount Sinai is no less fictional than that of the conquest of Canaan. The Ten Commandments were not boomed from a thunderstorm. Whatever we may believe about divine inspiration, the biblical texts are incontrovertibly the work of human authors and shaped by human purposes to at least some degree.

Similarly, not all who spoke in the name of the Lord can be accepted as truly uttering divine words. The prophet Jeremiah is caustic about prophets who "speak visions from their own minds, not from the mouth of the Lord" (23:16). If we accept an oracle of Jeremiah or Amos as truly a word of the Lord, what this means is that we think it is right and good. But this is a human judgment, informed, to be sure, by the whole biblical tradition and by much else, but a human judgment nonetheless, for which we must take responsibility. Critics have rightly objected to ascribing agency to the Bible, to claiming that "the Bible says" this or that. A greater problem is the tendency to ascribe divine authority to it indiscriminately, regardless of its content.

THE BIBLE AS TRADITION

The Bible, in its different forms, is the deepest layer of Jewish and Christian tradition. As such, it has a major role in shaping these traditions. A person who found nothing to affirm in the

Bible would have no reason to identify as Jewish or Christian. But those who stand in the Jewish or Christian tradition do not necessarily have to affirm everything in their respective scriptures. Rather, what a tradition does is provide a context for thought and argument that shapes the questions we consider important. It also urges basic principles on us, but these must be conceived broadly and not reduced to dogmatic stands on specific issues.

Far from being a systematic, unified treatise, the Bible has the character of a running argument. Beginning with the opening chapters of Genesis, different viewpoints are juxtaposed and not resolved. The Pentateuch/Torah binds together quite different theologies in Leviticus and Deuteronomy. The New Testament embraces different attitudes toward Jewish law and many other topics. This is not simply a matter of juxtaposing different viewpoints: they are often in conflict. The prophets are sharply critical even of long-standing traditions. Amos suggests that the Exodus is no different from the movements of other peoples (9:8). Jeremiah mocks those who place their trust in the temple of the Lord (7:4) and says that the Law of the Lord has been turned into falsehood by the lying pens of scribes (8:8). In the Sermon on the Mount, Jesus freely supersedes that which "was said to them of old."

Criticism of received tradition is itself a biblical value. Some of the most fruitful work on biblical theology in recent years has used dialogical models to capture this sense of ongoing debate.[11] The Bible is not a book of definitive answers. Ethical issues always depend on context. That is why the sweeping commandments of the Decalogue are followed by laws that take specific circumstances into account: if X, then Y, but if Z, the decision may be different. As Qoheleth (Ecclesiastes) says, there is a season for everything, a time to kill as well as a time to heal, a time to hate as well as a time to love (3:1–8). The tradition informs our decisions by illustrating options, but it does not make our decisions for us.

Equally, criticism of one's own society is a biblical value. The Hebrew prophets provide a blistering critique of Israelite and Judean society. Amos saw northern Israel as a sinful kingdom that God would wipe off the face of the earth (9:9). His contemporary Isaiah saw in the southern kingdom of Judah a "sinful nation, people laden with iniquity, offspring who do evil, children who deal corruptly" (1:4), and he saw the devastation of the land by the Assyrians as divine punishment. The blessings of the covenant were predicated on righteous behavior. It is ironic, then, that some Christians brook no criticism of modern Israel and that the Billy Graham Evangelistic Association considers support for the state of Israel a basic biblical principle. No doubt, people who care about the Bible should wish Israel well, but if they are guided by biblical principles, they should insist that the welfare of Israel, and its claim to its land, depends on the practice of justice.[12] There is nothing biblical about unconditional support for Israel or for any other government or state.

Much in the Bible can inspire and challenge the modern world. It remains a relevant resource on political and social issues if it is used judiciously. But the mere fact that something is found in the Bible is in itself no guarantee of right conduct or justice or anything else. Interpreters remain responsible for what they take from the Bible. Biblical values must be sifted and evaluated, and the Bible itself provides broad criteria by which to do so. To treat the Bible as a magical book of answers to modern problems amounts to a refusal to grapple with it seriously.

Critics of the Old Testament accuse its defenders of cherry-picking the good parts to offset the parts used as warrants for intolerance and violence. The cherry-picking is not arbitrary, however. It is based on priorities that are affirmed within the Bible itself and that also accord with humanistic principles.

Walter Benjamin famously said that there is no document of civilization that is not at the same time a document of barbarism.[13] This is as true of the Bible as it is of any other document. Even the Exodus is the prelude to the conquest of Canaan. But cultural documents should not be discarded for that reason. Given the reverence in which the Bible has been held for two thousand years, it is an exceptionally powerful source of effective rhetoric. That rhetoric can be used "for the cause of truth and to defend the right" (Psalm 45:4); it should not be abandoned to those who would use it in the cause of bigotry. And if the Bible also reminds us of the barbarism in our past, and even in our present, this, too, can be salutary. The Bible is important as a reminder that our history, and indeed our present, is flawed, even as it also reminds us of the higher ideals to which we should aspire.

Notes

Citations from Philo, Josephus, and other classical authors are from the Loeb Classical Library unless otherwise indicated.

WHAT ARE BIBLICAL VALUES?

1. *Wall Street Journal*, October 18, 2012.

2. Compare Friedman and Dolansky, *The Bible Now;* Flannery and Werline, *The Bible in Political Debate.* Friedman and Dolansky confine their analysis to the Hebrew Bible.

3. For excellent such studies, see Barton, *Ethics in Ancient Israel;* Hays, *The Moral Vision of the New Testament.*

4. For a fuller discussion see my book, *The Bible after Babel*, 1–25.

5. Martin, *The Pedagogy of the Bible*, 31; Martin, *Sex and the Single Savior,* 1. See now Martin, *Biblical Truths*, 95, on the problem of speaking of the Bible as an agent.

6. See especially Fish, *Is There a Text in This Class?*

7. Martin, *The Pedagogy of the Bible*, 70.

8. See further my essay "Historical-Critical Methods."

9. Even the authors of *The Postmodern Bible* allow that "deconstructive reading relies necessarily on traditional historical criticism as 'an indispensable guardrail' or 'safeguard' for reading. If it were not so, Derrida cautions, 'one could say just anything at all.' " Aichele et al., *The Postmodern Bible*, 64, with reference to Derrida, *Limited Inc.*, 141.

10. See, e.g., Sherwood, *A Biblical Text and Its Afterlives.*

11. Alter, *The Pleasures of Reading*, 224.

12. Martin, *Sex and the Single Savior*, 16.

13. See Setzer and Shefferman, eds., *The Bible and American Culture*, 101–9.

14. Compare Matthew 22:34–40; Luke 10:25–28. Translations of biblical texts follow the New Revised Standard Version unless otherwise indicated.

15. The degree of continuity is disputed. See the thorough discussion by Meier, *A Marginal Jew*, 4:499–522.

16. Philo, *Special Laws* 2.63 (trans. F. H. Colson, *Philo VII*, Loeb Classical Library [Cambridge: Harvard University Press, 1937], 347).

17. Yarbro Collins, "The Reception of the Torah in Mark," 237.

18. Meier, *A Marginal Jew*,, 4:513.

19. Sifra, *Qedoshim*, 4; Meier, *A Marginal Jew*, 4:514.

20. See the sensitive discussion in Barton, *Ethics in Ancient Israel*.

21. See Coogan, *The Ten Commandments*, 113–26, on the selective observance of the commandments.

22. Sommer, *Revelation and Authority*, 146.

23. Ibid., 147–87.

24. See, e.g., D. Wright, *Inventing God's Law*.

25. Hayes, *What's Divine about Divine Law?*

26. Matthew 5, passim.

27. Berman, "The History of Legal Theory"; LeFebvre, *Collections, Codes, and Torah*, 1–54.

28. Jackson, *Wisdom-Laws*.

29. For a humorous treatment of the difficulties of "living biblically" in a modern city see Jacobs, *The Year of Living Biblically*.

30. Gustafson, "The Place of Scripture in Christian Ethics," 141: "there is a dialectic between more intuitive moral judgments and both scriptural and nonscriptural principles and values."

31. Farley, *Just Love*, 194.

32. Ricoeur, *Essays in Biblical Interpretation*, 95. See Farley, *Just Love*, 195.

33. Trible, *Texts of Terror*, 65–91.

34. Galatians 3:16, usually translated as "faith in Jesus Christ."

35. See now Morgan, *Roman Faith and Christian Faith*, 212–306.

36. Hays, *The Faith of Jesus Christ*. See the nuanced discussion in Morgan, *Roman Faith and Christian Faith*, 265–82.

37. 1 Corinthians 6:9–10.

38. Sanders, *Paul, the Law, and the Jewish People*, 95.
39. Hays, *The Faith of Jesus Christ*, 211.

CHAPTER 1. FRAMES OF REFERENCE

1. Clifford, *Creation Accounts*, 73–98.
2. The classic work is Gunkel, *Creation and Chaos*. See also Day, *God's Conflict with the Dragon and the Sea*; Scoggins Ballentine, *The Conflict Myth and the Biblical Tradition*.
3. Clifford, *Creation Accounts*, 74–82.
4. Harlow, "After Adam," especially 184.
5. Clifford, *Creation Accounts*, 106.
6. E.g., Carlson and Longman, *Science, Creation, and the Bible*, 121.
7. See further Yarbro Collins, *The Combat Myth*.
8. Levenson, *Creation and the Persistence of Evil*, 27.
9. See my essay "The Biblical Precedent for Natural Theology."
10. For a sampling of nineteenth-century polemics on the subject of evolution see Setzer and Sheffernan, *The Bible and American Culture*, 158–73. See also the overview in Hendel, *The Book of Genesis*, 145–95.
11. D. Wilkinson, "Reading Genesis 1–3," especially 132–41.
12. Ibid., 130.
13. Enns, *The Evolution of Adam*, 137: "literalism is not an option."
14. D. Wilkinson, "Reading Genesis 1–3," 136.
15. Robinson, *The Death of Adam*, 39.
16. See, e.g., W. Brown, *The Seven Pillars of Creation*, 49–59.
17. Ibid., 57. David Wilkinson, in "Reading Genesis 1–3," 138–39, also considers this possibility. John Haught, in *Science and Religion*, 106, comments: "A great deal of ink has been spilled in attempts to show that big bang physics has made the theological idea of creation intellectually respectable once again."
18. Stephen Hawking, in *A Brief History of Time*, 140–41, entertains the possibility that "the universe is completely self-contained, having no boundary or edge," leaving no place for a creator.
19. Polkinghorne, *Serious Talk*, 64.
20. For a good exposition, see Smith, *The Priestly Vision of Genesis 1*.
21. Römer, *The Invention of God*, 141–59.
22. This point will be important when we discuss the creation of humanity as "male and female," in Chapter 4.

23. Barr, *The Garden of Eden*, 1–20.

24. Lanfer, *Remembering Eden*, 7.

25. Barr, *The Garden of Eden*, 11.

26. Kugel, *The Traditions of the Bible*, 94.

27. Meyers, *Rediscovering Eve*, 63.

28. Levenson, *Sinai and Zion*, 15–86.

29. Levenson, *The Love of God*, 1–58.

30. Sanders, *Paul and Palestinian Judaism*, 75.

31. For a sensitive discussion see Kaminsky, *Yet I Loved Jacob*.

32. Philo, *On the Migration of Abraham*, 89–93; Collins, *The Invention of Judaism*, 134–42.

33. Barr, *Biblical Faith and Natural Theology*.

34. Philo, *On the Decalogue*, 58.

35. Collins, *The Apocalyptic Imagination*, 53–106.

36. Ibid., 107–42.

37. *2 Esdras* 7:30–31; Collins, *The Apocalyptic Imagination*, 242–64.

38. Collins, *Apocalypticism in the Dead Sea Scrolls*, 91–129.

39. Reynolds and Stuckenbruck, *The Jewish Apocalyptic Tradition*.

40. German: *Endzeit gleicht Urzeit*.

41. Yarbro Collins, *The Combat Myth*.

42. See, e.g., Boyer, *When Time Shall Be No More*.

CHAPTER 2. A RIGHT TO LIFE?

1. Hunt, *Inventing Human Rights*, 20.

2. Wolterstorff, *Justice*, 65.

3. Wolterstorff, *Justice*, 53–64; Ishay, *The History of Human Rights*, 15–62.

4. See especially Moyn, *The Last Utopia*.

5. Wolterstorff, *Justice*, 90.

6. Cassin, "Religions et droits de l'homme," 4:98, translated in Ishay, *The History of Human Rights*, 19. For an attempt by a biblical scholar to find a precedent for human rights in the Hebrew Bible, specifically in Deuteronomy, see Otto, "Human Rights."

7. Barr, "Ancient Biblical Laws," especially 24–25.

8. Exodus 20:13; Deuteronomy 5:17. In the Catholic, Anglican, and Lutheran traditions, this is the fifth commandment. In the Hebrew Bible and other Protestant traditions, it is the sixth.

9. Coogan, *The Ten Commandments*, 80; Miller, *The Ten Command-ments*, 223. The verb does not have a single specific meaning "to murder." The translation of the word has to be determined by context rather than purely by philology.

10. De Vaux, *Studies in Old Testament Sacrifice*, 71.

11. So Levenson, *The Death and Resurrection*, 9.

12. See further my essay "Faith without Works."

13. See the classic essay of Phyllis Trible, "The Daughter of Jephtah."

14. See the discussion of this passage in Levenson, *The Death and Resurrection*, 5–8.

15. Friedman and Dolansky, *The Bible Now*, 126–28.

16. Philo, *Hypothetica* 7.1–2 (trans. F. H. Colson, *Philo IX*, Loeb Classical Library [Cambridge: Harvard University Press, 1967], 423). Compare Josephus, *Against Apion* 2.215–17: "the penalty for most of-fences against the Law is death" (trans. H. St. J. Thackeray, *Josephus 1. The Life. Against Apion*, Loeb Classical Library [Cambridge: Harvard University Press, 1976], 379).

17. Riddle, *Eve's Herbs*, 35–36; Friedman and Dolansky, *The Bible Now*, 54.

18. Biggs, "Conception, Contraception, and Abortion in Ancient Mesopotamia"; Friedman and Dolansky, *The Bible Now*, 54.

19. Pritchard, *Ancient Near Eastern Texts*, 185; Matthews and Benja-min, *Old Testament Parallels*, 129; Friedman and Dolansky, *The Bible Now*, 54.

20. Compare Job 3:3–16, where Job wishes he had been stillborn.

21. Friedman and Dolansky, *The Bible Now*, 55–63.

22. Schiff, *Abortion in Judaism*, 1–12.

23. Friedman and Dolansky, *The Bible Now*, 44–46. Similar laws from the Code of Hammurabi, Middle Assyrian laws, and Hittite laws are cited here.

24. Schiff, *Abortion in Judaism*, 13–14.

25. Philo, *Special Laws* 3.117 (trans. F. H. Colson, *Philo VII*, Loeb Classical Library [Cambridge: Harvard University Press, 1937]). The view that the fetus is part of the mother is associated with the Stoics.

26. Ricks, "Abortion in Antiquity."

27. Ibid., 32.

28. Schiff, *Abortion in Judaism*, 27.

29. Ibid., 58.

30. Hays, *The Moral Vision of the New Testament*, 453; Ricks, "Abortion in Antiquity," 33–34.

31. Ricks, in "Abortion in Antiquity," 33–34, says that the fetus was viewed as having the same rights that a neighbor would have, including the right to life, but the language of rights is anachronistic.

32. Peerbolte, "Ending a Life," 50.

33. Peerbolte, "Ending a Life," 56; J. Elliott, *The Apocryphal New Testament*, 605.

34. Hays, *The Moral Vision of the New Testament*, 450.

35. Ibid., 454.

36. Ibid., 450.

37. Prior to the 1970s, abortion was perceived in the United States primarily as a Roman Catholic issue. It was developed as an evangelical issue by the Republican strategist Paul Weyrich as part of the political process of building a "moral majority." See Balmer, *Evangelicalism in America*, 109–21, especially 119–21.

CHAPTER 3. THE BIBLE AND GENDER

1. Garr, *In His Own Image*, 144.

2. See Bird, " 'Male and Female He Created Them,' " especially 134–36.

3. Ibid., 142.

4. *BeReshith Rabbah* 8.1.

5. Plato, *Symposium*, trans. Benjamin Jowett, Great Books of the Western World, 7. *Plato* (London: Encyclopaedia Britannica, 1952), 189.

6. Garr, *In His Own Image*, 128.

7. On biological essentialism, gender polarization, and androcentrism see Bem, *The Lenses of Gender*. The author discusses the influence of Genesis on 43–49.

8. The essentialist view that sexuality is genetically determined is assumed by John Boswell in *Christianity, Social Tolerance, and Homosexuality* and vigorously defended by Michael B. Regele in *Science, Scripture, and Same-Sex Love*, 31–62. For the constructivist view, that ideas of gender are socially constructed, see Foucault, *The History of Sexuality*, vol. 1; Halperin, *One Hundred Years of Homosexuality*, 41–53; Halperin, Winkler, and Zeitlin, *Before Sexuality*, 5–7.

9. In contrast, a Roman physiognomist, Polemo, wrote in the second century CE: "You may obtain physiognomic indications of masculinity and femininity from your subject's glance, movement, and voice, and then, from among these signs, compare one with another until you determine to your satisfaction which of these two sexes prevails. For in the masculine there is something feminine to be found, and in the feminine something masculine, but the name masculine or feminine is assigned according to which of the two prevails." Polemo, *Physiognomy* 2,1.192F, cited in Nissinen, *Homoeroticism in the Biblical World*, 15.

10. D. Petersen, "Genesis and Family Values," especially 16–17, on Abraham, Sarah, and Hagar.

11. See Bem, *Lenses of Gender*, 87–101; D. Greenberg, *The Construction of Homosexuality*, 301–454; Regele, *Science, Scripture, and Same-Sex Love*, 34–60.

12. Halperin, *One Hundred Years of Homosexuality*, 15.

13. Foucault, *The History of Sexuality*, 1:43.

14. D. Greenberg, *The Construction of Homosexuality*, 397–433.

15. Freud in a Viennese newspaper in 1903, quoted in Bem, *Lenses of Gender*, 90.

16. Bem, *Lenses of Gender*, 101.

17. Nissinen, *Homoeroticism in the Biblical World*, 5–10.

18. Plato, *Symposium* 192, trans. Benjamin Jowett. See further Thorp, "The Social Construction of Homosexuality."

19. Halperin, *One Hundred Years of Homosexuality*, 19–21.

20. Friedman and Dolansky comment that "offering your daughters for rape is far beyond what almost anyone in any culture would consider to be an obligation of hospitality." *The Bible Now*, 7.

21. Philo, *Hypothetica* 7.1 (trans. F. H. Colson, *Philo IX*, Loeb Classical Library [Cambridge: Harvard University Press, 1967]).

22. Robert A. J. Gagnon, in *The Bible and Homosexual Practice*, 91, infers that Jesus would have been aware of the homoerotic dimension of the story, but the inference is gratuitous.

23. Other references can be found in 1 Kings 15:12; 2 Kings 23:7; Job 36:14. See Nissinen, *Homoeroticism in the Biblical World*, 41.

24. Nissinen, *Homoeroticism in the Biblical World*, 55.

25. Olyan, *Social Inequality in the World of the Text*, 85–100, especially 85–88. See the classic article of William L. Moran, "The Ancient

Near Eastern Background of the Love of God in Deuteronomy." An example of this kind of language is found in the Vassal Treaty of Esarhaddon, which is widely thought to have influenced the Book of Deuteronomy.

26. Heacock, *Jonathan Loved David*, 35–55, provides a good overview of scholarship.

27. Nissinen, *Homoeroticism in the Biblical World*, 56.

28. McKenzie, *King David*, 85.

29. Olyan, *Social Inequality in the World of the Text*, 57–83, especially 63.

30. Friedman and Dolansky, *The Bible Now*, 22.

31. Middle Assyrian Law 20; Friedman and Dolansky, *The Bible Now*, 31.

32. Douglas, *Purity and Danger*.

33. Boswell, *Christianity, Social Tolerance, and Homosexuality*, 100.

34. D. Greenberg, *The Construction of Homosexuality*, 195.

35. On the distinction between moral and ritual impurity see Klawans, *Impurity and Sin in Ancient Judaism*, 21–42. The distinction is not always satisfactory when applied to sexual matters.

36. Gagnon, *The Bible and Homosexual Practice*, 119. The word certainly signifies disapproval, but Gagnon's characterization of the abhorrent quality of the acts in question is overstated.

37. Gagnon, in his zeal to affirm a biblical condemnation of homosexuality, can only say that "Jesus did not overturn any prohibitions against immoral sexual behavior in Leviticus or anywhere else." *The Bible and Homosexual Practice*, 227. But Jesus did not affirm them, either.

38. Brooten, *Love between Women*, 273. Aristotle records same-sex contact between animals in *History of Animals* 6.680–81.

39. Brooten, *Love between Women*, 251.

40. See further Hays, "Relations Natural and Unnatural," especially 192–93.

41. Van der Horst, *The Sayings of Pseudo-Phocylides*, 237–41.

42. Brooten, *Love between Women*, 246–47.

43. Josephus, *Against Apion* 2.199 (trans. H. St. J. Thackeray, *Josephus 1. The Life. Against Apion*, Loeb Classical Library [Cambridge: Harvard University Press, 1976]).

44. Hays, *The Moral Vision of the New Testament*, 387.

45. Brooten, *Love between Women*, 248–51.

46. Boswell, *Christianity, Social Tolerance, and Homosexuality*, 109; McNeill, *The Church and the Homosexual*, 53–56.

47. Scroggs, *The New Testament and Homosexuality*, 117; Furnish, *The Moral Teaching of Paul*, 52–83.

48. Winkler, "Unnatural Acts," 17.

49. Martin, "*Arsenokoites* and *Malakos*," 44.

50. Boswell, *Christianity, Social Tolerance, and Homosexuality*, 341–53.

51. Hays, *The Moral Vision of the New Testament*, 382. Robin Scroggs, in *The New Testament and Homosexuality*, 107–8, suggests that the word is derived from the Hebrew expression used for male homosexual relations in rabbinic literature, *mishkav zakur*, "lying with a male," but it is doubtful that that expression would have been known to Paul.

52. Martin, *Sex and the Single Savior*, 40.

53. 1 Timothy is one of the Pastoral Epistles, written perhaps in the second century but almost certainly not by Paul.

CHAPTER 4. MARRIAGE AND FAMILY

1. Rollston, "The Marginalization of Women."

2. Rollston, "Women, the Bible, and the Nineteenth Amendment," 161.

3. He is now professor at George Washington University in Washington, DC.

4. Meyers, "Was Ancient Israel a Patriarchal Society?" The address was delivered on November 23, 2013.

5. Ibid., 27.

6. Ibid.

7. See the discussion in my book *The Bible after Babel*, 75–98.

8. Trible, *God and the Rhetoric of Sexuality*; Trible, *Texts of Terror*; Schüssler Fiorenza, *In Memory of Her*.

9. Trible, "Depatriarchalizing in Biblical Interpretation," 31.

10. Meyers, *Rediscovering Eve*.

11. Aichele et al., *The Postmodern Bible*, 245–46. Feminist scholarship has moved on since these pioneering works. See Yvonne Sherwood, *The Bible and Feminism*.

12. Aichele et al., *The Postmodern Bible*, 247–48.

13. Schüssler Fiorenza, *In Memory of Her*.

14. Schüssler Fiorenza, *Jesus and the Politics of Interpretation*, 48–49.

15. Ibid., 50.

16. Schüssler Fiorenza, "The Ethics of Biblical Interpretation," 15. Compare the argument of Dale Martin, discussed in the Introduction to this volume, that the Bible is available for instrumental use to support whatever position we wish to endorse.

17. Trible, *God and the Rhetoric of Sexuality*, 98.

18. Fewell and Gunn, *Gender, Power, and Promise*, 28: "flying in the face of what every reader knows to be reality, he [the author of Genesis 2] claims that woman comes out of man—claims for himself, that is, woman's biological function of child-bearing."

19. See the comments in Clines, *What Does Eve Do to Help?*, 30–31.

20. Von Rad, *Genesis*, 101.

21. Ben Sira 25:24. This statement is anomalous even in Ben Sira and may be a secondary addition.

22. See, e.g., Ackerman, *Warrior, Dancer, Seductress, Queen*; Alice Bach, *Women in the Hebrew Bible*; Chapman, *The House of the Mother*.

23. For a concise list of examples, see Rollston, "Women, The Bible, and the Nineteenth Amendment," 161–62.

24. Lemos, *Marriage Gifts and Social Change in Ancient Palestine*.

25. De Vaux, *Ancient Israel*, 1:26–29; Satlow, *Jewish Marriage in Antiquity*, 200.

26. Lemos, "Were Israelite Women Chattel?," especially 232–35; Evans-Pritchard, "An Alternative Term for 'Bride-Price.'"

27. See further my article "Marriage, Divorce, and Family," 113–15; Satlow, *Jewish Marriage*, 200–216.

28. The Hebrew phrase for "something objectionable" is *erwat dabar*.

29. Collins, "Marriage, Divorce, and Family," 115–16.

30. Josephus, *Jewish Antiquities* 15.259 (Herod's sister Salome), 18.136 (Herodias, Agrippa's daughter).

31. Josephus, *Jewish Antiquities* 15.259, 18.136.

32. Josephus, *Life*, 414–15.

33. Josephus, *Life*, 426.

34. Collins, "Marriage, Divorce, and Family," 120.

35. Ibid., 122–27.

36. This reading is found in the *Scroll of the Minor Prophets* found among the Dead Sea Scrolls. See Fuller, "Text-Critical Problems in Malachi 2:10–16."

37. See further Claudia Camp, "Understanding a Patriarchy": Camp, *Ben Sira and the Men Who Handle Books*, especially 82–99.

38. Weems, "Gomer." See further her book *Battered Love*.

39. Setel, "Prophets and Pornography"; Exum, "Prophetic Pornography."

40. So Martin, *Sex and the Single Savior*, 104–5.

41. The nonconformist expositor Matthew Henry (1662–1714) cited this passage as evidence of Jesus' approval of married life.

42. So Martin, *Sex and the Single Savior*, 105.

43. Baumgarten, "Celibacy."

44. See the decisive discussion in Meier, *A Marginal Jew*, 4:74–181.

45. 1 Corinthians 7:12–16; Meier, *A Marginal Jew*, 4:101–2; Fitzmyer, *First Corinthians*, 296–304.

46. For the details and arguments see my article "Divorce and Remarriage in the Damascus Document."

47. Schüssler Fiorenza, *In Memory of Her*, 140–51.

48. Matthew 10:1–4; Mark 3:13–19; Luke 6:12–16.

49. Fitzmyer, *First Corinthians*, 272–87.

50. Deming, *Paul on Marriage and Celibacy*, 213.

51. M. MacDonald, "Reading Real Women," 211–13.

52. Betz, *Galatians*, 184.

53. Martyn, *Galatians*, 376.

54. Schüssler Fiorenza, *In Memory of Her*, 211.

55. See the commentary of Fitzmyer, *First Corinthians*, 404–25.

56. On what it meant for women to uncover their hair, see Schüssler Fiorenza, *In Memory of Her*, 227–28; M. MacDonald, "Reading Real Women," 215.

57. See M. MacDonald, "Reading Real Women," 216. Schüssler Fiorenza, in *In Memory of Her*, 231, tries to resolve the contradiction by proposing that 1 Corinthians 14 only applies to married women.

58. Balch, *Let Wives Be Submissive*; Balch, "Household Codes."

59. See Balch, "Household Codes," 318; Schüssler Fiorenza, *In Memory of Her*, 255.

60. Aristotle, *Politics* 1.1259b (trans. H. Rackham, Loeb Classical Library [Cambridge: Harvard, 1932]). Aristotle allowed an exception in cases where the wife was an heiress (*Nicomachean Ethics* 8.1160b).

61. Philo, *Special Laws* 3.170–71 (trans. F. H. Colson, *Philo VII*, Loeb Classical Library [Cambridge: Harvard University Press, 1937]).

62. Josephus, *Against Apion* 2.201 (trans. H. St. J. Thackeray, *Josephus 1. The Life. Against Apion*, Loeb Classical Library [Cambridge: Harvard University Press, 1976]).

63. D. MacDonald, *The Legend and the Apostle*; M. MacDonald, "Rereading Paul," 249. For a translation of the Acts of Paul and Thecla see J. Elliott, *The Apocryphal New Testament*, 372–74.

64. Yarbro Collins, "The Female Body as Social Space."

CHAPTER 5. THE BIBLE AND THE ENVIRONMENT

1. White, "The Historical Roots of Our Ecological Crisis."

2. Ibid., 1205.

3. See Friedman and Dolansky, *The Bible Now*, 172–73; Horrell, *The Bible and the Environment*, 15–17; Flannery, "Senators, Snowballs, and Scripture."

4. Coulter, "Oil Good; Democrats Bad."

5. Grove, "Hellfire Is the Real Global Warming."

6. Beisner, *Where Garden Meets Wilderness*, 107.

7. Horrell, *The Bible and the Environment*, 11–19. See especially Habel, *Readings from the Perspective of the Earth;* and subsequent volumes in the Earth Bible series from the same publisher: Habel and Wurst, *The Earth Story in Genesis* (2000); Habel and Wurst, *The Earth Story in Wisdom Traditions* (2001); and Habel, *The Earth Story in the Psalms and the Prophets* (2001). Note, too, White, "An Evangelical Declaration on the Care of Creation," 17–22, and the ensuing discussion in Berry, *The Care of Creation*, 31–42, in which White's essay is included.

8. *The Green Bible;* Bauckham, *The Bible and Ecology*.

9. See especially Horrell, *The Bible and the Environment*.

10. Beisner, *Where Garden Meets Wilderness*, 103; compare Rogerson, "The Old Testament and the Environment," 155; Norman C. Habel, "Geophany: The Earth Story in Genesis 1," in Habel and Wurst, *The Earth Story in Genesis*, 46–47.

11. Barr, "Man and Nature." Compare the remarks of Cyril Rodd in *Glimpses of a Strange Land*, 248, on the hardships of farming in the ancient Near East.

12. Wybrow, *The Bible, Baconianism, and Mastery over Nature*, 153–59.

13. Davis, *Scripture, Culture, and Agriculture*, 64–65.

14. The agrarian focus of the Hebrew Bible is emphasized especially in Davis, *Scripture, Culture, and Agriculture*. Compare Hiebert, *The Yahwist's Landscape*, 141–49.

15. See, e.g., Berry, *Environmental Stewardship*.

16. Reumann, *Stewardship and the Economy of God*, 7; Horrell, *The Bible and the Environment*, 29.

17. Tucker, "Rain on a Land," especially 17.

18. The prophetic books belong to a different stream of tradition and allow that the earth may be cursed because of human behavior. See Marlow, *Biblical Prophets*.

19. Bauckham, *The Bible and Ecology*, 64–72; Horrell, *The Bible and the Environment*, 55–60.

20. Patrick, "Divine Creative Power and the Decentering of Creation."

21. Terence Fretheim, in *God and the World*, 267–78, lists some fifty texts in which nature praises God.

22. Bauckham, *The Bible and Ecology*, 79.

23. Barton, "Reading the Prophets from an Environmental Perspective," 55.

24. Dell, "The Significance of the Wisdom Tradition," 67.

25. Rodd, *Glimpses of a Strange Land*, 249.

26. Bauckham, "Reading the Synoptic Gospels Ecologically," 70–82.

27. This passage is highlighted by Pope Francis in *Laudato Si*, paragraphs 95–98. See also Leske, "Matthew 6:25–34"; Bauckham, *The Bible and Ecology*, 72–76.

28. Pope Francis, *Laudato Si*, paragraph 98. For other references, see Horrell, *The Bible and the Environment*, 64.

29. McDonagh, *The Greening of the Earth*, 158.

30. Horrell, *The Bible and the Environment*, 65.

31. Byrne, "An Ecological Reading," especially 88–89.

32. Martin, *The Corinthian Body*, 104–36.

33. Horrell, *The Bible and the Environment*, 78–80.

34. Tonstad, "Creation Groaning in Labor Pains."

35. Bauckham, *The Bible and Ecology*, 100: "we cannot achieve the liberation of creation, but we can anticipate it."

36. Balabanski, "Critiquing Anthropocentric Cosmology."

37. Richard Bauckham, in *The Bible and Ecology*, 159, says that Paul claims that Christ has pacified the destructive elements in the created world, but they seem to persist nonetheless.

38. Compare Horrell, *The Bible and the Environment*, 83–85.

39. So N. T. Wright, *New Heavens, New Earth*.

40. For an excellent overview, see E. Adams, *The Stars Will Fall from Heaven*. See also E. Adams, "Retrieving the Earth from the Conflagration."

41. Horrell, *The Bible and the Environment*, 113.

42. Maier, "There's a New World Coming!," especially 170–71.

43. See especially Yarbro Collins, *Crisis and Catharsis*. Barbara Rossing, in "Alas for Earth!," argues that Revelation laments Rome's exploitation of the entire world.

44. Rossing, "River of Life in God's New Jerusalem."

45. Maier, "There's a New World Coming!," 177–78.

CHAPTER 6. SLAVERY AND LIBERATION

1. Isaiah 40:3; 43:19; 51:9–11; Hosea 2:14, etc.

2. Tombs, *Latin American Liberation Theology*; Gutiérrez, *A Theology of Liberation*; Gottwald and Horsley, *The Bible and Liberation*; Dussel, "Exodus as a Paradigm in Liberation Theology"; Lohfink, *Option for the Poor*.

3. Levenson, *The Hebrew Bible*, 151–52.

4. Brueggemann, "Pharaoh as Vassal."

5. Croatto, *Exodus*, 15.

6. The same Hebrew word, *ᶜabadim*, can mean "slaves" or "servants."

7. Levenson acknowledges this in *The Hebrew Bible*, 152–53.

8. So Hoffmeier, *The Immigration Crisis*.

9. For the view that the biblical laws prioritize compassionate treatment of aliens, see Carroll R., *Christians at the Border*; F. Houston, *You Shall Love the Stranger as Yourself*.

10. Ezra 9–10; Avalos, "Diasporas 'R' Us," 43.

11. As implied in Avalos, "Diasporas 'R' Us," 40.

12. Mendelsohn, *Slavery in the Ancient Near East*, 1–33; Dandamaev, "Slavery: Ancient Near East," 59–60. See also Snell, "Slavery in the Ancient Near East."

13. D. Wright, " 'She Shall Not Go Free as Male Slaves Do,' " 131; and in more detail, D. Wright, *Inventing God's Law*, 123–49.

14. Translated by Martha Roth, in Roth, *Law Collections*, 103.

15. Joshua Berman, in *Created Equal*, 106, says that the Hebrew word ʿ*ebed* does not connote ownership of the person. The word may not always connote ownership, but it clearly does when the ʿ*ebed* in question has been purchased. See the criticism of Berman in Avalos, *Slavery, Abolitionism*, 6, with reference to Leviticus 25:44–46: If buying and inheriting an ʿ*ebed* does not connote ownership of a person, then what does?

16. Berman, *Created Equal*, 105; D. Wright, *Inventing God's Law*, 150.

17. Berman, in *Created Equal*, 105, tries to give a theological explanation for this custom: "The slave's preference for servitude represents a rejection of the freedom he has been accorded by the Exodus; he must therefore declare his desire to remain in servitude 'before God.' " In fact, choosing servitude hardly implies a preference for it, but rather a desire to remain with his wife and children.

18. According to one estimate, the number of slaves owned by private persons averaged from one to four. Mendelsohn, *Slavery in the Ancient Near East*, 121.

19. Van Houten, *The Alien in Israelite Law*.

20. Botta, "Slaves, Slavery"; Hezser, *Jewish Slavery in Antiquity*.

21. Gropp, "Slavery."

22. Glancy, *Slavery in Early Christianity*, 102–28. My concern is with Jesus as portrayed in the Gospels, not necessarily with the historical Jesus.

23. Bartchy, "Slavery: New Testament," 68.

24. Payne, *Man and Woman*, 79.

25. Galatians 4:21–31. See Glancy, "Early Christianity, Slavery, and Women's Bodies," 147.

26. Bartchy, *Mallon Chresai*, 119.

27. Harrill, *The Manumission of Slaves*, 122. A third option is proposed by S. Scott Bartchy, in *Mallon Chresai*, 128. He thinks the object of "use" is the Christian calling: if you are freed, you should nonetheless live according to the calling.

28. Bartchy, *Mallon Chresai*, 180.

29. We find a similar emphasis on spiritual freedom in the philosopher Epictetus. See Bradley, *Slavery and Society at Rome*, 175.

30. Bartchy, "Slavery: New Testament," 66.

31. Patterson, *Slavery and Social Death*, 13.

32. Glancy, *Slavery in Early Christianity*, 21–26.

33. Saller, "Corporal Punishment," 160.

34. Bradley, *Slavery and Society at Rome*, 178–79.

35. E.g., Barclay, "Paul, Philemon."

36. See the overviews in Fitzmyer, *The Letter to Philemon*, 17–23; Harrill, *Slaves in the New Testament*, 6–16; Kreitzer, *Philemon*, 38–69.

37. Winter, "Paul's Letter to Philemon"; Kreitzer, *Philemon*, 63–65.

38. So Callahan, *Embassy of Onesimus*, a view endorsed enthusiastically in Horsley, "Paul and Slavery," 181–82.

39. See the comments in Fitzmyer, *The Letter to Philemon*, 19.

40. Pliny to Sabinianus (Epistle 9.21), cited in Fitzmyer, *The Letter to Philemon*, 21–22.

41. J. Albert Harrill, in *Slaves in the New Testament*, 7, dismisses the parallel too hastily because of the differences.

42. N. Petersen, *Rediscovering Paul*, 98–101.

43. Colossians 4:9 implies that Philemon set Onesimus free and that he became a coworker of Paul's. Fitzmyer, *The Letter to Philemon*, 24.

44. Luther, *Werke: Kritische Gesamtausgabe: Die Deutsche Bibel* 7, 292–93, cited in Fitzmyer, *The Letter to Philemon*, 36.

45. See Martin, *Slavery as Salvation*, 50–85.

46. Ibid., 147.

47. Horsley, "The Slave Systems of Classical Antiquity," 59.

48. Stringfellow, *Scriptural and Statistical Views*, cited in Setzer and Shefferman, *The Bible in American Culture*, 103. Stringfellow was a minister in Virginia.

49. Stuart, *Conscience and Constitution*, 36–37, cited in Powery, "The Bible, Slavery, and Political Debate," 143–44. Moses Stuart's views on slavery were complex. He favored gradual emancipation.

50. Douglass, "Slavery's Northern Bulwarks," cited in Avalos, *Slavery, Abolitionism*, 263.

CHAPTER 7. VIOLENCE AND ZEAL

1. See, e.g., Collins, *Does the Bible Justify Violence?*; Ellens, *The Destructive Power of Religion*; Avalos, *Fighting Words*. The connection between religion, specifically the Bible, and violence had already been the

subject of major studies before 9/11—e.g., Schwartz, *The Curse of Cain;* and Assmann, *Moses the Egyptian.*

2. R. Brown, *Religion and Violence,* 8.

3. Arendt, *On Violence,* 46, 79.

4. Dever, *Who Were the Early Israelites?,* 227–28. To be sure, some conservative scholars still defend the historicity of the biblical account. See my critique in *The Bible after Babel,* 27–51.

5. Dozeman, *Joshua 1–12,* 27–31.

6. Barr, *Biblical Faith and Natural Theology,* 209. In contrast, David A. Bernat and Jonathan Klawans, in *Religion and Violence,* 7–10, seem to think that the violence in the text is inconsequential if it was not historically perpetrated.

7. Kant, *The Conflict of the Faculties,* 115.

8. Collins, *Does the Bible Justify Violence?,* 17–20.

9. See Bainton, *Christian Attitudes towards War and Peace,* 151, 168. Amalek was a tribe that attacked the Israelites when they were wandering in the wilderness (Deuteronomy 25:17–18: "Remember what Amalek did to you on your journey out of Egypt, how he attacked you on the way, when you were faint and weary, and struck down all who lagged behind you"). See also Exodus 17:8.

10. The phrase of Michael Walzer, in *Exodus and Revolution,* 141–43.

11. E.g., G. Wright, *The Book of the Acts of God,* 109.

12. E.g., Anderson, "What about the Canaanites?," 282. The argument dates back at least to Calvin.

13. Albright, *From the Stone Age to Christianity,* 280–81.

14. Said, "Michael Walzer's *Exodus and Revolution.*"

15. Whitelam, *The Invention of Ancient Israel.*

16. Calvin, *Commentaries on the Book of Joshua,* 163.

17. Wolterstorff, "Comments on 'What About the Canaanites?,' " 284.

18. M. Greenberg, "On the Political Use of the Bible."

19. For a full analysis of the passage, see Levine, *Numbers 21–36,* 279–303. Verses 1–5, where the issue concerns Moabite women, are usually attributed to the Yahwist (J) or combined Yahwist-Elohist strand of Pentateuchal narrative. The remainder of the story, which concerns a Midianite woman, is priestly.

20. Janzen, *Old Testament Ethics,* 108.

21. Pakkala, *Intolerant Monolatry.*

22. See, e.g., Smith, *The Origins of Biblical Monotheism.*

23. For a nuanced discussion, see Schwartz, *The Curse of Cain.*

24. Soloveichik, "The Virtue of Hate."

25. Ibid., 42. The contrast between Judaism and Christianity on this point is overdrawn. In fall 2018 a Roman Catholic bishop, Robert Morlino of Madison, Wisconsin, a critic of Pope Francis, declared: "There is too much talk of love in the church and too little hatred of evil" (reported by the *National Catholic Reporter,* November 2–15, 2018, 26).

26. Soloveichik, "The Virtue of Hate,"46.

27. Ibid., 43–44.

28. Whether there was religious persecution in the Maccabean era has been questioned. See my essay "Temple or Taxes?"

29. See my essay "Cognitive Dissonance and Eschatological Violence," 310–14.

30. Gyges reigned as king of Lydia from 716 to 678 BCE. He was the subject of several legendary stories preserved by the Greek historian Herodotus and also by Plato.

31. So Crossan, "Divine Violence in the Christian Bible," 209; similarly, Frankfurter, "The Legacy of Sectarian Rage." For a more balanced assessment see van Henten, "Violence in Revelation."

32. Stratton, "The Eschatological Arena."

33. See, e.g., Desjardins, *Peace, Violence, and the New Testament,* 62–110; Matthews and Gibson, *Violence in the New Testament.*

34. See Wessinger, "Apocalypse and Violence."

35. Tacitus, *Agricola* 30 (trans. M. Hutton, revised by R. Ogilvie, Loeb Classical Library [Cambridge: Harvard University Press, 1958], 81).

36. Lawrence, *Apocalypse,* 87–88.

37. Schüssler Fiorenza, *Invitation to the Book of Revelation,* 173; Schüssler Fiorenza, *The Book of Revelation.*

38. See Appleby, "The Unholy Uses," 75.

39. Revelation 13:10. The text of this passage is uncertain. See Yarbro Collins, "The Political Perspective," 206.

40. Stendahl, "Hate, Non-retaliation and Love," 344–45.

41. On apocalyptic fantasy as catharsis, see Yarbro Collins, *Crisis and Catharsis,* 141–63.

42. Ibid., 69–73.

43. See Gager with Gibson, "Violent Acts and Violent Language."

44. Josephus, *Jewish War* 2.259–60 (trans. H. St. J. Thackeray, Loeb Classical Library [Cambridge: Harvard University Press, 1927], 425).

45. Juergensmeyer, *Terror in the Mind of God*, 108–9.

46. See Appleby, "The Unholy Uses," 77.

47. Lincoln, "Symmetric Dualisms," republished as chapter 2 in Lincoln, *Holy Terrors*.

48. Hays, *The Moral Vision of the New Testament*, 332. David J. Neville, in *A Peaceable Hope*, argues for a *shalom*-oriented canonical trajectory in the Bible.

49. See the balanced discussion in Desjardins, *Peace, Violence, and the New Testament*.

50. Aslan, *Zealot*, 144.

51. Martin, "Jesus in Jerusalem."

52. See the refutation of Martin's argument in Paula Fredriksen, "Arms and the Man."

53. Hays, *The Moral Vision of the New Testament*, 322–23.

54. See Yarbro Collins, "Jesus' Action in Herod's Temple."

55. Wink, *Jesus and Nonviolence*.

56. So Horsley, " 'By the Finger of God,' " 69. See also Horsley, *Jesus and the Spiral of Violence*.

57. Horsley, " 'By the Finger of God,' " 70.

58. John P. Meier, in *A Marginal Jew*, 5:261, regards the mixture of good and bad in this world as a typically Matthean theme.

59. See the thorough discussion in Meier, *A Marginal Jew*, 4:532–51.

60. So Williams, *The Bible, Violence, and the Sacred*, 243. Williams bases his approach on the work of the French philosopher René Girard.

CHAPTER 8. SOCIAL JUSTICE IN THE HEBREW BIBLE

1. Pritchard, *Ancient Near Eastern Texts*, 164.

2. Ibid., 178.

3. See especially Weinfeld, *Social Justice in Ancient Israel*.

4. Ibid., 77; Nardoni, *Rise Up, O Judge*, 1–20.

5. A city northwest of the junction of the Euphrates and Tigris in modern Iraq.

6. Weinfeld, *Social Justice in Ancient Israel*, 78.

7. Ibid., 81.

8. Ibid., 79.

9. W. Houston, *Contending for Justice*, 14: "The class that claims to direct society must, in order to make good their claim, present themselves as guardians of the common interest."

10. Ibid., 138–59.

11. Whitelam, *The Just King*, 30–32.

12. Birch, *Let Justice Roll Down*, 259–69; Pleins, *The Social Visions of the Hebrew Bible*, 213–416; W. Houston, *Contending for Justice*, 52–98.

13. Brueggemann, *Theology of the Old Testament*, 736–37.

14. *Pace* the ingenious critique of David Clines, in "Metacommenting Amos."

15. O'Donovan, *The Desire of the Nations*, 39. See the discussion by Nicholas Wolterstorff in *Justice*, 68–75.

16. O'Donovan, *The Desire of the Nations*, 39.

17. See especially Barton, *Ethics in Ancient Israel*, 94–126; Barr, *Biblical Faith and Natural Theology*, 58–101. The view that justice lies in the right order of creation is characteristic of wisdom books such as Proverbs. The classic treatment is that of Gerhard von Rad, in *Wisdom in Israel*, 74–96.

18. Untermann, *Justice for All*, 85–108.

19. Berman, *Created Equal*. Berman focuses especially on Deuteronomy.

20. Gottwald, *A Sociology of the Religion of Liberated Israel*.

21. Levinson, "The Reconceptualization of Kingship."

22. Untermann, *Justice for All*, 44–65.

23. Van Houten, *The Alien in Israelite Law*.

24. Wolterstorff, *Justice*, 90.

25. Lohfink, *Option for the Poor*.

26. Wolterstorff, *Justice*, 77.

27. Despite the title, Miranda, *Marx and the Bible*, does not offer a Marxist interpretation of the Bible. The author only argues that Marx and the Bible share a basic concern for social justice.

28. Anderson, *Charity*, 1–2.

29. Daniel 4:24. The word translated as "almsgiving" here is *tsidqah*, the Aramaic equivalent of the Hebrew *tsedaqah*.

30. Anderson, *Charity*, 41–52.

31. See, e.g., *1 Enoch* 96–97.

32. Bowler, *Blessed*. See also Strawn, *The Old Testament Is Dying*, 131–55.

33. B. Wilkinson, *The Prayer of Jabez*.

CHAPTER 9. SOCIAL JUSTICE IN THE SHADOW
OF THE APOCALYPSE

1. Hauerwas, *After Christendom*, chapter 2.

2. See Hauerwas, "Jesus: The Justice of God," especially 83–84.

3. For an excellent critique of Hauerwas, see Wolterstorff, *Justice*, 96–98.

4. Nygren, *Agape and Eros*, 70.

5. For a full discussion of this issue see Wolterstorff, *Justice in Love*.

6. LaHaye and Jenkins, *Left Behind*.

7. Boyer, *When Time Shall Be No More*.

8. On the progressive heritage of American Evangelicism, see Balmer, *Evangelicalism in America*, especially 29–64.

9. Boyer, *When Time Shall Be No More*, 88.

10. Scofield, *Addresses on Prophecy*, 26; Boyer, *When Time Shall Be No More*, 298.

11. Walvoord, "Why Must Christ Return?."

12. Lindsey, "The Great Cosmic Countdown."

13. See, e.g., Schüssler Fiorenza, *The Book of Revelation*; Schüssler Fiorenza, *Revelation*.

14. Kraybill, *Imperial Cult and Commerce*; Royalty, *The Streets of Heaven*.

15. Yarbro Collins, *Crisis and Catharsis*, 126–27; Kraybill, *Imperial Cult and Commerce*, 138–39.

16. Donahue, *Seek Justice That You May Live*, 181–85.

17. Horsley, *Paul and Empire*; Horsley, *Jesus and Empire*: Carter, *The Roman Empire and the New Testament*; Crossan, *God and Empire*.

18. N. Elliott, "The Anti-Imperial Message of the Cross."

19. Romans 13:1–7, here verse 1. See the discussion of this passage in N. Elliott, *Liberating Paul*, 217–26.

20. J. A. Fitzmyer, in *Romans*, 664, reviews the arguments and finds no evidence of an interpolation.

21. So Dunn, *Romans 9–16*, 773.

22. Horsley, "1 Corinthians."

23. E.g., Horsley, *The Prophet Jesus and the Renewal of Israel;* Horsley, *Jesus and the Politics of Roman Palestine.*

24. Schweitzer, *The Quest of the Historical Jesus;* Allison, *Jesus of Nazareth;* Ehrman, *Jesus, Apocalyptic Prophet.*

25. Johnson, *Sharing Possessions,* 12.

26. Josephus, *Jewish Antiquities* 15.299–316.

27. Josephus, *Jewish Antiquities* 20.101; Acts 11:27–30.

28. Horsley with Hanson, *Bandits, Prophets, and Messiahs.*

29. It is used in this way in the scroll 11QMelchizedek, in the Dead Sea Scrolls.

30. Hays, *The Moral Vision of the New Testament,* 116.

31. Wolterstorff, *Justice,* 110–13.

32. The adjective *epiousios,* which is usually translated as "daily," is not attested otherwise in classical or Hellenistic Greek literature.

33. Anderson, *Sin,* 27–39.

34. S. Adams, *Social and Economic Life in Second Temple Judea,* 171–82.

35. The claim in Horsley, *Jesus and Empire,* 99, that Jesus' statement would have been understood as a denial of the legitimacy of the tax, is gratuitous.

36. Yarbro Collins, *Mark,* 555.

37. Yarbro Collins, "Jesus' Action in Herod's Temple."

38. See Collins, *The Scepter and the Star,* 215–37.

39. Johnson, *Sharing Possessions,* 15.

40. Mark 10:17–31. The parallel accounts in Matthew 19:16–30 and Luke 18:18–30 do not have the statement that Jesus loved him.

41. Bassler, *God and Mammon,* 37–59; Johnson, *Sharing Possessions,* 16.

42. Mark 6:8–9. Cf. Luke 9:3–5.

43. Matthew 10:8–9; Luke 10:4.

44. Matthew 10:8.

45. Matthew 10:46–48.

46. Johnson, *Sharing Possessions,* 21–23.

47. On the motif of "treasure in heaven," see Anderson, *Charity,* 123–35.

48. Johnson, *Sharing Possessions,* 17–20; see, more broadly, Anderson, *Charity.*

49. Donahue, *Seek Justice That You May Live,* 179. The author inclines toward the "discipleship" interpretation.

50. "John Hagee: " 'Nasty' Welfare Recipients Don't Deserve to Eat," RWW News, August 6, 2014, https://www.youtube.com/watch?v=zoj5dpme9UA.2014. See Werline, "Work, Poverty, and Welfare," 76. A position similar to Hagee's was articulated by Texas Republican Jodey Arrington, as reported on CNN, March 31, 2017.

51. See the excellent overview in Krentz, "Thessalonians," especially 518–22.

THE AUTHORITY OF THE BIBLE

1. The comments of Sessions and Colbert are cited from CNN.com, June 15, 2018.

2. Mark 12:28–34; Matthew 22:34–40; Luke 10:25–28.

3. Romans 13:9.

4. Dawkins, *The God Delusion*, 237.

5. Wolterstorff, "Reading Joshua," 236.

6. Untermann, *Justice for All*.

7. Dawkins, *The God Delusion*, 250.

8. Babylonian Talmud, tractate Shabbath 31a. More generally see Gensler, *Ethics and the Golden Rule*.

9. See Betz, *The Sermon on the Mount*, 509–16. Copious examples from several cultures can be found in the Wikipedia article "Golden Rule" (consulted in the form edited on June 9, 2018).

10. Wolterstorff, "Comments on 'What about the Canaanites?,' " 284.

11. Newsom, "Bakhtin, the Bible, and Dialogic Truth"; Brueggemann, *Theology of the Old Testament*.

12. Simon, *Seek Peace and Pursue It*.

13. Benjamin, *Theses on the Philosophy of History*, Thesis 7, in Benjamin, *One-Way Street*, 359.

Bibliography

Ackerman, Susan. *Warrior, Dancer, Seductress, Queen: Women in Judges and Biblical Israel*. Anchor Reference Library. New York: Doubleday, 1998.

Adams, Edward. "Retrieving the Earth from the Conflagration: 2 Peter 3.5–13 and the Environment." In Horrell, Hunt, Southgate, and Stavrakopoulou, *Ecological Hermeneutics*, 108–20.

———. *The Stars Will Fall from Heaven: Cosmic Catastrophe in the New Testament and Its World*. Library of New Testament Studies 347. London: T&T Clark, 2007.

Adams, Samuel L. *Social and Economic Life in Second Temple Judea*. Louisville, KY: Westminster John Knox, 2014.

Aichele, George, et al. (The Bible and Culture Collective). *The Postmodern Bible*. New Haven: Yale University Press, 1995.

Albright, William Foxwell. *From the Stone Age to Christianity*. Garden City, NY: Doubleday, 1957.

Allison, Dale C. *Jesus of Nazareth: Millenarian Prophet*. Minneapolis: Fortress, 1998.

Alter, Robert. *The Pleasures of Reading in an Ideological Age*. New York: Simon and Schuster, 1989.

Amanat, Abbas, and John J. Collins, eds. *Apocalypse and Violence*. New Haven: The MacMillan Center for International and Area Studies and the Council on Middle East Studies, 2002.

Anderson, Gary. *Charity: The Place of the Poor in the Biblical Tradition.* New Haven: Yale University Press, 2013.

———. *Sin: A History.* New Haven: Yale University Press, 2009.

———. "What about the Canaanites?" In Bergmann, Murray, and Rea, *Divine Evil?*, 269–91.

Appleby, R. Scott. "The Unholy Uses of Apocalyptic Imagination: Twentieth-Century Patterns." In Amanat and Collins, *Apocalypse and Violence*, 69–87.

Arendt, Hannah. *On Violence.* New York: Harcourt, Brace & World, 1969.

Aslan, Reza. *Zealot: The Life and Times of Jesus of Nazareth.* New York: Random House, 2013.

Assmann, Jan. *Moses the Egyptian: The Memory of Egypt in Western Monotheism.* Cambridge: Harvard University Press, 1997.

Avalos, Hector. "Diasporas 'R' Us: Attitudes toward Immigrants in the Hebrew Bible." In Flannery and Werline, *Bible in Political Debate*, 33–46.

———. *Fighting Words: The Origins of Religious Violence.* Amherst, NY: Prometheus, 2005.

———. *Slavery, Abolitionism, and the Ethics of Biblical Scholarship.* Sheffield, UK: Sheffield Phoenix, 2011.

Bach, Alice, ed. *Women in the Hebrew Bible: A Reader.* London: Routledge, 1999.

Bainton, Roland H. *Christian Attitudes towards War and Peace: A Historical Survey and Critical Re-evaluation.* Nashville, TN: Abingdon, 1960.

Balabanski, Vicky. "Critiquing Anthropocentric Cosmology: Retrieving a Stoic 'Permeation Cosmology' in Colossians 1:15–20." In Habel and Trudinger, *Exploring Ecological Hermeneutics*, 151–59.

Balch, David L. "Household Codes." Pages 318–20 in vol. 3 of Freedman, *The Anchor Bible Dictionary.*

———. *Let Wives Be Submissive: The Domestic Code in 1 Peter.* Society of Biblical Literature Monograph Series 26. Chico, CA: Scholars Press, 1981.

Balmer, Randall. *Evangelicalism in America.* Waco, TX: Baylor University Press, 2016.

Barclay, J. M. G. "Paul, Philemon, and the Dilemma of Christian Slave Ownership." *New Testament Studies* 37 (1991): 161–86.

Barr, James. "Ancient Biblical Laws and Modern Human Rights." Pages 21–33 in *Justice and the Holy: Essays in Honor of Walter Harrelson*. Edited by Douglas A. Knight and Peter J. Paris. Atlanta: Scholars Press, 1989.

———. *Biblical Faith and Natural Theology*. Oxford: Clarendon, 1993.

———. *The Garden of Eden and the Hope of Immortality*. Minneapolis: Fortress, 1992.

———. "Man and Nature—The Ecological Controversy and the Old Testament." *Bulletin of the John Rylands Library* 55 (1972): 9–32.

Bartchy, S. Scott. *Mallon Chresai: First-Century Slavery and the Interpretation of 1 Corinthians 7:21*. Society of Biblical Literature Dissertation Series 11. Missoula, MT: Scholars Press, 1973.

———. "Slavery: New Testament." Pages 65–73 in vol. 6 of Freedman, *The Anchor Bible Dictionary*.

Barton, John. *Ethics in Ancient Israel*. Oxford: Oxford University Press, 2014.

———. "Reading the Prophets from an Environmental Perspective." In Horrell, Hunt, Southgate, and Stavrakopoulou, *Ecological Hermeneutics*, 46–55.

Barton, Stephen C., and David Wilkinson, eds. *Reading Genesis after Darwin*. Oxford: Oxford University Press, 2009.

Bassler, Jouette M. *God and Mammon: Asking for Money in the New Testament*. Nashville, TN: Abingdon, 1991.

Bauckham, Richard. *The Bible and Ecology: Rediscovering the Community of Creation*. Waco, TX: Baylor, 2010.

———. "Reading the Synoptic Gospels Ecologically." In Horrell, Hunt, Southgate, and Stavrakopoulou, *Ecological Hermeneutics*, 70–82.

Baumgarten, Joseph M. "Celibacy." In Schiffman and VanderKam, *Dead Sea Scrolls*, 122–25.

Beisner, E. Calvin. *Where Garden Meets Wilderness: Evangelical Entry into the Environmental Debate*. Grand Rapids, MI: Eerdmans, 1997.

Bem, Sandra L. *The Lenses of Gender: Transforming the Debate on Sexual Inequality*. New Haven: Yale University Press, 1993.

Benjamin, Walter. *One-Way Street and Other Writings*. London: New Left, 1979.

Bergmann, Michael, Michael J. Murray, and Michael C. Rea, eds. *Divine Evil? The Moral Character of the God of Abraham.* Oxford: Oxford University Press, 2011.

Berman, Joshua. *Created Equal: How the Bible Broke with Ancient Political Thought.* New York: Oxford University Press, 2008.

———. "The History of Legal Theory and the Study of Biblical Law." *Catholic Biblical Quarterly* 76 (2014): 19–39.

Bernat, David A., and Jonathan Klawans, eds. *Religion and Violence: The Biblical Heritage.* Sheffield, UK: Sheffield Phoenix, 2007.

Berry, R. J., ed. *Environmental Stewardship: Critical Perspectives Past and Present.* London: Clark, 2006.

Betz, H. D. *Galatians.* Hermeneia. Philadelphia: Fortress, 1979.

———. *The Sermon on the Mount.* Hermeneia. Minneapolis: Fortress, 1995.

Biggs, R. D. "Conception, Contraception, and Abortion in Ancient Mesopotamia." Pages 1–14 in *Wisdom, Gods and Literature: Studies in Assyriology in Honour of W. G. Lambert.* Edited by A. R. George and I. L. Finkel. Winona Lake, IN: Eisenbrauns, 2000.

Birch, Bruce C. *Let Justice Roll Down: The Old Testament, Ethics, and Christian Life.* Louisville, KY: Westminster John Knox, 1991.

Bird, Phyllis. " 'Male and Female He Created Them': Genesis 1:27b in the Context of the Priestly Account of Creation." Pages 123–54 in Bird, *Missing Persons and Mistaken Identities: Women and Gender in Ancient Israel.* Minneapolis: Fortress, 1997.

Boswell, John. *Christianity, Social Tolerance, and Homosexuality.* Chicago: University of Chicago Press, 1980.

Botta, Alejandro F. "Slaves, Slavery." Pages 1232–33 in *The Eerdmans Dictionary of Early Judaism.* Edited by John J. Collins and Daniel C. Harlow. Grand Rapids, MI: Eerdmans, 2010.

Bowler, Kate. *Blessed: A History of the American Prosperity Gospel.* New York: Oxford University Press, 2013.

Boyer, Paul S. *When Time Shall Be No More: Prophecy Belief in Modern American Culture.* Cambridge: Harvard University Press, 1992.

Bradley, Keith. *Slavery and Society at Rome.* Cambridge: Cambridge University Press, 1994.

Brooten, Bernadette, ed. *Beyond Slavery: Overcoming Its Religious and Sexual Legacies.* New York: Palgrave Macmillan, 2010.

————. *Love between Women*. Chicago: University of Chicago Press, 1996.

Brown, Robert McAfee. *Religion and Violence*. 2nd ed. Philadelphia: Westminster, 1987.

Brown, William P. *The Seven Pillars of Creation: The Bible, Science, and the Ecology of Wonder*. Oxford: Oxford University Press, 2010.

Brueggemann, Walter. "Pharaoh as Vassal: A Study of a Political Metaphor." *Catholic Biblical Quarterly* 57 (1995): 27–51.

————. *Theology of the Old Testament: Testimony, Dispute, Advocacy*. Minneapolis: Fortress, 1997.

Byrne, Brendan, S.J. "An Ecological Reading of Rom. 8.19–22: Possibilities and Hesitations." In Horrell, Hunt, Southgate, and Stavrakopoulou, *Ecological Hermeneutics*, 83–93.

Callahan, Allen D. *Embassy of Onesimus: The Letter of Paul to Philemon*. Valley Forge, PA: Trinity Press International, 1997.

Callahan, Allen D., Richard A. Horsley, and Abraham Smith, eds. *Slavery in Text and Interpretation*. Semeia 83–4. Atlanta: Society of Biblical Literature, 1998.

Calvin, Jean [John]. *Commentaries on the Book of Joshua*. Translated by H. Beveridge. Grand Rapids, MI: Eerdmans, 1949.

Camp, Claudia. *Ben Sira and the Men Who Handle Books: Gender and the Rise of Canon-Consciousness*. Sheffield, UK: Sheffield Phoenix, 2013.

————. "Understanding a Patriarchy: Women in Second-Century Jerusalem through the Eyes of Ben Sira." Pages 1–39 in *"Women Like This": New Perspectives on Jewish Women in the Greco-Roman World*. Edited by A. J. Levine. Atlanta: Scholars Press, 1991.

Carlson, Richard F., and Tremper Longman III. *Science, Creation, and the Bible: Reconciling Rival Theories of Origins*. Downers Grove, IL: Intervarsity, 2010.

Carroll R., M. Daniel. *Christians at the Border: Immigration, the Church, and the Bible*. Grand Rapids, MI: Baker, 2008.

Carter, Warren. *The Roman Empire and the New Testament: An Essential Guide*. Nashville, TN: Abingdon, 2006.

Cassin, René. "Religions et droits de l'homme." Pages 97–104 in vol. 4 of *Amicorum discipulorumque liber: Methodologie des droits de l'homme*. Edited by René Cassin. Paris: Pedone, 1972.

Chapman, Cynthia R. *The House of the Mother: The Social Roles of Maternal Kin in Biblical Hebrew Narrative and Poetry*. Anchor Yale Bible Reference Library. New Haven: Yale University Press, 2016.

Clifford, Richard J. *Creation Accounts in the Ancient Near East and in the Bible*. Catholic Biblical Quarterly Monograph Series 26. Washington, DC: Catholic Biblical Association of America, 1994.

Clines, David J. A. "Metacommenting Amos." Pages 76–93 in *Interested Parties: The Ideology of Writers and Readers of the Hebrew Bible*. Journal for the Study of the Old Testament Supplements 205. Sheffield, UK: Sheffield Academic, 1995.

———. *What Does Eve Do to Help? And Other Readerly Questions to the Old Testament*. Journal for the Study of the Old Testament Supplements 94. Sheffield, UK: Sheffield Academic, 1990.

Collins, John J. *The Apocalyptic Imagination: An Introduction to Jewish Apocalyptic Literature*. 3rd ed. Grand Rapids, MI: Eerdmans, 2016.

———. *Apocalypticism in the Dead Sea Scrolls*. London: Routledge, 1997.

———. *The Bible after Babel: Historical Criticism in a Postmodern Age*. Grand Rapids, MI: Eerdmans, 2005.

———. "The Biblical Precedent for Natural Theology." In Collins, *Encounters with Biblical Theology*, 91–104.

———. "Cognitive Dissonance and Eschatological Violence: Fantasized Solutions to a Theological Dilemma in Second Temple Judaism." Pages 308–25 in Collins, *Apocalypse, Prophecy, and Pseudepigraphy: On Jewish Apocalyptic Literature*. Grand Rapids, MI: Eerdmans, 2015.

———. "Divorce and Remarriage in the Damascus Document." Pages 81–93 in *The Faces of Torah: Studies in the Texts and Contexts of Ancient Judaism in Honor of Steven Fraade*. Edited by Christine Hayes, Tzvi Novick, and Michal Bar-Asher Siegal. Journal of Ancient Judaism Supplements. Göttingen: Vandenhoeck & Ruprecht, 2017.

———. *Does the Bible Justify Violence?* Minneapolis: Fortress, 2004.

———. *Encounters with Biblical Theology*. Minneapolis: Fortress, 2005.

———. "Faith without Works: Biblical Ethics and the Sacrifice of Isaac." In Collins, *Encounters with Biblical Theology*, 47–58.

———. "Historical-Critical Methods." Pages 129–45 in *The Cambridge Companion to the Hebrew Bible/Old Testament*. Edited by Stephen B. Chapman and Marvin A. Sweeney. Cambridge: Cambridge University Press, 2016.

———. *The Invention of Judaism: Torah and Jewish Identity from Deuter-onomy to Paul.* Oakland: University of California Press, 2017.

———. "Marriage, Divorce, and Family in Second Temple Judaism." Pages 104–62 in Leo G. Perdue, Joseph Blenkinsopp, John J. Collins, and Carol Meyers, *Families in Ancient Israel.* Louisville, KY: Westminster John Knox, 1997.

———. *The Scepter and the Star: Messianism in Light of the Dead Sea Scrolls.* 2nd ed. Grand Rapids, MI: Eerdmans, 2010.

———. "Temple or Taxes? What Sparked the Maccabean Revolt?" Pages 189–201 in *Revolt and Resistance in the Ancient Classical World and the Near East: In the Crucible of Empire.* Edited by John J. Collins and J. G. Manning. Culture and History of the Ancient Near East 85. Leiden: Brill, 2016.

Coogan, Michael. *The Ten Commandments: A Short History of an Ancient Text.* New Haven: Yale University Press, 2014.

Coomber, Matthew J. M., ed. *Bible and Justice: Ancient Texts, Modern Challenges.* London: Equinox, 2011.

Croatto, J. Severino. *Exodus: A Hermeneutics of Freedom.* Maryknoll, NY: Orbis Books, 1978.

Crossan, John Dominic. "Divine Violence in the Christian Bible." Pages 208–36 in *The Bible and the American Future.* Edited by R. L. Jewett, W. L. Alloway, Jr., and J. G. Lacy. Eugene, OR: Cascade, 2009.

———. *God and Empire: Jesus against Rome, Then and Now.* San Francisco: HarperSanFrancisco, 2007.

Dandamaev, Muhammad. "Slavery: Ancient Near East." Pages 58–62 in vol. 6 of Freedman, *Anchor Bible Dictionary* 6:58–62.

Davis, Ellen F. *Scripture, Culture, and Agriculture: An Agrarian Reading of the Bible.* Cambridge: Cambridge University Press, 2009.

Dawkins, Richard. *The God Delusion.* Boston: Houghton Mifflin, 2006.

Day, John. *God's Conflict with the Dragon and the Sea: Echoes of a Canaanite Myth in the Old Testament.* University of Cambridge Oriental Publications 35. Cambridge: Cambridge University Press, 1985.

Dell, Katharine J. "The Significance of the Wisdom Tradition in the Ecological Debate." In Horrell, Hunt, Southgate, and Stavrakopoulou, *Ecological Hermeneutics*, 56–69.

Deming, Will. *Paul on Marriage and Celibacy: The Hellenistic Background of 1 Corinthians 7.* 2nd ed. Grand Rapids, MI: Eerdmans, 2004.

Derrida, Jacques. *Limited Inc.* Evanston, IL: Northwestern University Press, 1988.

Desjardins, Michael. *Peace, Violence, and the New Testament.* Sheffield, UK: Sheffield Academic, 1997.

Dever, William. *Who Were the Early Israelites and Where Did They Come From?* Grand Rapids, MI: Eerdmans, 2003.

Donahue, John R. *Seek Justice That You May Live: Reflections and Resources on the Bible and Social Justice.* Mahwah, NJ: Paulist, 2014.

Douglas, Mary. *Purity and Danger: An Analysis of Concepts of Pollution and Taboo.* London: Praeger, 1966.

Douglass, Frederick. "Slavery's Northern Bulwarks . . . 12 January, 1851." Page 284 in vol. 2 of *The Frederick Douglass Papers, Series One—Speeches, Debates, and Interviews.* Edited by John W. Blassingame and John R. McKivigan. New Haven: Yale University Press, 1982.

Dozeman, Thomas. *Joshua 1–12.* Anchor Yale Bible 6B. New Haven: Yale University Press, 2014.

Dunn, James D. G. *Romans 9–16.* Word Biblical Commentary 38. Dallas, TX: Word, 1988.

Dussel, Enrique. "Exodus as a Paradigm in Liberation Theology." Pages 83–92 in *Exodus: A Lasting Paradigm.* Edited by Bas van Iersel and Anton Weiler. Edinburgh: T&T Clark, 1987.

Ehrman, Bart D. *Jesus, Apocalyptic Prophet of the New Millennium.* New York: Oxford University Press, 1999.

Ellens, J. Harold, ed. *The Destructive Power of Religion: Violence in Judaism, Christianity, and Islam.* Westport, CT: Praeger, 2004.

Elliott, James Keith, ed. *The Apocryphal New Testament: A Collection of Apocryphal Christian Literature in an English Translation.* Oxford: Clarendon, 1993.

Elliott, Neil. "The Anti-Imperial Message of the Cross." In Horsley, *Paul and Empire*, 167–83.

———. *Liberating Paul: The Justice of God and the Politics of the Apostle.* Sheffield, UK: Sheffield Academic, 1995.

Enns, Peter. *The Evolution of Adam: What the Bible Does and Doesn't Say about Human Origins.* Grand Rapids, MI: Brazos, 2012.

Evans-Pritchard, E. E. "An Alternative Term for 'Bride-Price.'" *Man* 31 (1931): 36–39.

Exum, J. Cheryl. "Prophetic Pornography." Pages 105–31 in *Plotted, Shot, and Painted: Cultural Representations of Biblical Women*. 2nd ed. Edited by Cheryl J. Exum. Sheffield, UK: Phoenix, 2012.

Farley, Margaret. *Just Love: A Framework for Christian Sexual Ethics*. New York: Continuum, 2006.

Fewell, Danna Nolan, and David M. Gunn. *Gender, Power, and Promise: The Subject of the Bible's First Story*. Nashville, TN: Abingdon, 1993.

Fish, Stanley. *Is There a Text in This Class? The Authority of Interpretive Communities*. Cambridge: Harvard, 1980.

Fitzmyer, Joseph A., S.J. *First Corinthians*. Anchor Yale Bible 32. New Haven: Yale University Press, 2008.

———. *The Letter to Philemon*. AB 34C. New York: Doubleday, 2000.

———. *Romans*. AB 33. New York: Doubleday, 1992.

Flannery, Frances. "Senators, Snowballs, and Scripture: The Bible and Climate Change." In Flannery and Werline, *The Bible in Political Debate*, 61–73.

Flannery, Frances, and Rodney A. Werline, eds. *The Bible in Political Debate: What Does It Really Say?* London: Bloomsbury, 2016.

Foucault, Michel. *The History of Sexuality*. Vol. 1, *An Introduction*. New York: Pantheon, 1978.

Francis, Pope. *Laudato Si: On Care for Our Common Home*. Vatican City: Libreria Editrice, 2015.

Frankfurter, David. "The Legacy of Sectarian Rage: Vengeance Fantasies in the New Testament." In Bernat and Klawans, *Religion and Violence*, 114–28.

Fredriksen, Paula. "Arms and the Man: A Response to Dale Martin's 'Jesus in Jerusalem: Armed and Not Dangerous.' " *Journal for the Study of the New Testament* 37 (2015): 312–25.

Freedman, D. N., ed. *The Anchor Bible Dictionary*. 6 vols. New York: Doubleday, 1992.

Fretheim, Terence. *God and the World in the Old Testament: A Relational Theology of Creation*. Nashville, TN: Abingdon, 2005.

Friedman, Richard Elliott, and Shawna Dolansky. *The Bible Now*. New York: Oxford University Press, 2011.

Frymer-Kensky, Tikva. *Reading the Women of the Bible*. New York: Schocken, 2002.

Fuller, Russell. "Text-Critical Problems in Malachi 2:10–16." *Journal of Biblical Literature* 110 (1991): 47–57.

Furnish, Victor Paul. *The Moral Teaching of Paul*. Nashville, TN: Abingdon, 1979.

Gager, John G., with E. Leigh Gibson. "Violent Acts and Violent Language in the Apostle Paul." In Matthews and Gibson, *Violence in the New Testament*, 13–21.

Gagnon, Robert A. J. *The Bible and Homosexual Practice: Texts and Hermeneutics*. Nashville, TN: Abingdon, 2001.

Garr, W. Randall. *In His Own Image and Likeness: Humanity, Divinity, and Monotheism*. Leiden: Brill, 2003.

Gensler, Harry J. *Ethics and the Golden Rule*. New York: Routledge, 2013.

Glancy, Jennifer A. "Early Christianity, Slavery, and Women's Bodies." In Brooten, *Beyond Slavery*, 143–58.

———. *Slavery in Early Christianity*. New York: Oxford University Press, 2002.

Gottwald, Norman K. *A Sociology of the Religion of Liberated Israel, 1250–1050 B.C.* Maryknoll, NY: Orbis Books, 1979.

Gottwald, Norman K., and Richard Horsley, eds. *The Bible and Liberation: Political and Social Hermeneutics*. Maryknoll, NY: Orbis Books, 1993.

Greenberg, David F. *The Construction of Homosexuality*. Chicago: University of Chicago Press, 1988.

Greenberg, Moshe. "On the Political Use of the Bible in Modern Israel: An Engaged Critique." Pages 461–71 in *Pomegranates and Golden Bells: Studies in Biblical, Jewish, and Near Eastern Ritual, Law, and Literature in Honor of Jacob Milgrom*. Edited by David P. Wright, David Noel Freedman, and Avi Hurvitz. Winona Lake, IN: Eisenbrauns, 1995.

The Green Bible. New York: HarperOne, 2008.

Gropp, Douglas M. "Slavery." In Schiffman and VanderKam, *Dead Sea Scrolls*, 884–86.

Grove, Jim. "Hellfire Is the Real Global Warming." *York Daily Record*, 2008, https://www.ydr.com/.

Gunkel, Hermann. *Creation and Chaos in the Primeval Era and in the Eschaton*. Translated by K. William Whitney, Jr. 1895; Grand Rapids, MI: Eerdmans, 2006.

Gustafson, James M. "The Place of Scripture in Christian Ethics." *Interpretation* 24 (1970): 430–55.

Gutiérrez, Gustavo. *A Theology of Liberation.* Maryknoll, NY: Orbis Books, 1973.

Habel, Norman C., ed. *The Earth Story in the Psalms and the Prophets.* Sheffield, UK: Sheffield Academic, 2001.

———. *Readings from the Perspective of the Earth.* Sheffield, UK: Sheffield Academic, 2000.

Habel, Norman C., and Vicky Balabanski, eds. *The Earth Story in the New Testament.* Sheffield, UK: Sheffield Academic, 2002.

Habel, Norman C., and Peter Trudinger, eds. *Exploring Ecological Hermeneutics.* SBL Symposium Series 46. Atlanta, GA: Society of Biblical Literature; Leiden: Brill, 2008.

Habel, Norman C., and Shirley Wurst, eds. *The Earth Story in Genesis.* Sheffield, UK: Sheffield Academic, 2000.

———, eds. *The Earth Story in Wisdom Traditions.* Sheffield, UK: Sheffield Academic, 2001.

Halperin, David M. *One Hundred Years of Homosexuality and Other Essays on Greek Love.* London: Routledge, 1990.

Halperin, David M., John J. Winkler, and Froma I. Zeitlin, eds. *Before Sexuality: The Construction of Erotic Experience in the Ancient Greek World.* Princeton, NJ: Princeton University Press, 1990.

Harlow, Daniel C. "After Adam: Reading Genesis in an Age of Evolutionary Science." *Perspectives on Science and Christian Faith* 62 (2010): 179–95.

Harrill, J. Albert. *The Manumission of Slaves in Early Christianity.* Tübingen: Mohr Siebeck, 1995.

———. *Slaves in the New Testament: Literary, Social, and Moral Dimensions.* Minneapolis: Fortress, 2006.

Hauerwas, Stanley. *After Christendom: How the Church Is to Behave if Freedom, Justice, and a Christian Nation Are Bad Ideas.* Nashville, TN: Abingdon, 1991.

———. "Jesus: The Justice of God." In Coomber, *Bible and Justice,* 20-90.

Haught, John F. *Science and Religion: From Conflict to Conversation.* Mahwah, NJ: Paulist, 1995.

Hawking, Stephen. *A Brief History of Time.* New York: Bantam, 1988.

Hayes, Christine. *What's Divine about Divine Law? Early Perspectives.* Princeton, NJ: Princeton University Press, 2015.

Hays, Richard B. *The Faith of Jesus Christ: The Narrative Substructure of Galatians 3:1–4:11.* Grand Rapids, MI: Eerdmans, 2002.

———. *The Moral Vision of the New Testament.* San Francisco: Harper-SanFrancisco, 1996.

———. "Relations Natural and Unnatural: A Response to John Boswell's Exegesis of Romans 1." *Journal of Christian Ethics* 14 (1986): 184–215.

Heacock, Anthony. *Jonathan Loved David: Manly Love in the Bible and the Hermeneutics of Sex.* Sheffield, UK: Sheffield Phoenix, 2011.

Hendel, Ronald. *The Book of Genesis: A Biography.* Princeton, NJ: Princeton University Press, 2013.

Henten, Jan Willem van. "Violence in Revelation." Pages 50–77 in *New Perspectives on the Book of Revelation.* Edited by Adela Yarbro Collins. Bibliotheca Ephemeridum Theologicarum Lovaniensium 291. Leuven, Belgium: Peeters, 2017.

Hezser, Catherine. *Jewish Slavery in Antiquity.* Oxford: Oxford University Press, 2006.

Hiebert, Theodore. *The Yahwist's Landscape: Nature and Religion in Early Israel.* New York: Oxford University Press, 1996.

Hoffmeier, James K. *The Immigration Crisis: Immigrants, Aliens, and the Bible.* Wheaton, IL: Crossway, 2009.

Horrell, David G. *The Bible and the Environment: Towards a Critical Ecological Biblical Theology.* London: Equinox, 2010.

Horrell, David G., Cherryl Hunt, Christopher Southgate, and Francesca Stavrakopoulou, eds. *Ecological Hermeneutics: Biblical, Historical and Theological Perspectives.* London: T&T Clark, 2010.

Horsley, Richard A. " 'By the Finger of God': Jesus and Imperial Violence." In Matthews and Gibson, *Violence in the New Testament,* 51–80.

———. *Jesus and Empire.* Minneapolis: Fortress, 2003.

———. *Jesus and the Politics of Roman Palestine.* Columbia: University of South Carolina Press, 2014.

———. *Jesus and the Spiral of Violence.* San Francisco: Harper and Row, 1987.

———. "1 Corinthians: A Case Study of Paul's Assembly as an Alternative Society." In Horsley, *Paul and Empire,* 242–52.

————. *Paul and Empire: Religion and Power in Roman Imperial Society.* Harrisburg, PA: Trinity Press International, 1997.

————. "Paul and Slavery: A Critical Alternative to Recent Readings." In Callahan, Horsley, and Smith, *Slavery in Text and Interpretation,* 153–200.

————. *The Prophet Jesus and the Renewal of Israel: Moving Beyond a Diversionary Debate.* Grand Rapids, MI: Eerdmans, 2012.

————. "The Slave Systems of Classical Antiquity and Their Reluctant Recognition by Modern Scholars." In Callahan, Horsley, and Smith, *Slavery in Text and Interpretation,* 19–66.

Horsley, Richard A., with John S. Hanson. *Bandits, Prophets, and Messiahs: Popular Movements in the Time of Jesus.* Harrisburg, PA: Trinity Press International, 1999.

Horst, P. W. van der. *The Sayings of Pseudo-Phocylides.* Leiden: Brill, 1978.

Houston, Fleur S. *You Shall Love the Stranger as Yourself: The Bible, Refugees, and Asylum.* New York: Routledge, 2015.

Houston, Walter J. *Contending for Justice: Ideologies and Theologies of Social Justice in the Old Testament.* Library of Hebrew Bible/Old Testament Studies 428. London: T&T Clark, 2006.

Houten, Christiana van. *The Alien in Israelite Law.* Journal for the Study of the Old Testament Supplements 107. Sheffield, UK: JSOT Press, 1991.

Hunt, Lynn. *Inventing Human Rights: A History.* New York: Norton, 2007.

Ishay, Micheline R. *The History of Human Rights: From Ancient Times to the Globalization Era.* Berkeley: University of California Press, 2004.

Jackson, Bernard S. *Wisdom-Laws: A Study of the Mishpatim of Exodus 21:1–22:16.* Oxford: Oxford University Press, 2006.

Jacobs, A. J. *The Year of Living Biblically.* New York: Simon & Schuster, 2007.

Janzen, Waldemar. *Old Testament Ethics: A Paradigmatic Approach.* Louisville, KY: Westminster John Knox, 1994.

Johnson, Luke Timothy. *Sharing Possessions.* Philadelphia: Fortress, 1981.

Juergensmeyer, Mark. *Terror in the Mind of God.* Berkeley: University of California Press, 2003.

Kaminsky, Joel. *Yet I Loved Jacob: Reclaiming the Biblical Concept of Election*. Nashville, TN: Abingdon, 2007.

Kant, Immanuel. *The Conflict of the Faculties*. Translated by Mary Gregor. New York: Abaris, 1979.

Klawans, Jonathan. *Impurity and Sin in Ancient Judaism*. New York: Oxford University Press, 2000.

Kraybill, J. Nelson. *Imperial Cult and Commerce in John's Apocalypse*. Sheffield, UK: Sheffield Academic, 1996.

Kreitzer, Larry J. *Philemon*. Sheffield, UK: Sheffield Phoenix, 2008.

Krentz, Edgar M. "Thessalonians, First and Second Epistles to the." Pages 515–23 in vol. 6 of Freedman, *The Anchor Bible Dictionary*.

Kugel, James L. *The Traditions of the Bible*. Cambridge: Harvard University Press, 1998.

LaHaye, Tim, and Jerry B. Jenkins. *Left Behind: A Novel of the Earth's Last Days*. Wheaton, IL: Tyndale, 1995.

Lanfer, Peter. *Remembering Eden: The Reception History of Genesis 3:22–24*. New York: Oxford University Press, 2012.

Lawrence, D. H. *Apocalypse*. New York: Viking, 1932.

LeFebvre, Michael. *Collections, Codes, and Torah: The Re-characterization of Israel's Written Law*. New York: Clark, 2006.

Lemos, Tracy M. *Marriage Gifts and Social Change in Ancient Palestine: 1200 BCE to 200 CE*. New York: Cambridge University Press, 2010.

———. "Were Israelite Women Chattel? Shedding New Light on an Old Question." Pages 227–41 in *Worship, Women, and War: Essays in Honor of Susan Niditch*. Edited by J. J. Collins, T. M. Lemos, and S. M. Olyan. Brown Judaic Studies 357. Providence, RI: Brown University Press, 2015.

Leske, Adrian M. "Matthew 6:25–34: Human Anxiety and the Natural World." In Habel and Balabanski, *Earth Story in the New Testament*, 15–27.

Levenson, Jon D. *Creation and the Persistence of Evil: The Jewish Drama of Divine Omnipotence*. San Francisco: Harper, 1988.

———. *The Death and Resurrection of the Beloved Son*. New Haven: Yale University Press, 1993.

———. *The Hebrew Bible, the Old Testament, and Historical Criticism*. Louisville, KY: Westminster John Knox, 1993.

———. *The Love of God: Divine Gift, Human Gratitude, and Mutual Faithfulness in Judaism*. Princeton, NJ: Princeton University Press, 2016.

———. *Sinai and Zion: An Entry into the Jewish Bible*. Minneapolis: Winston, 1985.

Levine, Baruch A. *Numbers 21–36*. Anchor Bible 4A. New York: Doubleday, 2000.

Levinson, Bernard M. "The Reconceptualization of Kingship in Deuteronomy and the Deuteronomistic History's Reconceptualization of Torah." *Vetus Testamentum* 51 (2001): 511–34.

Lincoln, Bruce. *Holy Terrors: Thinking about Religion after September 11*. Chicago: University of Chicago, 2003.

———. "Symmetric Dualisms: Bush and Bin Laden on Oct. 7, 2001." In Amanat and Collins, *Apocalypse and Violence*, 89–112.

Lindsey, Hal. "The Great Cosmic Countdown: Hal Lindsey on the Future." *Eternity* (1977): 21.

———. *The Late Great Planet Earth*. Grand Rapids, MI: Zondervan, 1970.

Lohfink, Norbert F., S.J. *Option for the Poor: The Basic Principle of Liberation Theology in the Light of the Bible*. Berkeley, CA: Bibal, 1987.

Luther, Martin. *D. Martin Luthers Werke: Kritische Gesamtausgabe: Die deutsche Bibel 7*. Weimar: Böhlaus Nachfolger, 1931.

MacDonald, Dennis Ronald. *The Legend and the Apostle: The Battle for Paul; Story and Canon*. Philadelphia: Westminster, 1983.

MacDonald, Margaret Y. "Reading Real Women through the Undisputed Letters of Paul." Pages 199–220 in *Women and Christian Origins*. Edited by Ross Shepard Kraemer and Mary Rose D'Angelo. New York: Oxford University Press, 1999.

———. "Rereading Paul: Early Interpreters of Paul on Women and Gender." Pages 236–53, ibid.

Maier, Harry O. "There's a New World Coming! Reading the Apocalypse in the Shadow of the Canadian Rockies." In Habel and Balabanski, *Earth Story in the New Testament*, 166–79.

Marlow, Hilary. *Biblical Prophets: Contemporary Environmental Ethics*. Oxford: Oxford University Press, 2009.

Martin, Dale B. "*Arsenokoites* and *Malakos*: Meanings and Consequences." Pages 37–50 in *Sex and the Single Savior: Gender and Sexuality in Biblical Interpretation*. Louisville, KY: Westminster John Knox, 2006.

————. *Biblical Truths: The Meaning of Scripture in the Twenty-First Century*. New Haven: Yale University Press, 2017.

————. *The Corinthian Body*. New Haven: Yale University Press, 1995.

————. "Jesus in Jerusalem: Armed but Not Dangerous." *Journal for the Study of the New Testament* 37 (2014): 3–24.

————. *The Pedagogy of the Bible: An Analysis and Proposal*. Louisville, KY: Westminster John Knox, 2008.

————. *Sex and the Single Savior: Gender and Sexuality in Biblical Interpretation*. Louisville, KY: Westminster John Knox, 2006.

————. *Slavery as Salvation: The Metaphor of Slavery in Pauline Christianity*. New Haven: Yale University Press, 1990.

Martyn, J. L. *Galatians*. Anchor Bible 33A. New York: Doubleday, 1997.

Matthews, Shelly, and E. Leigh Gibson, eds. *Violence in the New Testament*. New York: T&T Clark, 2005.

Matthews, Victor H., and Don C. Benjamin. *Old Testament Parallels: Laws and Stories from the Ancient Near East*. Mahwah, NJ: Paulist, 2007.

McDonagh, Sean. *The Greening of the Earth*. Maryknoll, NY: Orbis Books, 1990.

McKenzie, Steven L. *King David: A Biography*. New York: Oxford University Press, 2000.

McNeill, John J. *The Church and the Homosexual*. 3rd ed. Boston: Beacon, 1988.

Meier, John P. *A Marginal Jew*. Vol. 4, *Law and Love*. Anchor Yale Bible Reference Library. New Haven: Yale University Press, 2009.

————. *A Marginal Jew*. Vol. 5, *Probing the Authenticity of the Parables*. Anchor Yale Bible Reference Library. New Haven: Yale University Press, 2016.

Mendelsohn, Isaac. *Slavery in the Ancient Near East*. Westport, CT: Greenwood, 1949.

Meyers, Carol. *Rediscovering Eve: Ancient Israelite Women in Context*. New York: Oxford University Press, 2013.

————. "Was Ancient Israel a Patriarchal Society?" *Journal of Biblical Literature* 133 (2014): 8–27.

Miller, Patrick D. *The Ten Commandments*. Louisville, KY: Westminster John Knox, 2009.

Miranda, José P. *Marx and the Bible*. Maryknoll, NY: Orbis Books, 1974.

Moran, William L. "The Ancient Near Eastern Background of the Love of God in Deuteronomy." *Catholic Biblical Quarterly* 25 (1963): 77–87.

Morgan, Teresa. *Roman Faith and Christian Faith: Pistis and Fides in the Early Roman Empire and Early Churches.* Oxford: Oxford University Press, 2015.

Moyn, Samuel. *The Last Utopia: Human Rights in History.* Cambridge: Belknap Press of Harvard University Press, 2010.

Nardoni, Enrique. *Rise Up, O Judge: A Study of Justice in the Biblical World.* Peabody, MA: Hendrickson, 2004.

Neville, David J. *A Peaceable Hope: Contesting Violent Eschatology in New Testament Narratives.* Grand Rapids, MI: Baker, 2013.

Newsom, Carol A. "Bakhtin, the Bible, and Dialogic Truth." *Journal of Religion* 76 (1996): 290–306.

Nissinen, Martti. *Homoeroticism in the Biblical World.* Minneapolis: Fortress, 1998.

Nygren, Anders. *Agape and Eros.* London: Society for the Promotion of Christian Knowledge, 1953.

O'Donovan, Oliver. *The Desire of the Nations.* Cambridge: Cambridge University Press, 1996.

Olyan, Saul. *Social Inequality in the World of the Text: The Significance of Ritual and Social Distinctions in the Hebrew Bible.* Journal of Ancient Judaism Supplements 4. Göttingen: Vandenhoeck & Ruprecht, 2011.

Otto, Eckart. "Human Rights: The Influence of the Hebrew Bible," *Journal of Northwest Semitic Languages* 25 (1999): 1–20.

Pakkala, Juha. *Intolerant Monolatry in the Deuteronomistic History.* Göttingen: Vandenhoeck & Ruprecht, 1999.

Patrick, Dale. "Divine Creative Power and the Decentering of Creation: The Subtext of the Lord's Addresses to Job." Pages 103-15 in Habel and Wurst, *The Earth Story in Wisdom Traditions.*

Patterson, Orlando. *Slavery and Social Death.* Cambridge: Harvard University Press, 1982.

Payne, Philip B. *Man and Woman: One in Christ.* Grand Rapids, MI: Zondervan, 2009.

Peerbolte, Bert Jan Lietaert. "Ending a Life That Has Not Begun—Abortion in the Bible." In Flannery and Werline, *The Bible in Political Debate,* 47–60.

Petersen, David. "Genesis and Family Values." *Journal of Biblical Literature* 124 (2005): 5–23.

Petersen, Norman R. *Rediscovering Paul: Philemon and the Sociology of Paul's Narrative World.* Philadelphia: Fortress, 1985.

Pleins, J. David. *The Social Visions of the Hebrew Bible: A Theological Introduction.* Louisville, KY: Westminster John Knox, 2001.

Polkinghorne, John. *Serious Talk: Science and Religion in Dialogue.* Valley Forge, PA: Trinity Press International, 1995.

Powery, Emerson B. "The Bible, Slavery, and Political Debate." In Flannery and Werline, *Bible in Political Debate*, 141–53.

Pritchard, James B. *Ancient Near Eastern Texts Relating to the Old Testament.* 3rd ed. Princeton, NJ: Princeton University Press, 1969.

Rad, Gerhard von. *Genesis.* Old Testament Library. Philadelphia: Westminster, 1972.

———. *Wisdom in Israel.* Nashville, TN: Abingdon, 1972.

Regele, Michael B. *Science, Scripture, and Same-Sex Love.* Nashville, TN: Abingdon, 2014.

Reumann, John. *Stewardship and the Economy of God.* Grand Rapids, MI: Eerdmans, 1992.

Reynolds, Benjamin E., and Loren T. Stuckenbruck, eds. *The Jewish Apocalyptic Tradition and the Shaping of New Testament Thought.* Minneapolis: Fortress, 2017.

Ricks, Stephen D. "Abortion in Antiquity." Pages 31–35 in vol. 1 of Freedman, *The Anchor Bible Dictionary.*

Ricoeur, Paul. *Essays in Biblical Interpretation.* Philadelphia: Fortress, 1980.

Riddle, John M. *Eve's Herbs: A History of Contraception and Abortion in the West.* Cambridge: Harvard University Press, 1997.

Robinson, Marilynne. *The Death of Adam: Essays on Modern Thought.* Boston: Houghton Mifflin, 1998.

Rodd, Cyril. *Glimpses of a Strange Land: Studies in Old Testament Ethics.* Edinburgh: Clark, 2001.

Rogerson, John W. "The Old Testament and the Environment." In Coomber, *The Bible and Justice*, 147–57.

Rollston, Christopher. "The Marginalization of Women: A Biblical Value We Don't Like to Talk About." *Huffington Post*, October 31, 2012. https://www.huffingtonpost.com/christopher-rollston/the-marginalization-of-women-biblical-value-we-dont-like-to-talk-about_b_1833648.html.

———. "Women, the Bible, and the Nineteenth Amendment to the U.S. Constitution." In Flannery and Werline, *The Bible in Political Debate*, 155–66.

Römer, Thomas. *The Invention of God*. Cambridge: Harvard University Press, 2015.

Rossing, Barbara. "Alas for Earth! Lament and Resistance in Revelation 12." In Habel and Balabanski, *Earth Story in the New Testament*, 180–92.

———. "River of Life in God's New Jerusalem: An Ecological Vision for Earth's Future." Pages 205–26 in *Christianity and Ecology*. Edited by Rosemary Radford Ruether and Dieter Hessel. Cambridge: Harvard University Center for World Religions, 1998.

Roth, Martha. *Law Collections from Mesopotamia and Asia Minor*. 2nd ed. Writings from the Ancient World 6. Atlanta, GA: Society of Biblical Literature, 1997.

Royalty, Robert M. *The Streets of Heaven: The Ideology of Wealth in the Apocalypse of John*. Macon, GA: Mercer, 1998.

Said, Edward. "Michael Walzer's *Exodus and Revolution*: A Canaanite Reading." *Grand Street* 5 (1986): 86–106.

Saller, Richard. "Corporal Punishment, Authority, and Obedience in the Roman Household." Pages 145–65 in *Marriage, Divorce and Children in Ancient Rome*. Edited by Beryl Rawson. Oxford: Clarendon, 1991.

Sanders, E. P. *Paul and Palestinian Judaism*. Philadelphia: Fortress, 1977.

———. *Paul, the Law, and the Jewish People*. Philadelphia: Fortress, 1983.

Satlow, Michael. *Jewish Marriage in Antiquity*. Princeton, NJ: Princeton University Press, 2001.

Schiff, Daniel. *Abortion in Judaism*. Cambridge: Cambridge University Press, 2002.

Schiffman, Lawrence H., and James C. VanderKam, eds. *The Oxford Encyclopedia of the Dead Sea Scrolls*. New York: Oxford University Press, 2000.

Schüssler Fiorenza, Elisabeth. *The Book of Revelation: Justice and Judgment*. Philadelphia: Fortress, 1985.

———. "The Ethics of Biblical Interpretation: De-centering Biblical Scholarship." *Journal of Biblical Literature* 107 (1988): 3–17.

———. *In Memory of Her: A Feminist Theological Reconstruction of Christian Origins.* 2nd ed. New York: Crossroad, 1995.

———. *Invitation to the Book of Revelation.* New York: Doubleday, 1981.

———. *Jesus and the Politics of Interpretation.* New York: Continuum, 2000.

———. *Revelation: Vision of a Just World.* Minneapolis: Fortress, 1991.

Schwartz, Regina M. *The Curse of Cain: The Violent Legacy of Monotheism.* Chicago: University of Chicago Press, 1997.

Schweitzer, Albert. *The Quest of the Historical Jesus: A Critical Study of Its Progress.* London: Black, 1910.

Scofield, Cyrus I. *Addresses on Prophecy.* New York: Gaebelin, 1910.

———. *The Scofield Reference Bible.* Oxford: Oxford University Press, 1917.

Scoggins Ballentine, Debra. *The Conflict Myth and the Biblical Tradition.* New York: Oxford University Press, 2015.

Scroggs, Robin. *The New Testament and Homosexuality: Contextual Background for Contemporary Debate.* Philadelphia: Fortress, 1983.

Setel, T. Drorah. "Prophets and Pornography: Female Sexual Imagery in Hosea." Pages 86–95 in *Feminist Interpretation of the Bible.* Edited by Letty M. Russell. Philadelphia: Westminster, 1985.

Setzer, Claudia, and David A. Shefferman, eds. *The Bible and American Culture: A Sourcebook.* London: Routledge, 2011.

Sherwood, Yvonne, ed. *The Bible and Feminism: Remapping the Field.* Oxford: Oxford University Press, 2017.

———. *A Biblical Text and Its Afterlives: The Survival of Jonah in Western Culture.* Cambridge: Cambridge University Press, 2000.

Simon, Uriel. *Seek Peace and Pursue It.* Tel Aviv: Yediot Aharonot, 2002 [Hebrew].

Smith, Mark S. *The Origins of Biblical Monotheism: Israel's Polytheistic Background and the Ugaritic Texts.* Oxford: Oxford University Press, 2001.

———. *The Priestly Vision of Genesis 1.* Minneapolis: Fortress, 2010.

Snell, Daniel C. "Slavery in the Ancient Near East." Pages 4–21 in *The Cambridge World History of Slavery.* Vol. 1, *The Ancient Mediterranean World.* Edited by Keith Bradley and Paul Cartledge. Cambridge: Cambridge University Press, 2011.

Soloveichik, Meir Y. "The Virtue of Hate." *First Things* 130 (2003): 41–46.

Sommer, Benjamin D. *Revelation and Authority: Sinai in Jewish Scripture and Tradition.* Anchor Yale Bible Reference Library. New Haven: Yale University Press, 2015.

Stendahl, Krister. "Hate, Non-retaliation and Love: 1QS X 17–20 and Rom 12:19–21." *Harvard Theological Review* 55 (1962): 343–55.

Stratton, Kimberly B. "The Eschatological Arena: Reinscribing Roman Violence in Fantasies of the End Times." Pages 45–76 in *Violence, Scripture, and Textual Practice in Early Judaism and Christianity.* Edited by Ra'anan S. Boustan, Alex P. Jassen, and Calvin J. Roetzel. Leiden: Brill, 2010.

Strawn, Brent A. *The Old Testament Is Dying: A Diagnosis and Recommended Treatment.* Grand Rapids, MI: Baker, 2017.

Stringfellow, Thornton. *Scriptural and Statistical Views in Favor of Slavery.* Pamphlet, 1856. University Library, University of North Carolina at Chapel Hill, Documenting the American South, http://docsouth.unc.edu.

Stuart, Moses. *Conscience and Constitution.* Boston: Crocker & Brewster, 1850.

Thorp, John. "The Social Construction of Homosexuality." *Phoenix 46* (1992): 54–65.

Tombs, David. *Latin American Liberation Theology.* Leiden: Brill, 2002.

Tonstad, Sigve. "Creation Groaning in Labor Pains." In Habel and Trudinger, *Exploring Ecological Hermeneutics,* 141–50.

Trible, Phyllis. "The Daughter of Jephtah: An Inhuman Sacrifice." In Trible, *Texts of Terror,* 93–116.

———. "Depatriarchalizing in Biblical Interpretation." *Journal of the American Academy of Religion* 41 (1973): 30–48.

———. *God and the Rhetoric of Sexuality.* Philadelphia: Fortress, 1978.

———. *Texts of Terror: Literary-Feminist Readings of Biblical Narratives.* Philadelphia: Fortress, 1984.

Tucker, Gene M. "Rain on a Land Where No One Lives: The Hebrew Bible on the Environment." *Journal of Biblical Literature* 116 (1997): 3–17.

Untermann, Jeremiah. *Justice for All: How the Jewish Bible Revolutionized Ethics.* Philadelphia: Jewish Publication Society; Lincoln: University of Nebraska Press, 2017.

Vaux, Roland de, O.P. *Ancient Israel*. 2 vols. New York: McGraw-Hill, 1965.

———. *Studies in Old Testament Sacrifice*. Cardiff: University of Wales Press, 1964.

Walvoord, John F. "Why Must Christ Return?" Page 43 in *Prophecy and the Seventies*. Edited by Charles Lee Feinberg. Chicago: Moody, 1971.

Walzer, Michael. *Exodus and Revolution*. New York: Basic Books, 1984.

Weems, Renita J. *Battered Love: Marriage, Sex, and Violence in the Hebrew Prophets*. Minneapolis: Fortress, 1995.

———. "Gomer: Victim of Violence or Victim of Metaphor?" *Semeia* 49 (1989): 87–104.

Weinfeld, Moshe. *Social Justice in Ancient Israel and in the Ancient Near East*. Jerusalem: Magnes; Minneapolis: Fortress, 1995.

Werline, Rodney A. "Work, Poverty, and Welfare." In Flannery and Werline, *The Bible in Political Debate*, 75–86.

Wessinger, Catherine. "Apocalypse and Violence." Pages 422–40 in *The Oxford Handbook of Apocalyptic Literature*. Edited by John J. Collins. New York: Oxford University Press, 2014.

White, Lynn, Jr. "An Evangelical Declaration on the Care of Creation." Pages 17–22 in *The Care of Creation: Focusing Concern and Action*. Edited by R. J. Berry. Downer's Grove, IL: Intervarsity, 2000.

———. "The Historical Roots of Our Ecological Crisis." *Science* 155 (1967): 1203–7.

Whitelam, Keith W. *The Invention of Ancient Israel: The Silencing of Palestinian History*. London: Routledge, 1996.

———. *The Just King: Monarchical Judicial Authority in Ancient Israel*. Journal for the Study of the Old Testament Supplements 12. Sheffield, UK: University of Sheffield Press, 1979.

Wilkinson, Bruce. *The Prayer of Jabez: Breaking Through to the Blessed Life*. Portland, OR: Multnomah, 2000.

Wilkinson, David. "Reading Genesis 1–3 in Light of Modern Science." In Barton and Wilkinson, *Reading Genesis after Darwin*, 127–44.

Williams, James G. *The Bible, Violence, and the Sacred: Liberation from the Myth of Sanctioned Violence*. San Francisco: HarperSanFrancisco, 1991.

Wink, Walter. *Jesus and Nonviolence: A Third Way*. Minneapolis: Fortress, 2003.

Winkler, John J. "Unnatural Acts: Erotic Protocols in Artemidoros' *Dream Analysis.*" Pages 17–44 in *The Constraints of Desire: The Anthropology of Sex and Gender in Ancient Greece.* London: Routledge, 1990.

Winter, Sara B. C. "Paul's Letter to Philemon." *New Testament Studies* 33 (1987): 1–15.

Wolterstorff, Nicholas. "Comments on 'What about the Canaanites?' " In Bergmann, Murray, and Rea, *Divine Evil?*, 283–88.

———. *Justice: Rights and Wrongs.* Princeton, NJ: Princeton University Press, 2008.

———. *Justice in Love.* Grand Rapids, MI: Eerdmans, 2011.

———. "Reading Joshua." In Bergmann, Murray, and Rea, *Divine Evil?*, 236–56.

Wright, David P. *Inventing God's Law: How the Covenant Code of the Bible Used and Revised the Laws of Hammurabi.* Oxford: Oxford University Press, 2009.

———. " 'She Shall Not Go Free as Male Slaves Do': Developing Views about Slavery and Gender in the Laws of the Hebrew Bible." In Brooten, *Beyond Slavery*, 125–42.

Wright, G. E. *The Book of the Acts of God: Christian Scholarship Interprets the Bible.* London: Duckworth, 1960.

Wright, N. T. *New Heavens, New Earth: The Biblical Picture of Christian Hope.* Cambridge: Grove, 1999.

Wybrow, Cameron. *The Bible, Baconianism, and Mastery over Nature: The Old Testament and Its Modern Misreading.* New York: Lang, 1991.

Yarbro Collins, Adela. *The Combat Myth in the Book of Revelation.* Harvard Dissertations in Religion 9. Missoula, MT: Scholars Press, 1976.

———. *Crisis and Catharsis: The Power of the Apocalypse.* Philadelphia: Westminster, 1984.

———. "The Female Body as Social Space in 1 Timothy." *New Testament Studies* 57 (2011): 155–75.

———. "Jesus' Action in Herod's Temple." Pages 45–61 in *Antiquity and Humanity: Essays on Ancient Religion and Philosophy Presented to Hans Dieter Betz on His 70th Birthday.* Edited by Adela Yarbro Collins and Margaret M. Mitchell. Tübingen: Mohr Siebeck, 2001.

———. *Mark: A Commentary.* Hermeneia. Minneapolis: Fortress, 2007.

———. "The Political Perspective of the Revelation to John." Pages 198–217 in Yarbro Collins, *Cosmology and Eschatology in Jewish and Christian Apocalypticism*. Journal for the Study of Judaism Supplements 50. Leiden: Brill, 1996.

———. "The Reception of the Torah in Mark: The Question about the Greatest Commandment." Pages 227–42 in *Pentateuchal Traditions in the Late Second Temple Period*. Edited by Akio Moriya and Gohei Hata. Journal for the Study of Judaism Supplements 158. Leiden: Brill, 2012.

General Index

Abel and Cain, 31
abolition movement, 145–46
abortion, 50–58
Abraham, 45, 63, 151, 180, 201
Achilles, 69
Adam and Eve, 29–31, 32, 59–63, 86–88
Adapa, 30
adultery, 48–49, 51, 89, 91
Agamemnon, 46
agape, love, 190
agriculture, 112–13, 117–18
Ahab (king), 177
Ahaz (king), 46
Akiba, Rabbi, 10, 92
Albright, William Foxwell, 151
aliens, 128–30, 180
almsgiving, 207–8, 209, 240n29
Alter, Robert, 6
Amalek, 237n9
American Psychiatric Association, 64
Amos, 174–75, 178, 182, 217–19
Ananias, 205
androcentrism, 61, 84, 94–96
androgynes, 62
Antichrist, 192
Antiochus Epiphanes, 157
Anum, 171

apocalypticism: and environmental protection, 121–25; as frame of reference, 21, 35–39; and new Jerusalem, 124, 183, 191; and social justice, 189–211; and terrorism, 160–66; and violence, 158–66
apodictic laws, 11
Apsu, 22
Aristophanes, 64–65
Aristotle, 53, 104–5, 176, 228n38, 231n60
Armageddon, 192
Arrington, Jodey, 243n50
arsenokoitai (sodomites), 79–81
Assyrians: and abortion, 50, 225n23; attacks on Israel, 129, 156–57, 219; and same-sex relations, 71–72; siege warfare conducted by, 113; *Vassal Treaty of Esarhaddon*, 34, 228n25
Atrahasis myth (Babylonian), 22–23, 28, 29
Augustine, 26

Babylonian Exile period, 29, 71, 129, 157
Babylonian mythology, 22, 60
Balaam, 164–65
Barr, James, 30

Index of Ancient Sources